Thoreau MacDonald

Thoreau MacDonald

A CATALOGUE OF DESIGN AND ILLUSTRATION · MARGARET E. EDISON

UNIVERSITY OF TORONTO PRESS

Toronto and Buffalo
Printed in Canada
Reprinted in 2018
ISBN 0-8020-1959-5
ISBN 978-1-4875-7213-6 (paper)
ISBN Special Edition 0-8020-1989-7
LC 72-95462

Permission to reproduce his memoirs, drawings, and designs has been given by the artist and by the following publishers, publications, institutions, galleries, and individuals.
Clarke, Irwin & Company Limited, for material from *Noranda* by Leslie Roberts, copyright Canada 1956 by Clarke, Irwin & Company Limited, used by permission; J.M. Dent & Sons (Canada) Limited; Hodder & Stoughton, Limited; Holt, Rinehart and Winston, Inc., New York, NY, for material from *Northern Farm* by Henry Beston, illustrated by Thoreau MacDonald, copyright 1948 by Holt, Rinehart and Winston, Inc., reproduced by permission of Holt, Rinehart and Winston, Inc., and from *The Mackenzie* by Leslie Roberts, illustrated by Thoreau MacDonald, copyright 1949 by Holt, Rinehart and Winston, Inc., reproduced by permission of Holt, Rinehart and Winston, Inc.; Longman Canada Limited; McClelland and Stewart Limited; McGraw-Hill Ryerson Limited; Macmillan Company of Canada Limited; Oxford University Press Canadian Branch; the Stinehour Press, Lunenburg, Vermont; *The Canadian Forum*; *Print: America's Graphic Design Magazine*; *Queen's Quarterly*; The Federation of Ontario Naturalists; Victoria College, the University of Toronto; The London Public Library and Art Museum; Department of Rare Books and Special Collections of the McGill University Libraries; Metropolitan Toronto Central Library; Yale University Library; Agnes Etherington Art Centre, Queen's University; Art Gallery of Ontario for 'March Wind,' 'The Burnished Plow,' 'Horse in Farm Landscape,' 'Kitchen Window,' 'Sunflower in Winter,' 'The Manger,' 'Armistice Silence,' and 'The Plain,' from *West by East* (B16); the McMichael Canadian Collection; Department of Prints and Drawings, The National Gallery of Canada, Ottawa, for illustrations from B28 and B62; The Vancouver Art Gallery; Allan Burton, esquire; members of the Dunlap family; Barker Fairley and the McMichael Canadian Collection (for the poem 'Wild Geese'); E.R. Hunter, esquire (for the Lawren Harris portrait of TM); the late Norman Kent, esquire; members of the family of the honourable Albert Matthews; C.A.G. Matthews, esquire; Professor Ray Nash; members of the family of Dr E.M. Walker; several private collectors.

Every care has been exercised to trace ownership of material, but omissions may be found; the publishers will be pleased to receive information that may enable them to rectify any errors in subsequent editions or printings.

For John and Rob, and for Thoreau

Foreword

Thoreau MacDonald, born near Toronto in 1901, is the gifted son of J.E.H. MacDonald, a member of the Group of Seven. He shared the Severn Street studio with his father until the latter's death in 1932 and continued to use it for his commercial work until 1949. Since then he has lived and worked in his family house in Thornhill, not far from Toronto. This is a record of his work as a designer and illustrator in black and white, with particular reference to books, a field in which he is unexcelled in Canada. His retiring nature and dislike of publicity have prevented his remarkable accomplishment from being more widely known. Love of, and respect for, the rural way of life illuminates much of his work and is clearly shown in the themes of his private press books, many of which constitute section A of the catalogue.

The research for the catalogue has taken some years to complete and was done for pleasure. It grew out of a natural interest in books and the artists who made them attractive. The nucleus of the collection which is the basis of this catalogue was formed in the early thirties. In the sixties I suggested to the artist that I would like to compile a catalogue of his work which would be as definitive as possible; the suggestion was agreeably received by him and, although he has kept no written records, I have discussed all the material with him. His comments and recollections, often humorous, sometimes astringent, have been as generously given as have his autobiographical notes. Of particular value was his help in sorting out the work that he and his father did jointly. Section E of the catalogue records the result.

Once embarked on the search for more books, pamphlets, and printed material, I found the Ryerson Press archives of great assistance, for it contains a complete collection of Ryerson Press books and a meticulously kept record. Interested friends added to my collection and advanced my knowledge with theirs. Members of the Antiquarian Book Sellers Association of Canada and others were most helpful. Individuals in libraries, archives, and art galleries, as well as collectors both in Canada and the United States, seemed to share my enthusiasm and I owe a great debt of gratitude to them.

I am most grateful to several good friends who have helped me in a variety of ways. One of these is E.R. Hunter, Director of the Norton Gallery of Art, West Palm Beach, Florida. Born and educated in Toronto, a graduate of the Courtauld Institute of Art, University of London, and well known as a writer and art historian, he became the recognized authority on the work of Thoreau MacDonald with the publication in 1942 of his critical appreciation of the artist, a book which is now out of print. I am indebted to him both for his generous permission to quote from this book and for his continuing interest and counsel.

Barker Fairley, German scholar at the University of Toronto, artist, literary critic, and friend of both the MacDonalds, has written a prefatory note in the form of a letter to the artist. For this charming and original contribution, so full of affection and reminiscence, I give him my grateful thanks.

Professor Ray Nash, professor of art, Dartmouth College, Hanover, New Hampshire, holds Thoreau MacDonald in high esteem as both an artist and a friend. He invited me to spend time in the Hopkins Center Gallery and the Baker Library and made his large and well-loved collection available for as much research and study as time allowed. For this privilege and for his patience with my many questions I thank him most warmly.

Mrs Northrop Frye has taken a personal interest in this book. She accompanied me to Hanover to share my pleasure in the Nash collection. I have greatly appreciated her persistent encouragement and many helpful suggestions.

I am also indebted to the late Mr Norman Kent, editor emeritus of *American Artist*, who gave me permission to quote from his written material. Well known in the world of design and illustration, his two articles in *American Artist* and his prompt answers to my letters showed an artist's understanding and admiration of the work of Thoreau MacDonald.

The Master of Massey College, Robertson Davies, encouraged me to undertake this book, and he and Mr Douglas Lochhead, librarian of the College and professor of English at University College, made me a frequent and always welcome visitor in the Massey College Library. This was of great value for many reasons, not the least of which is that jackets are kept on the books in this collection.

It is a pleasure to express my appreciation to Miss Patricia Norman of the Reference Department of the University of Toronto Library and to Mr Alan Suddon of the Fine Arts Section of the Metropolitan Toronto Central Library. Both had tireless enthusiasm and great imagination.

It also gives me pleasure to thank Mrs L.M. Haddad of the Department of Rare Books and Special Collections, McGill University, with whom I have had a lively and most helpful correspondence in connection with the Colgate Collection of Printing. Another lengthy and helpful correspondence was with Mr William F.E. Morley, curator of Special Collections, Douglas Library, Queen's University, and, through his kindness, with Mrs Frances K. Smith, assistant to the director of the Agnes Etherington Art Centre.

Mrs Vinetta Lunn and Miss J. Hunter of the library of the National Gallery of Canada have kept a friendly eye on my research and I have been the beneficiary of their kindness in producing well-documented information unavailable elsewhere. I am also indebted to Mrs Joan Murray, curator of Canadian Art, Art Gallery of Ontario, who provided the list of *Forum* drawings for section D of the catalogue, and to Miss Sybille Pantazzi of the library of the Art Gallery of Ontario for her assistance in the compilation of section E of the catalogue.

Mr Richard Landon, research and administrative assistant to the Rare Books and Special Collections Department, University of Toronto Library, prepared the catalogue and the index and I am most appreciative of his expertise in working out with me a form of listing for the variety of material in my collection.

My grateful thanks go to the trustees of the McLean Foundation who have shown by the gift of a generous grant their affirmation of the value of this piece of research. Without this grant it would have been difficult to produce a book of sufficient quality to demonstrate the essential skill of the artist.

MARGARET E. EDISON

Contents

Introduction

A Letter

Dear Thoreau

I promised long ago to write some prefatory words to this volume and now I find myself addressing you in person instead of addressing the reader. This may surprise you because you don't realize how much you are in my mind and have been in my mind all through the long years in which, it seems, we never meet. It goes back to the winter of 1917-18 when your father was bedridden with some sort of breakdown; perhaps, as you once said to me, a mild stroke anticipating the one that took him away some fifteen years later. I had just made his acquaintance in the fall of the year at the Arts and Letters Club and was so drawn to him as a man like no one I had ever met that, when I heard soon after of his illness, I at once ran out to see him, stranger or near-stranger that I was, and then went to see him again and again in the following months. You were living at that time in the Usher cottage at York Mills in the valley bottom east of the highway.

The memory of those visits is printed indelibly on my mind, your father sitting up in bed, not suffering enough to make conversation a strain, me sitting on a chair by the bedside, and you standing very upright, almost at attention, at the foot of the bed, saying nothing, while he and I chatted. Not being able to paint, he was writing verses and I got hold of some of them to be printed in *The Rebel*, a not very responsible little publication at University College, jointly edited by a group of staff and students. If I am not mistaken, it was the beginning of his verse-writing or nearly so. You were the silent watcher.

Whoever reads this letter may be saying to himself that I was supposed to be writing a word on Thoreau MacDonald, not on his father. But it is the close bond between you and your father, signalized by this quiet picture of the three of us together, that I want to commemorate, more for your sake than for his. So let me continue in this vein. I remember a day in the early spring when his long confinement was over and he sat in front of the house, or rather at the back of the house, and made a sketch of some of us planting potatoes behind the plough, the Club having rented the Usher farm to grow vegetables as a war economy. I have seen two such sketches, probably made on the same day. And it was about this time, or a little earlier, that he made sketches of fields and trees in the Thornhill neighbourhood. Somehow these sketches made such an appeal to me that I felt, and have felt ever since, that this was where he belonged and that he was swept north with the others into the land of rocks and rapids long before he had fully expressed the pastoral vein that was deepest in him. Or, to put it another way, I think of him now as the painter of the tangled garden first of all and only then, and less exclusively, as the painter of the solemn land. I wish he could have lingered in the cultivated area a little longer.

But there is no need to hang our heads, because it now seems as if he simply pulled out and left it to you to carry on where he stopped and to do the fuller justice to the home environment of farmyards and fallow fields that he might well have spent his life on. So this is where you come in, and this is why I had to say a word or two about him to begin with, before saying what I want to say about you.

I recall Alec Jackson telling me once, or telling it in my company, that he refused to sketch within less than sixty miles of Toronto, and a long story could be written round this remark. It is curious how slight has been the appeal of the nearer environment to our more gifted artists. It may be the spell of Tom Thomson or it may be the sheer excitement of the northern granite and its autumn splendour that has kept people in Ontario less alive to the beauty of the farming country that surrounds them than they ought to be.

You are not the only artist who has tried to correct the bias. There are others as well, Carl Schaefer among them, but you are the one who has stayed longest and most devotedly with this worthy endeavour. Working almost entirely in black-and-white with pen and paper you can never have expected to make as much of a splash as those who work in bright colours – the notion of Thoreau MacDonald making a splash is ridiculous in any case, isn't it? – but what you have done is there, and there to stay, and this book, I have no doubt, will demonstrate it conclusively. I like to think that I had a hand in your career at an early stage, because it was through me and my closeness to the group – you know which group I mean – that you became Art Editor of *The Canadian Forum*, a journal set going by some of us in 1920 when *The Rebel* stopped, and in consequence made that long series of frontispieces and illustrations which gave such distinction to the journal in its opening years. Was it here that you first found your true direction or had you found it sooner than that? Anyhow, the *Forum* connection must have helped. For our part we all grieved when you suddenly pulled out for reasons of your own which I never asked you about.

Well, here you are now, turned seventy, with this rich achievement behind you, and more to come. You may wonder whether I am not viewing this achievement too narrowly when I identify you with rural Ontario. But I can't help it. I know your range is wider. I know that you cultivated the art of lettering and made yourself a secure niche there in the small company of the best, alongside of Carl Dair. You looked at Quebec and illustrated *Maria Chapdelaine* and those may be right who consider this your top performance. When you travelled north into remoter country you seem to me to have been as much at home there as any of them. And yet, notwithstanding all these distinctions, when I say your name or think of you I see old gates and fences and farmyards and early cottages, farm implements, domestic animals, wild animals, birds flying, not many people. Strange how lonely the Canadian landscape is, even in southern Ontario, even when it is you who depict it with all the warmth and affection that gets into everything you do.

I hope this book will make you happy, as it most certainly should. What all artists dream of is that their work should finally hang together, that it should carry its own signature without having to be signed. And of whom can we say this more confidently than of you, whose handwriting is present in every line you draw?

Here's to you, Thoreau, and greetings

BARKER FAIRLEY

Autobiographical Note

My earliest memory is of being wheeled in a go-cart along High Park Avenue through the pines and oaks. It was a rough ride as the sidewalk was of pine planks laid crossways. My nurses were twins of about ten years who helped my mother around the house. But how happy I was bumping along through the sunny open woods full of flowers and bushes never seen now. There were only three houses on the street then, Thompson's and Cook's on the east, Murdoch's on the west. The Murdoch house was almost like a farm with a wooden windmill tower and barn. Of the family I remember only Lloyd and Marjory, teenagers of exceptional gentleness and kindness. At the end of the Avenue was Bloor Street, another sandy trail through the bush, and beyond that High Park, the most beautiful and unique area in the world, without exception. It was a real foretaste of Heaven and only a few realized the wonders of this piece of land. One was Professor E.M. Walker, who was later a firm friend to me. He said that a German had made a study of the Park, never translated. Bloor Street between Dundas and the Humber River was a sandy three-track trail, one for the horse and two for the wheels. As I remember, there were not more than four houses in that whole distance, mostly small cabins in the woods though there was a little farm on the south side of Bloor with a few cleared fields. High Park itself showed traces of old furrows but must have proved too sandy for farming. The open spaces were covered thick with lupines, many acres of them, a beautiful poor-land flower.

West of High Park Avenue was another sandy trail, Quebec Avenue, running through more oak and mostly red pine. About half a mile north of the Park was a neat little roughcast house on an acre of land where my parents lived after their marriage, complete with a collie dog and cat and rent of $12 monthly. They lived there when I was born though that event took place in the Toronto General hospital. My mother always said that by ten months I could walk and talk and was already exploring the woods with my father. I said I wasn't tired but loved it out there with the trees and little flowers and leaves. And no wonder, with the fields of lupines and, among the trees, columbines, wild geraniums, anemones, hepaticas, blood root and, under the pine shade, yellow moccasin flowers.

After a few years my father bought a lot a few rods farther north on the east side of the road. I remember watching while he cut a few trees that were in the way. He designed the house himself and a local carpenter built it for $500. It was torn down for apartments about 1968. A little to the north was an old house and small red barn, a real miniature farm with two cows, lots of chickens and ducks and a potato patch. Here lived a very old couple, Mr Tomlinson, a veteran of the war between the States, and Mrs T, a tiny but fiery and determined old lady with advanced religious notions. She spent lots of time in the woods gathering pine cones for fuel. While our house was building we lived in a tent. It had a floor and was warm and I remember how the roof was weighed down by the snow. But we were soon in our first house with a furnace and even running water. However, local people didn't like to drink the water as it came from the lake and they knew Toronto's sewage discharged there. We children were sent to one of the fine springs nearby and carried home water in covered tin pails. I went with a young girl neighbour who kept a maternal eye on me and she once impressed me by whirling the full pail around her head minus the cover and without spilling a drop. When my father came home he explained how centrifugal force pressed the water into the pail.

All this time my father was working at Grip Ltd, walking through the woods to Dundas Street where a car ran out to Toronto Junction, a little town in itself. I should have said how carefully my father answered childish questions on all sorts of subjects, among them Halley's Comet which was passing about that time. I remember him explaining evolution and how features are developed by use and need. I said, 'But I thought everyone knew that.' It seemed so obvious and we could almost see it happening.

Directly opposite lived an English plasterer and his daughter, a gentle oppressed young woman and a friend of my mother. The father once needlessly shot an owl in front of the house and so started my lifelong prejudice against the English. Westward through the woods, on what is called Gothic Avenue, a family named Peel was living in a little shack while they built themselves a fine solid brick house. Mr Peel did most of the work himself on weekends, hammering and sawing on Sunday, and this wasn't approved by some neighbours. Besides he was said to be a socialist but my father seemed to approve both these activities. Anyhow, Mrs P and the three children were all fine people and I still think of them with affection wherever they may be. Before going further west I should speak of Scott's Bush, a very beautiful piece of level land with trees, mostly pine and just thick enough to let grass and flowers grow beneath. It was about one-half by one-quarter mile in area and just east of High Park Avenue. It belonged to the Scott family who had a few cows and sold milk. Their pretty daughter Maggie often herded the cattle, elegantly dressed in white and assisted by a couple of experienced cattle dogs. Near their place on Pacific Avenue was our only store where we went when we were allowed a cent (never more) to spend. Either a long bag of popcorn with a prize or else a licorice plug were the best values.

When I was about three we spent two years in England. Some young Canadians started a commercial art business in London, The Carlton Studio. It was very successful and they persuaded my father to work with them for a time. We lived in Loughton near Epping Forest and the ancient trees and Roman remnants were impressive. But we were all glad to return to Canada, and when at last we were driving home from Toronto Junction how I rejoiced at the sight of a little snow and thin ice by the roadside.

My father returned to Grip Ltd and to his weekend attempts at painting and I to the company of the loved pine, oak, and sassafras trees. These last were common and we children ate the leaves like young moose. I never saw them elsewhere in the Toronto area and I think High Park to be near their northern limit in America.

At Christmas an uncle in the States sent me what would now be called a comic book, the title, *Little Johnnie and the Teddy Bears.* Every page had six pictures and a verse for each. By the association of verse and picture I soon learned to read and began to look around for other literature. The largest in sight were some big black volumes of Carlyle's *French Revolution* but I made no progress there. Then I made a start on Tolstoi's *Death of Ivan Ilyitch.* Once past the gloomy title story I really got going on 'Ivan the Fool,' 'Where Love Is, God Is,' and so on. This was the first book I remember reading and to me it has remained Scripture ever since.

Then I found an old school prize of my father's, called *The Three Trappers* and though it was nothing as literature I read it many times. If children want to read try to get them something worthwhile. About this time another power came into our life: music, one of the few signs of the divine in man. We had had a Bowmanville Organ on which my mother played hymns, but now my father bought, second-hand, a little gramophone with a horn and fox terrier pictured on it, also a few old records. By some miracle one of these happened to be *La Marseillaise*, the first real music I ever heard. What sounds to break forth in our kitchen and how pleased Rouget de Lisle must have been at the effect on us. The old records also included Schubert's *Erl König*, and they were my introduction to music. I could never learn to play or even understand music; I'm only a listener but still a good one.

By now I had started to attend Annette Street School but can't remember learning anything there though the teachers were conscientious and kind. My whole being was taken up in wandering through the beautiful country soon to be destroyed forever – although I didn't realize this. My father and grandfather and I nearly always took Sunday walks to the Humber and seldom met anyone the whole way from our house to the Old Mill, then in such a shakey state that my father wouldn't let me enter its high roofless walls, though the cows did and came to no harm.

On the way we passed the old Kennedy Farm, a mysterious tract of perhaps one hundred acres, and completely surrounded by a high board fence, the board set diagonally. We never once entered though in many places we could have crawled under. But in those days a fence meant keep out. A little stream ran the whole length of the farm and there had been a mill-pond where tradition said someone had drowned. But the dam was long since washed out in what I now think must have been the great Galveston storm of September 1900. Along the creek I found great chunks of masonry that looked as mysterious as ruined castles in the forest. Probably they were remains of bridges and culverts washed there by the same storm. This creek emptied into the north end of Grenadier Pond, a body of water worth a whole book to itself. We had a good view from Bloor Street, down the length of the Pond and beyond to the boundless horizon of Lake Ontario.

By the Humber we hunted for fossils and in spring watched the sucker fishers with their dip nets. In the river valley was a little abandoned farm house, quite fancy in design with porches and lattice work. We always took a peek in but it was empty except that on a shelf stood one of those sloping covered dishes for holding cheese, all gilded blue and gold. It stayed there as long as I remember and I never saw a window broken or anything damaged. How different it would be now.

A good part of my indoor life was a hunt for something to read. The few books I owned were second-rate classics like *Black Beauty*, or *Bevis*, and a volume or two of the *Boys Own* paper. Other kids lent me *Chatterbox* and other odds and ends. My grandfather MacDonald gave me an informative and well-illustrated book, thick and solid, called *All About Ships* and I often consult it still.

All this time since I was about two I had been drawing, filling hundreds of Eaton's 2 for 5¢ scribblers and this not because I liked drawing but because I wanted pictures of horses and boats even if I had to make them myself. Ninety per cent of all my drawings were horses. My ambition was to own a real horse but I never did though I got to know what they looked like and what they were thinking. My early drawings were no better than average but interest in the subject, observation, and practice improved them.

But by now the shadow of the population increase began to darken the sunny open woods, so my parents decided to move farther east where the land was settled and built up and my mother wouldn't have to watch the trees and flowers destroyed. I didn't like this move and returned nearly every day to see the woods and my old friends. I kept contact with some of them for many years and often wish I could find them again but haven't been able to do so.

Our new house stood high on a big lot and far to the southwest I could see a favourite red pine in High Park. I read more and more and coaxed my father to bring books from the library in the city. There were none locally. We had an old *Cassell's Concise Encyclopedia.* I studied all it contained on pulleys, levers, lenses, and telescopes, but more reading was coming my way. I had started at Western Avenue School but seemed to get nowhere. My father heard of a private school run on modern lines by a French lady, Miss Elise Guillet, and sent me there hoping I would learn some French as well as ordinary subjects. Miss Guillet was a kind and advanced teacher, a great lover of nature and some relation to H.D. Thoreau. She had a library of nature books as well as stories by Charles G.D. Roberts, and Ernest Thompson Seton. This was a paradise for me and I began going to school earlier and earlier, then spending the time reading. Miss Guillet encouraged me in this and never seemed to think my early attendance a nuisance. Of the other pupils I remember best a brother and sister, Bruce and Helen. Their last name I'm sorry to have forgotten. Helen, an intense little blonde, took a great interest in nature and had a passion for knowing and learning. She was full of reckless daring and would climb trees or ride her sleigh down the steepest, most dangerous hills, missing the trees by inches. All this time I was getting through Miss Guillet's nature books, especially Seton's. He lasted by far the best, and is popular even in Russia. What an achievement is his *Life Histories of Northern Animals*, the best book of its kind ever written.

About this time my father thought it might be good for me to live in a larger family and not as an only child. I went to cousins of my mother's, the Hardy family on a farm near Oakwood. Four of the boys and two girls were still at home so with the parents and hired man we were ten in all. It was a real old time Ontario household, family prayers, hard work, and a few simple pleasures. Profanity was never heard except perhaps from Jack James in the seclusion of the horse stable. Smoking and drinking were never even thought of.

In the fall, I and the youngest boy Willy, just my age, started off for school, a walk of about a mile and a half, along a snake-fenced road with many stone piles and big limestone erratics. There were about thirty children in school and our teacher was Miss Pepper, a girl in her first year of teaching and an idealistic and conscientious teacher who had a good effect on us all. She made us keep a daily weather record and from her I learned systematic observation and kept up my record for about forty years. We often forgot to notice the wind direction and relied on a little girl named Ruby from a farm just across the road: 'Ruby, which way was your windmill pointing?'

But we had Miss Pepper with us only one winter for next summer she went on a holiday to BC and was drowned. About this time my father got to know Dr J.M. MacCallum and we began to visit Georgian Bay where he had a couple of houses and several big islands. This was an important part of my life and education. Dr MacCallum gave me my first rifle, a single shot 22 Stevens model 1915. I fired thousands of rounds but not at living targets and though I retained my liking for firearms I never killed anything. But I could hit a cent at forty feet and probably no rifle was ever better cared for than that old Stevens. I learned a lot on the Bay and have drawn on that experience ever since, as well as the log drive on Gull River near Coboconk.

When I was about sixteen my father had a severe collapse and as he slowly recovered I tried to help him with his work in design, especially lettering. I learned from him and tried to teach myself by studying the Trajan Column, the work of Edward Johnston, W.A. Dwiggins, Eric Gill, F.W. Goudy, Percy Smith, and whatever else I could find. Practice was the main thing. I worked on in the old Studio Building for twenty-seven years and did designing of every kind, especially for the Ryerson Press, Toronto, and Dartmouth College in Hanover, NH, where I had been recommended by Carl Schaefer. I specialized in Roman Letters and always thought them the most noble and severe forms devised by man, well suited to express such ideas as 'All things noble are as difficult as they are rare.' After my father died I arranged and illustrated a few of his poems and had them privately printed in small paper books. They were followed by many more on different subjects and of varying merit. I also tried to do something in what is called Fine Art, such as painting, and a few of these are worth saving. A lot of early work, both drawing and painting, is pretentious and affected. It's well said that every one has a certain amount of nonsense they must get out of their system before starting their real work.

My twenty-seven years in the Studio Building were mostly long dreary stretches of T square and drawing board work but I made many good friends and saw the rise and decline of the Group of Seven, a piece of history.

Dr MacCallum was the first of the friends just mentioned who contributed to my life and education in various ways. Mr M. DesBrisay, our lawyer for many years, helped me along my way until his death in 1971. Professor Barker Fairley taught me more than any Arts course and directed my reading to such authors as Hardy, William Barnes, C.M. Doughty, and Cobbett. Dr Arnold Mason repaired my aching teeth and showed me a good example in every way. So did Mr Percy Robertson who also added to my joy in life by giving me a bicycle. I'm glad to have had such friends as Professor Ray Nash of Dartmouth College, C.W. Jefferys, Dr Fred Banting, and Dr Irving Cameron as well as more obscure rural neighbours, kind, upright, and capable. I thank them all.

THOREAU MACDONALD
1971

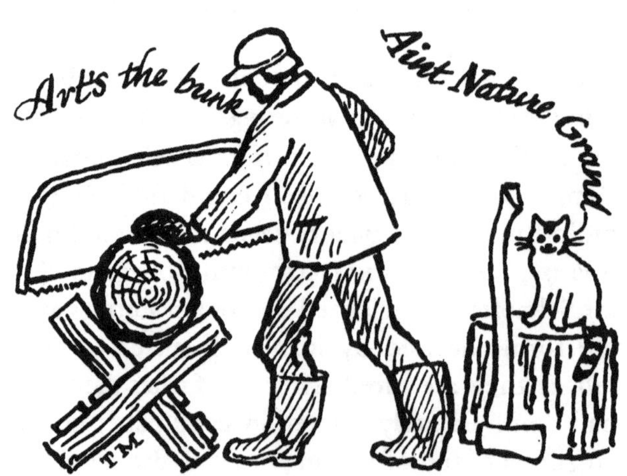

The Work of Thoreau MacDonald

To Thoreau MacDonald the twenty-seven years in the Studio Building may now seem to have been 'long dreary stretches' but the following account of his activity during these years indicates that a vigorous and versatile mind was hard at work.

He painted thirty or forty oils, many watercolours, and hundreds of wash drawings. He made a few woodcuts, many linocuts, some stencils, thousands of line and dry brush drawings, and one design for a steel engraving. Further, the scope of his work includes hundreds of hand-lettered presentation addresses on parchment, certificates of several kinds, labels, bookplates, Christmas cards, and stamp designs. It also includes designs for painted ceilings and mosaic decorations, wrought iron, furniture, lamps, candelabra, decorative stone work, cast bronze lettering, a baby carriage, a soap dispenser, a snow plough, and an invention for removing and replacing the blades of a swede saw. To add to this he has done bronze, wood, and aluminum sculpture, cover designs for garden, book, and art catalogues, posters, colophons, and letterheads including one for his father. In 1922 he designed a full-page Christmas greeting for an Eaton's newspaper advertisement. And during the last war the National Gallery commissioned seven pictures in colours suitable for reproduction within the limitations of the silk-screen process.

Thoreau MacDonald has already referred to the three years his father spent in one of the large commercial studios in London. These years were part of a period of intense interest in private press work and in the revival of calligraphy 'an art more totally lost than fine printing.' Edward Johnston was probably more responsible for this revival than anyone else. It is evident that J.E.H. MacDonald was attracted by these high standards of book decoration and noticeably so by Johnston's contribution. As he grew up Thoreau MacDonald was exposed to these contemporary trends and became highly skilled in all the technical problems of book design. By 1926 he had begun to be a leader in this field in Canada.

The achievements of the private presses in Great Britain and the continent eventually influenced the design of commercial books in Europe, the United States, and to a minor extent in Canada. In this country there was little private press work and the commercial houses varied in their design requirements and printing capabilities. Thoreau therefore had to survive on modest commissions not commensurate with the full scope of his remarkable abilities. Only in a few cases was he allowed the freedom of expression which is accorded to book designers today and even then he was restricted by very small budgets. I suppose it might be argued that in his *Forum* work, begun in 1922, he had plenty of freedom and no budget at all.

With the printing of an eight-page booklet of woodcuts in 1922 he began to experiment with private press work. Three of the woodcuts from that first book appear in his latest privately printed book, *Farm Drawings*, 1971. It is probable that the woodcuts shown in 1924 at the Art Gallery of Toronto were from this small booklet for he made fewer woodcuts than is generally thought. His next private press book, and the first to be produced in any quantity, was not undertaken until 1932, the year he retired from his *Forum* work. The Woodchuck Press books were a genuine participation in the private press movement where author, designer, artist, and printer all come together.

If it could be argued that Thoreau MacDonald was born at the right time but in the wrong place for the most rewarding use, in terms of recognition, of all his skills as a book designer, he was, without doubt born at the right place and at the right time to use his drawing abilities as a visual historian of times past and passing in rural life. These haunting, evocative small pictures of barns and birds, fields and woods, many, but not all, appearing in his private press books, may, in the final analysis, have given him more satisfaction as an artist than anything else he could have done. The tributes of Barker Fairley and E.R. Hunter appearing in other parts of this book seem to agree with this supposition.

However, private press work seldom pays the rent. Thoreau MacDonald had done some designing for many of the commercial publishing houses in Toronto, one in Montreal and another in Ottawa; he began to find that the late Lorne Pierce, editor of the Ryerson Press, was predisposed towards his decorative treatment of books. Despite the fact that he deplored its press work, a good deal of his Canadian work was done for this house, as a long list of titles in this catalogue demonstrates.

His designs for art catalogues had begun to attract attention. The first of these, entirely prepared by him, was for an exhibition in 1926 at the Art Gallery of Toronto entitled The Group of Seven and Art in French Canada. For this he used a stylized pine tree which he repeated as a motif for the label of the *Portfolio of Prints* by members of the Group of Seven. This design turned up again in the same year as the cover stamp for *A Canadian Art Movement* by F.B. Housser and still later in 1964 as the cover stamp for Lawren Harris' book on the Group of Seven. The usual device associated with the Group of Seven is a design by Carmichael – but in the Housser book both are used. The demand for catalogue covers increased

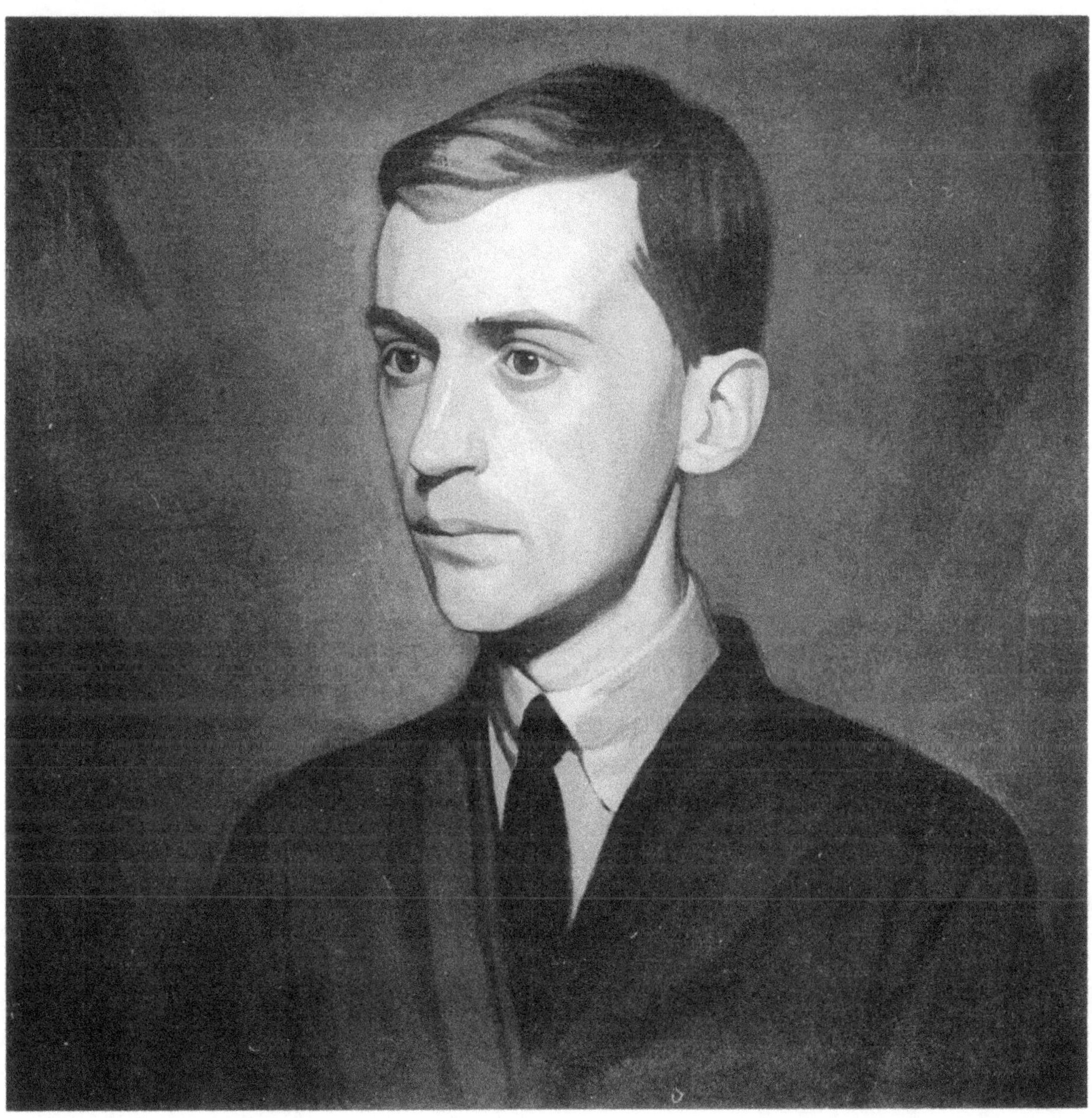

Lawren Harris: portrait of Thoreau MacDonald

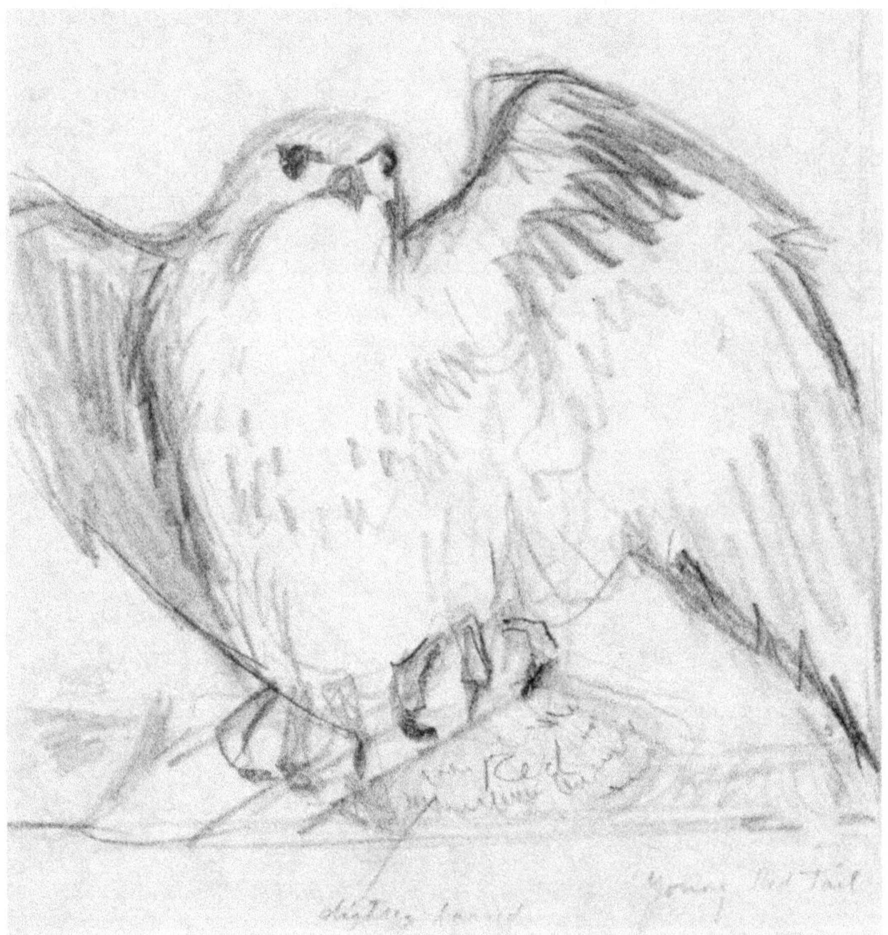

Young Red Tail, drawing, undated

and requests for periodical cover designs kept pace. These are listed and some are illustrated in sections B and D of the catalogue.

As an admirer (and namesake) of Henry David Thoreau he became interested in the thirties in a competition for an illustrated edition of *Walden.* He submitted a layout, ten illustrations and projections for more, eighteen decorated initials, one for each chapter, and the following observations: 'H.D. Thoreau's *Walden* has never yet been successfully illustrated and perhaps never will be. It is perhaps too good a book to illustrate, so packed with sense that the best drawings seem feeble in comparison ...' For some reason, not altogether surprising in the light of the above remarks, his work was not chosen and the whole portfolio is now in a private collection.

By 1934 he had completed three other Woodchuck Press books and at least one of these had come to the particular attention of Charles W. Jefferys. In a letter to him in that year Jefferys says, 'Looking at the little book *A Year on the Farm* again makes me think of our effort of the 1890's, The Art League Calendar. It is gratifying to find that something of the native spirit that led some of us to that venture, seems to reappear, with modern improvements in your booklets. There appears to be a renaissance of interest in *older* Ontario, the hardy north, the Rockies and the Prairies have had a good run: I think it time that Upper Canada should be rediscovered, before it disappears forever. Let the woodchuck continue to dig, and may he find a roomy and comfortable burrow in the New Year.'

In 1938 MacDonald designed and illustrated *Maria Chapdelaine* by Louis Hémon for the Macmillan Company. This he considers his finest book and in his notes are these observations: 'The designs for Maria Chapdelaine do not attempt to show dramatic movement in the story. When illustrating a book so fine as this the designer had better merely accompany the text as harmoniously and unobtrusively as he can and not interrupt the author and reader with his conceptions. The present drawings are an attempt to make a setting or background for the dignity and simplicity of the story and to give some of the feeling of that section of our country.'

Thoreau received many compliments for his work on this book and he had had the satisfaction of having his high standards of design and printing met by the equally high standards of Rous and Mann under the supervision of Albert Robson. There were letters from many parts of the world after the success of *Maria Chapdelaine* and one from his artist friend in England, Thomas Hennell, comments on its reception there and also on the reaction of artists in Britain to the exhibition in 1938 at the Tate Gallery called A Century of Canadian Art in which Thoreau's oil *Ermine*, purchased by the National Gallery of Canada in 1939, and *Owl and Jay*, in the collection of Ray Nash, New Hampshire, were shown. 'There was a bracing air about the exhibition ... and your paintings were greatly admired.'

In 1939 he was asked to design a special binding for *Canadian Landscape Painters* by A.H. Robson. Along with examples of fine binding from 11 other countries, this was shown at the Golden Gate International Exposition in San Francisco. For this event the Grabhorn Press issued the official catalogue. The design for the binding for the Robson book, handsome in its simplicity and with end papers of birch bark, was carried out by the Ryerson Press.

In the same year Thoreau designed the catalogue for an exhibition entitled Tom Thomson and J.E.H. MacDonald and wrote an introduction for it. He had also written an introduction for the 1933 Memorial Exhibition of the work of J.E.H. MacDonald shown at both the Art Gallery of Toronto and the National Gallery. In 1940 he designed E.R. Hunter's *J.E.H. MacDonald: A Biography and Catalogue of His Work.* For this he also wrote an introduction as he again would do for the J.E.H. MacDonald Exhibition in the Art Gallery in Hamilton in 1957.

In 1941 he was the subject of an article by E.R. Hunter in the Canadian periodical, *Maritime Art.* This was expanded in 1942 in book form with the title *Thoreau MacDonald* and, as I have already indicated, it represents the only critical appraisal of his work of any length. I felt that it would be useful here to quote some lengthy passages from this book for the kind of appraisal which only an art historian can give. Since 1942 Thoreau MacDonald has, of course, added substantially to his canon, as the catalogue reflects. A list of exhibitions and references to the artist in print further supplement Hunter's primary critical assessment.

> Much has been said about J.E.H. MacDonald's love for Henry David Thoreau and of his son's admiration for his namesake ... Thoreau MacDonald has never lost touch with the New Englander's teaching, and still reads and regards him as a source book of truth and inspiration. He loathes cant and artificiality, as did his namesake, and grows caustic over much that passes for Art and Society. That is not to say that he is shirking his chance to use his talents for the common good. On the contrary, he is a leader among those who try to show us what we are missing in rushing headlong from a simpler life, without having anything better to replace it. In a self-centred age, where everyone is ready to talk, but no one to listen, he has listened and profited thereby, for he recognizes in rural life and all that goes with it the real wealth and strength of our nation ...
>
> MacDonald's sensitive mind rebels at blatant propaganda, but in his work and particularly in his Woodchuck Press booklets, written and illustrated by himself, he has tried to save for us in telling form many fine elements of this passing life that he thinks are worth preserving. Nor is this mere conservatism, for he is in no way against progress; he merely protests against destruction and change for themselves alone. In the same way he is against the wanton slaughter of wild life. He has always been particularly interested in birds of prey, in hawks and owls, for he well understands their essential place in nature, and he revolts at the persecution of these valuable birds, now fast disappearing. Here again his sensitive drawings represent his protest against this wilful destruction. And so it happens that we have some of the loveliest drawings of bird life in Canada ...
>
> It has already been said that Thoreau MacDonald began his life as an artist in 1922. In February of that year there appeared in an issue of *The Canadian Forum* a series of three linoleum cuts showing a horse, a squirrel and a rabbit. His first published work, they are well designed and show a keen observation and, incidentally, form an interesting introduction to the work that follows. Some time after this, pen drawings began to appear in the *Forum*; it was not long before the cover was designed by him and a new drawing prepared

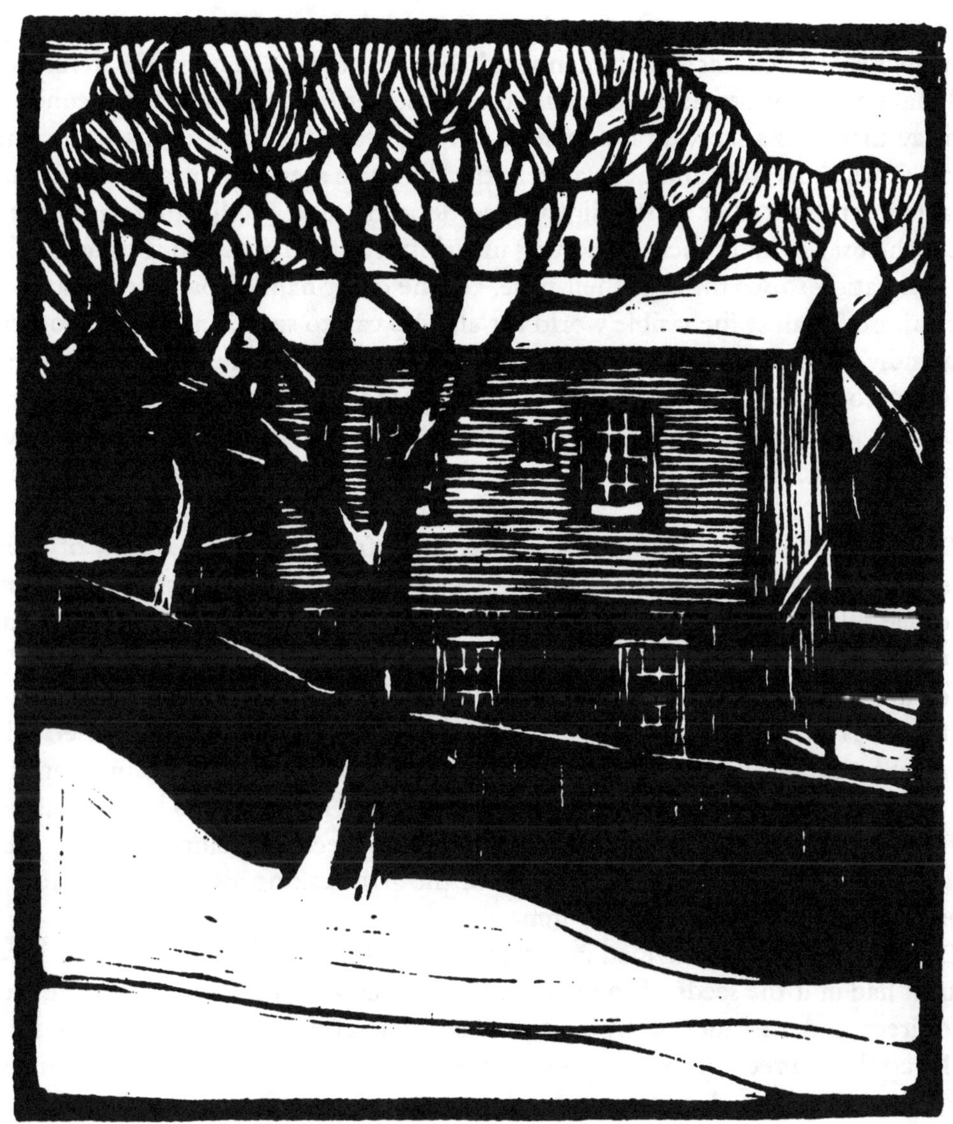

View from the Studio Building, linocut, undated

each month for it. A collection of these drawings is a fascinating record of the artist's development in thought and style, of the things that interested him and stimulated his creative powers. MacDonald says that he is an observer, and so he is. He will spend hours watching animals or birds, for a walk to him is one of the most interesting experiences in life, while his daily contacts with man yield countless details that appear in his drawings and make them authentic. MacDonald is an observer first and an artist second. This is not to say that he is a second-rate artist; it simply means that he uses his art as a means of putting down accurately and persuasively the things he sees and likes. He is not an intellectual painter, but rather an intelligent recorder of nature. Intellectual painters sometimes fool themselves and others by setting up arbitrary standards, and it usually takes another generation to see through their pose. On the other hand, a painter of nature measures himself against the visible world for all who can to see ... Integrity, good craftsmanship, individuality and good taste all help to make a good picture, but the power to stir the spectator, to tell him something worth knowing or to give him something stimulating to think about are all signs of a good artist as well. MacDonald has all these qualities and something more besides – a vitality and a singleness of purpose that place him near to genius.

MacDonald criticizes his own work almost entirely from the point of view of its accuracy of statement. This is what one would expect from so tireless and close an observer. He will discard drawings that have some minor inaccuracy, such as a badly described axe handle, even though its aesthetic qualities are perfectly good: to him it will not do. The subject comes first always. The art is incidental; it doesn't interest him, but he cannot escape it for it is inherent. Drawing and painting are to MacDonald, as he himself said they were to his father, simply handy ways of expressing his interest in things, or of recording what he wants to remember. Indeed, he says that he illustrates his various booklets with drawings rather than with photographs simply because a zinc block costs less than a half-tone. Here, I think, is an example of the artist taking his place in society without society having to make a place for him.

MacDonald's style can be divided into three parts. His first work was perhaps hardly a style, but it had in it the seeds of the two definite styles which followed, the one growing out of it direct, and the other returning to the beginning for its roots. At first he set down all that he could in direct outline, without any attempt to conventionalize. His instinct for design kept him from cluttering up his drawings with meaningless detail, and the rather attractive simplification that resulted was partly due also to his timidity in attempting anything beyond his means. One of his earliest drawings, *Shingled House*, illustrates this point. As MacDonald's style began to take form, somewhere about 1924, the influence of Rockwell Kent began to appear. It is not a superficial likeness, but an aesthetic kinship, perhaps a similarity of feeling. There is a certain deliberation in the designing, at this time, and a smooth stylization that stem from Kent's work. He left large areas of space and usually drew with a thin tenuous line which gave his work a slightly Oriental emphasis particularly in the design. Indeed, he often added a decorative border below the drawing to heighten the effect. In *Swans and New Snow* and *Loons* this particular phase is well shown. In *Farmhouse: Autumn*, done at the same time (1924), we find a link with his later style. It is still a simple statement of fact, but he has used a bolder line and has handled the house and corn shocks boldly and with distinction. This drawing is one of his finest. It combines the early economy of line with hardly a trace of the stylization that marked much of his work at this time. In fact, except for one or two minor details, it might well have been done ten years later.

Though MacDonald's style crystallized somewhere about 1924, we must realize that such drawings as *Swans and New Snow* were not necessarily the dominant type, but rather representative of one phase of his work, of which another comprises those akin to *Farmhouse: Autumn* and *Harvest*. Drawings of these two phases formed his contribution to the *Forum* covers for several years. In 1927 a dozen of them were selected and reprinted by J.M. Dent & Sons. Seen by themselves, one would hardly believe that they were the work of one who had been drawing less than four years. Indeed, some of the best ones were nearly three years old at the time they were reproduced in this portfolio.

Though pen and ink was his principal medium, even in these early days, he experimented a good deal with others. *Harvest*, for instance, is done with a brush. He also made some wood engravings and lino-cuts, and, while these are less well known, since they reached a smaller market, they show his ability to cut a design out of a dark mass.

Although MacDonald had made a good name for himself with these early drawings, he became tired of this manner and deliberately aimed at a more direct approach to nature. He was too independent to let any influence, however good, hold him long. The rest of the work of these years – the later twenties – shows the gradual development of his present style. Line drawings still predominate, with a few brush drawings and an occasional lino-cut. In his line drawings he began to use a thicker line, filling up his spaces more, and eschewing all traces of conventionalized detail. Henceforth he sought absolute realism, and about 1930 his new style had emerged. It is surer, more solid, and though his choice of subjects has broadened, he is still a defender of the simple life, and a believer in the right of all things to live in their own way. Good examples of this transitional style are such drawings as *Chickadees* and *Northern Cabin*. They are both reed pen drawings, done in 1928. In the former some of the old spacing is used, but the stylization has gone, while in the latter MacDonald has crowded a number of detailed observations and, although some stylization is evident, the whole drawing has a new feeling. It is darker, perhaps less precious. *Pioneer Graves* is a magnificent drawing which combines elements of MacDonald's two basic styles to perfection. The poplar leaves are drawn in the strong but sensitive way in which he did much of his earlier work, but the well-ordered mass of vegetation shows how he has learned to draw, and draw well. This drawing was made in 1930, and is therefore a valuable link in his development ...

His last *Forum* cover, *Rapids at Night*, appeared on the issue for June, 1932, and is one of the best of these later works. It has great freedom of line and a real grasp of the subject, together with a brooding sombreness which the artist himself likes ... When he dropped out of the *Forum* in June, 1932, he had no field for his work other than ordinary commercial work and commissions to design or illustrate books: fortunately these increased.

Shortly after this time the idea of supplying his own field took form, and The Woodchuck Press came into being. One of the first publications of this new venture was a pamphlet entitled *A Few of the Old Gates at Thornhill.* Although there are no figures in the full-page drawings of this booklet, one seems to feel the presence of human beings in each one. With no loss of artistic sensibility, these drawings are also a fine record of some of the best carpenter's skill, which at one time abounded in our country towns ... Another pamphlet, called *A Year on the Farm* (1934), contains a collection of old rural sayings once current in Ontario and elsewhere. There is one for each month, accompanied by a suitable drawing from farm life. Many a city dweller will smile as he recalls such old adages as 'A Year of snow makes Apples grow,' or 'All signs of Rain fail in a dry Spell.' But best of all are the little drawings which capture so exquisitely the scenes of farm life that many know so well. Still another pamphlet is *Some Tools of the Pioneers.* While it is more frankly a record of old implements once used on the farm, there is no loss of beauty in the general lay-out of the work. It contains a group of drawings of such equipment as could be found on any farm in former days, together with little vignettes showing how some of them were used. Here I think is the proof of the statement, already made, that MacDonald is using his art (his craft, as he calls it) to persuade us to pause and consider a little before sweeping away everything in the name of material progress ...

Thoreau MacDonald as a craftsman has a role of importance. His father found in E.J. Hathaway, an official of a Toronto printing concern, the challenge and encouragement that he needed to design outstanding books, and Thoreau has followed this lead in designing a series of books which stands out as a beacon in a sea of clumsy type, arty paper, hideous covers, and inept ornaments. His knowledge of types, paper, and layout has kept him abreast of the times, though he has never lost his individuality. A book designed by him is recognizable at a glance, yet rarely seems dated. One of his earliest commissions was to design and illustrate *The Chopping Bee, and other Laurentian Stories*, by M. Victorin (1925). For this book MacDonald made a dozen illustrations in wood-cut style which have a naive charm. They are particularly interesting today, not only for themselves and their position in MacDonald's work, but as an early experiment which culminated thirteen years later in the collection of drawings of French Canadian life which he made to illustrate *Maria Chapdelaine.* An even more comprehensive piece of work dates from the year 1925. MacDonald was called upon to design and illustrate a gift book of verses by D.A. Dunlap called *Shahwandagooze Days*, which was privately published under the supervision of Hathaway. It is a fine mature example of book production, and would be much better known were it not for its limited circulation.

In 1927 the Booksellers' and Stationers' Convention was held in Toronto and a Committee of Three was appointed to select the twelve best-produced Canadian books of the last few years. No less than four of these were the work of Thoreau MacDonald. Nor did this extraordinary feat include the book of verses mentioned above. The earliest of the four was *The Chopping Bee*, followed by *Lyrics of Earth*, by Archibald Lampman, also published in 1925. The design of Lampman's book is listed as the work of his father, to whom the commission was given, but it was in fact carried out by Thoreau. There are other instances of Thoreau helping his father with work of this kind, though there was much less of it than one might expect from two artists who shared their studio ... The third of these selected books, his best known of this time, is F.B. Housser's *A Canadian Art Movement*, which was first published in 1926. This book was designated by the Committee as the one which had achieved the greatest harmony and unity of design. For this book MacDonald made the jacket (which he adapted from A.Y. Jackson's bookplate for Mr Housser), the cover, end-papers, and title-page, together with the general layout and design. The last of these books was *The Poems of Duncan Campbell Scott*, published in 1927. There is no need to minimize this astonishing achievement by recalling the general state of book design in Canada at this time, for the books are still available for judgment ... It is also of interest to note that the portfolio of his pen drawings which was published in this year, 1927, received Honourable Mention from the same Committee of selection. The next book illustrated by him, *Indian Nights*, by Isabel Eccleston Mackay, included also ten illustrations and a frontispiece. When a few of his father's poems were published posthumously, in 1933, MacDonald had another opportunity to design and execute a book throughout, and *West by East* is the happy outcome of this tribute to his father. In the following years he designed and in some cases illustrated a few other volumes of verse, among the best of which are *The Iceberg* by Sir Charles G.D. Roberts, *The Leather Bottle* by Theodore Goodridge Roberts, and *The Complete Poems by Francis Sherman.* The change in his style which has already been discussed is noticeable in these last four books, and the final culmination can be seen in the illustrations for *Maria Chapdelaine*, published in 1938. The illustrations for this work have a great feeling and intensity and show profound grasp of the spirit of the book. They are exciting not only as illustrations, but as works of art in themselves. Another fine piece of book production is the writer's life of his father, published in 1940 ...

Thoreau MacDonald, as we have seen, has no aesthetic snobbery: quite the reverse. To him there is no distinction to be made between fine and commercial art. In fact, he doesn't worry about art at all. Commercial art is important to him because it helps to pay the bills, though his charges for his work would lead one to doubt the efficacy of this method of income. No commission is too insignificant for him, and each one receives his best care. His range has been wide, going from bottle labels to university diplomas, from business cards and soap-wrappers to memorial tablets, and from designs for wrought iron to mural decoration. His lettering in particular is to be noticed. He rarely fails to produce a beautiful effect with his lines of letters, and when necessary he works them into his design with unfailing grace. His cover for one of the catalogues for the Canadian Art Exhibit at the New York World Fair, in 1939, is a most arresting piece of design which illustrates this point to perfection.

The cartoons which he made for the lobby ceiling of the Concourse Building, Adelaide

Street, Toronto (Baldwin & Greene, Architects), were drawn up from small sketches, and they are now in the possession of Carl Schaefer, who carried out the actual painting on the ceiling. Unfortunately the final painting has been covered over and there is nothing now left to judge these works by except these cartoons.* The ceiling became dirty, and rather than clean them the authorities took the easiest way out and destroyed them. The various figures of animals and flowers that made up the design were more stylized than MacDonald usually made them at this time, but they were eminently suitable for their task. Somewhat earlier than this Thoreau MacDonald worked on a commission which had been given to his father to supervise – the designing and decorating of St Anne's Church in Toronto – and it included seven paintings for the chancel. Two of these, St Anne and St George, are the work of Thoreau MacDonald.

MacDonald's earlier work, as we have seen, pointed out the beauty of the subject for us, by underlining its design, while his later work assumes that we are able to see it for ourselves. In all his work, early or late, there is a fine balance of interests: nothing is out of place, and there is nothing too much. In his drawings, his line is not in itself sensitive, but in remarking this we simply remove him from that class of artists who gain their effects by the quality of their line, a class which harbours many a virtuoso. MacDonald draws his line firmly and it says exactly what he means it to say. Good design, a sure balance of masses, a flair for significant detail and capable handling all go to make up his pictures. They are not just representations of things we know, but things filtered through his subtle personality to become experiences we can share with him. Thoreau MacDonald is an individualist of considerable courage and singleness of purpose. He is not a modernist in the international sense, nor is he an archaic survival. He is an individual of remarkable strength and penetration, and his strength is not based on a search for novelty. He often reworks old subjects, for as a searcher for truth he depends on simple themes. He has never cared for a quick reputation, nor has he made any effort to acquire honours or recognition. He is not gregarious, though he enjoys good company and behind his apparent shyness there is a hard core of independence and integrity. He will retreat from superficial things, but his opinions are simple and definite, and he will never give in. These characteristics and the discipline of long work and observations have made him one of the most forceful, unassuming and genuine characters in the Canadian world of art. [E.R.H.]

By 1942 MacDonald was corresponding with two new artist friends in the United States: Ray Nash, professor of art at Dartmouth College, and the late Norman Kent, then editor of *American Artist.*

Ray Nash is undoubtedly responsible for the amount of work Thoreau MacDonald has done for circulation in the United States. It is evident that MacDonald's sense of design and lettering greatly appealed to this discriminating artist who commissioned drawings for a variety of purposes, including vignettes and heraldic designs for college publications. Some of

*TM's mosaics forming five of the seven soffit panels of the main entrance arch were undamaged in 1972. MEE

these are in use today. He was asked to design a commemorative bookplate for the hymnal in the College chapel; about this design Thoreau wrote, 'I am sending a couple of rough layouts for your bookplate. A rope is a difficult object – what to do with the ends.'

In 1946 an unsigned review of *A Specimen Book of Cuts used by the Woodchuck Press* appeared in *Print: Quarterly Journal of the Graphic Arts*: 'The small but growing band of enthusiastic collectors of The Woodchuck Press output will be delighted with this group of forty drawings from the pen and brush of Mr Thoreau MacDonald. But joy turns to consternation at the news that, when other furtive presses are emerging to relax in the free post-war air, the contrary Woodchuck is going underground to sleep. Mr MacDonald, the Toronto designer who seems to be the Woodchuck's sole channel of expression, gives a glimmer of hope. He writes of a possible reappearance "on some future Groundhog Day." The extraordinary skill of the artist in drawing for reproduction (his illustrations for *Maria Chapdelaine* published by Macmillan of Toronto a few years ago are outstanding examples) and his insight into the human meanings of commonplace things cast a spell over the tools, gates, farmyards, and animals which are the subjects of this little book without words (except for an occasional handsomely-lettered caption). The cover is a printed wrapper showing the Woodchuck alert, sprig of clover in mouth – a good augury.'

In 1962 the cover of the Dartmouth College Year Book, *Aegis*, was designed by MacDonald and two name plates for the undergraduate newspaper, *The Dartmouth*, were drawn of which one at least was used. Cover designs for *Print* were also commissioned. MacDonald was well suited to draw the American eagle and was again commissioned by Nash to produce it as a headpiece. This forceful design was used for several purposes and in 1950 it appeared on the cover of *Thoreau MacDonald's Drawings for Dartmouth*, a delightful small booklet with notes by Ray Nash which was, as he says, 'the first attempt of Roderick D. Stinehour, now Master of the Stinehour Press, Lunenburg, Vermont.'

To generations of students Professor Nash cited Thoreau MacDonald's drawings as an example of a quality that defies poor printing. As he wrote in *Drawings for Dartmouth*, 'Like all of Thoreau MacDonald's work in reproduction, it can hold its own in actual or reduced size and comes through clean and fresh no matter by what process.' There is an understandable empathy between these two artists and some of Thoreau MacDonald's most vivid lettering has been done for Ray Nash. Their correspondence is evidence of Nash's continuing encouragement long after the Severn Street Studio had been given up in 1949.

His exchange of ideas with Norman Kent, another expert in the field of design and illustration, resulted in Kent's major article in the January 1946 issue of *American Artist*: 'Thoreau MacDonald, Canadian Illustrator.' In 1965 Kent prepared a second article, beginning it by stating: 'For more than twenty years I have enjoyed an intermittent correspondence, an occasional exchange of printed items, with a Canadian whom I have never met, yet a man I feel I know. For when two artists find a community of interest, even if this mutuality is primarily restricted to a technical expression, in this case the decorative embellishment of the printed page, they can pyramid a lot of vicarious experience without getting bogged down in irrelevant trivia. This is the way it has been between Thoreau MacDonald and me, and because I am so sure that he has communicated a certain Northland spirit to those familiar with this work, I want to share at least an echo of it in this text.'

During the war years he finished thirty or so commissions for the Ryerson Press, two of striking effectiveness. One of these is *J.E.H. MacDonald* by E.R. Hunter, 1940, and the other is William Colgate's *Canadian Art*, 1943. It is unfortunate that at this stage in the war good paper had become difficult to find and the brittle and yellowing pages of *Canadian Art* attest to the fact. In 1944 MacDonald wrote *The Group of Seven*, now in its tenth edition. He produced no private press books during the war. In 1944 *Mountain Cloud* by Marius Barbeau was published by the Macmillan Company with thirty-two drawings some of which Thoreau MacDonald agrees are 'not bad.' Five of these are in the Agnes Etherington Art Centre at Queen's University, Kingston. Barbeau inscribed a copy, 'To Thoreau MacDonald who has made this book as I wished it. All my gratefulness.'

The Canadian poet, Duncan Campbell Scott, asked MacDonald to design and illustrate his *Village of Viger*, published in 1945, and to 'make it look as much like Maria Chapdelaine as possible.' An examination of the two books will show how similar in style they are. Two years later, in 1947, Duncan Campbell Scott suggested that MacDonald design another book for him. This was *Circle of Affection* with ten vignettes and a jacket design which again pleased both the artist and the writer.

MacDonald's work was by this time well known to members of the American Institute of Graphic Arts, some of whom had doubtless studied at Dartmouth. 'All my students are unfailing enthusiasts' Nash recently wrote in a note to the author. He had also brought Thoreau MacDonald to the attention of the American writer Henry Beston. In 1946 the American Institute of Graphic Arts held an exhibition of International Book Illustration (1935-45) in New York City. The catalogue shows the Canadian entry as *Wendigo Pursuing the Trespassing Hunter*, one of the Chapdelaine illustrations.

In 1949 the recently founded Book Jacket Designers Guild Inc. held its second annual exhibition in the A-D Gallery in New York. The work of all American book publishers and designers was eligible and Rinehart submitted their jacket for *Northern Farm* by Henry Beston which was designed by MacDonald and published in 1948. The exhibition was circulated in the United States by the American Federation of Arts in Washington. For *Northern Farm* Thoreau MacDonald had made forty-seven drawings; in the following year another fourteen illustrated *The McKenzie*, also published by Rinehart.

In 1949 Thoreau gave up his studio at Severn Street and made the house at Thornhill his base. He continued to provide layout and design for the Ryerson Press until the retirement of Lorne Pierce in 1960. Three examples of the work of this period should be mentioned. The first, *The Rocking Chair* by A.M. Klein, had already been designed by MacDonald. In 1951 the book was reprinted with the addition of vignettes. The artist enjoyed making these little semi-abstract designs so unlike the rest of his decorative work and has commented, 'the author liked them too.' The second is *Hurt Not the Earth* by E. Newton White, 1958; included in it are some illustrations published in *Woods and Fields*, 1951, in which there is a note 'the following drawings are from a set of forty for an unpublished book on Canada's resources.' The third is *Country Hours* by Clarke Locke, 1959. In this book there are sixty-three drawings, eighteen of which are in the Vancouver Art Gallery, the London Art Gallery, and the National Gallery, Ottawa.

A good friend, the late Dr E.M. Walker, at this time professor emeritus of Zoology, University of Toronto, and honorary curator, Royal Ontario Museum, wrote, in a letter following the publication of *Country Hours*:

> I certainly don't know of anyone else who can approach you in pen-and-ink drawing of farm scenes and the animals, wild and domestic, that are seen there. Cows coming along a road, foxes, groundhogs, or just a bit of winter landscape with a bird or two on a fence or stump. The dead winter grass, spring pools, I am not articulate enough to tell how I feel about all these things. But I know you are the only person whose work gives me complete satisfaction.
>
> Once you had the idea you only made drawings as records, factual records, that you wanted to have. I knew you were absolutely sincere but I didn't believe and still don't believe you were analysing your motives correctly. But never mind that. You can do it magnificently ...
>
> I just had to tell you how I feel about your work. It is finer than ever.

It should be noted that the following are regarded by the artist as 'some better designed and illustrated commercial books': *Maria Chapdelaine* 1938, *J.E.H. MacDonald* 1940, *Village of Viger* 1945, *Green Fields Afar* 1947, *Northern Farm* 1948, *The Mackenzie* 1949, *The Rocking Chair* 1951, *Hurt Not the Earth* 1958, and *Country Hours* 1959.

An unrecorded exhibition of bird and animal drawings by Thoreau MacDonald was shown in the Natural History Section of the Royal Ontario Museum. Carl Schaefer, then an instructor at the Ontario College of Art, took his students to see them because, as he later wrote: 'I considered these drawings to be of an extraordinary fine quality, universal in character, and as I pointed out to my class, no doubt they were anatomically accurate and shown in their natural environment, but ... they communicated life itself and should be considered as original and creative works of art, not to be confused with work by many popular wildlife artists of the time.'

There have been two major exhibitions of Thoreau MacDonald's work. One originated in London, Ontario, in 1952 at the London Public Library and Art Museum and from there toured a number of western Canadian cities. The other was held in Hanover, NH, in 1967 in honour of Canada's centennial year, at the Barrows Print Room in Hopkins Center, Dartmouth College. For the exhibition in London, Thoreau wrote the following prefatory remarks:

> Line drawing has one advantage over other means of graphic expression. It's cheaper to print. But it's limited, troublesome to execute, and to most people has little interest compared to halftone or colour. It's possible by very fine lines and other forms of minute penwork to almost equal a halftone or photo. But this is more or less a degradation of true

line drawing, which should be marked by the apparent simplicity and decision of a well handled axe or scythe.

A line drawing is something like a blueprint or like shorthand; it has its symbols and conventions and these should be accepted to get its meaning. The draftsman tries, with these few marks and lines to indicate all the forms and colours of land, water and sky, humans and animals, buildings, rocks, trees and snow, the variations in spruce and cedar, granite and limestone, elm and maple. He may use black areas, outline, parallel lines, cross-hatching and white paper, but with these elements he tries to represent the visible world.

The present drawings are shown only as a few chips left after thirty years of hacking away at the problems of line drawing. They are feeble reminders of reality, the farms and woods, swamps and brush of the author's native country.

In 1964 he designed and provided illustrations and a chapter of reminiscences for a privately printed book *Thornhill: An Ontario Village* by Doris M. FitzGerald and in 1970 he designed another book by Mrs FitzGerald, *Old Time Thornhill*, which included drawn illustrations and photographs taken by the artist. His Christmas card designs have been noticed in the *Forum*, September 1924, in *American Artist*, December 1966, and in an exhibit in Newfoundland at the Art Gallery, Memorial University, in 1970. Some of these designs are reproduced in the catalogue.

He is represented in the permanent collections of the following galleries: the National Gallery of Canada; the Art Gallery of Ontario; the McMichael Conservation Collection of Art; the Art Gallery of Hamilton; the London Public Library and Art Museum; the Winnipeg Art Gallery; the Vancouver Art Gallery; McGill University (Colgate Collection); the University of

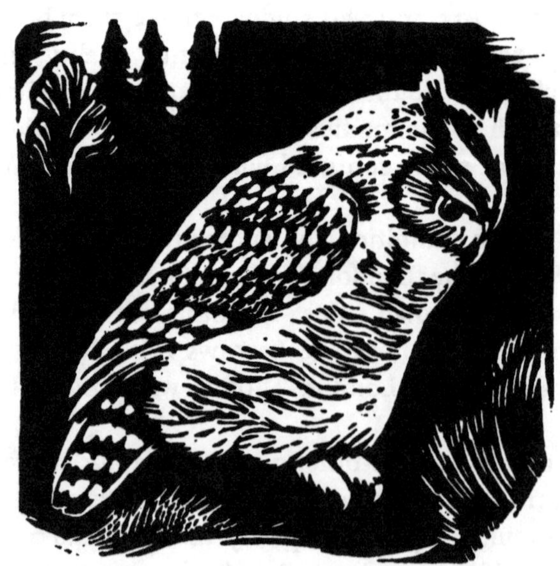

Toronto; Queen's University (Agnes Etherington Art Centre); Upper Canada College (Biriukova Gallery); the Victoria and Albert Museum, London. He is represented in private and corporate art collections, as well as in book collections, both in Canada and the United States.

E.R. Hunter has pointed out that MacDonald has never made any effort for honours or recognition and this is still true. When the Canadian Group of Painters was founded in 1933 with the idea of continuing the tradition of the Group of Seven he was for a short time a member. He resigned as Art Editor of the *Forum* when he felt that his job was done. In 1972 MacDonald was made an Honorary Life Member of the Society of Ontario Naturalists whose cause he has served all his life.

I believe that a pleasing end to this long list of activities and accomplishments, which the artist himself has not chosen to discuss, is to allow Thoreau MacDonald to have the final word. In his journal, 28 May 1946, he writes:

> Helping Mr. Jim Pearson plant spuds.
> A fine evening light on barn and lilacs.
> Team, barn and light seem of the past, also
> Jim himself. When they are gone there'll be
> no trace of that quiet old way of life and
> when I go, no memory of it even.
> So I tried to make some drawings of it
> though writing would be better if it could
> be done.

TM

The Catalogue

Notes on the Catalogue

This catalogue contains two hundred and seventy-six listings. This represents more than a thousand drawings and designs, some two hundred of which are illustrated on the following pages. All the drawings, decorated capital letters, maps, vignettes, and lettering referred to in the catalogue are by Thoreau MacDonald, unless another artist is named. Most of the books and catalogues can be seen in libraries but not, as yet, in one place. Every item listed has been checked with MacDonald. All material in my collection of books is signed and has notations of the particular work done by him. In some cases he has made his opinions quite clear and it is not always favourable.

The catalogue is divided into sections (their contents explained by their titles); entries are listed chronologically with the exception of the periodical section, D, which is listed alphabetically.

The entries are listed in a bibliographical format, but with the emphasis on illustration and decoration. Only a few of the books could be considered rare and there seemed no need to describe them in more detail. Although it will be noticed that there are binding variants, only a small number have been published in special editions or, indeed, in more than one edition. Of that small number Thoreau MacDonald's book, *The Group of Seven*, has sold more than 20,000 copies and has been reprinted nine times. In the case of all books, the edition number is given when known.

Books to which he only contributed the layout and no decoration have not been catalogued. In a few cases his name appears in a book as 'designer.' One example of this somewhat misplaced generosity is E.M. Pomeroy's *Sir Charles G.D. Roberts.* In my copy he has written 'shows no evidence of design.' Occasionally publishers gave him no credit. Sometimes he didn't sign his work with the familiar and very small TM and rarely did he date his work. In one sense it doesn't matter, for, as Barker Fairley has said, his style is so distinctive it doesn't need a signature – although many would agree that dates would have been useful. In many cases his drawings are untitled and the occasional change in the title of a drawing has added piquancy to my research.

Although an interesting study could be made of the colophon or publisher's mark designed by Thoreau MacDonald in such infinite variety, it seemed too detailed for a book of this kind. Devices for his own private press books are, however, reproduced; his preference being for the one with the motto 'ducit amor patriae' which he translates as 'love of country leads me on.'

Items in section A, entitled Artist and Writer, are those considered to be Thoreau MacDonald's own statement, whether drawn or written. Where there is a combination of illustration and written material both are reproduced. This section represents the point at which the eye of the viewer and the mind of the artist are in their closest conjunction and for this reason it is the most important section in the catalogue. Included in it are his own book, *Group of Seven*, 1944, and a chapter in *The History of an Ontario Village*, 1964, by Doris M. FitzGerald, as well as the brief essay *On Line Drawing* already quoted in the resumé. Other references to his written material are made throughout the catalogue but these three belong quite naturally in this section.

Section B represents the best of Thoreau MacDonald's commercial work and includes books wholly illustrated by him and exhibition catalogues with his cover designs. E.R. Hunter has already discussed many of them individually. Where another artist has made a contribution to the book this fact is recorded in the catalogue. In this section are eight private press books of which the design but not the content is Thoreau MacDonald's, and one, *Drawings for Dartmouth*, in which his designs are reproduced and in which he is quoted.

Section C contains one hundred and forty-three listings. These are books or printed work enhanced by his design in one way or another, especially by fine lettering: italic script with lively serifs ('I have never admired sans-serif' he once told me), the handsome classic Roman spoken of by MacDonald in his autobiographical notes, and an occasional example of Gothic style because 'it looks religious.' The drawn title page, repeated in many instances in the jacket and cover design, is a remarkable feature of Thoreau MacDonald's book designs and the following sentences from *The Making of Books* by Sean Jennett may be informative. 'The drawn title page is a comparative rarity ... An artist capable of the work must have an intimate knowledge of letter design and good taste in its use ... Few artists can both draw and letter well; fewer still know how their work will be reproduced, or how to make the most of their opportunities within the stringent limits of the printing processes.'

For section D I have located and listed all but one of the periodicals or pamphlets which Thoreau MacDonald has mentioned to me, and many others long forgotten by him. The omission is a magazine for children called *Peter Pan* which was 'published during the depression' and is thought to have only appeared in four or five issues. I have seen only one illustration for it. Included is a page from the *Forum* not widely known to have had any connection with MacDonald. This page in the issue of February 1924 consists of a poem by Barker Fairley with decorations by A.Y. Jackson. The lettering is by Thoreau. Generally speaking, drawings and designs re-used to add interest to a periodical are omitted from this list.

In section E the sixteen listings substantiate E.R. Hunter's opinion that there was less joint work than one might expect from two artists sharing a studio. There may be more shared work but I have not come across it. As far as I know no one has made a list of the book designs of J.E.H. MacDonald although it is well known that he excelled at this work. Thoreau has said that the three years in London at the Carlton Studio were spent principally on book design.

The material in the ephemera section of the catalogue is interesting and important but does not precisely fit into the specific categories already discussed and is not numbered. In this section there are examples of broadsides commissioned by Professor Nash for various purposes; one of these with the Webster quotation was used as the cover stamp for the Dartmouth College *Aegis*, 1962. The title page for the Honourable Albert Matthews' Guest Book, referred to by William Colgate in *Canadian Art*, is reproduced as is the hand-drawn explanatory note for the Queen's Rangers' flags, which hangs on a corridor wall of the Central Metropolitan Library, Toronto, between the two flags. MacDonald's hand-lettered nameplate used in the directory of the Studio Building is reproduced as is an example of his letterhead. Fourteen bookplates and a design for Yale University which rather resembles a bookplate, are reproduced on two pages in the Ephemera. The Yale design is made up of its motto, coat of arms, and the elm trees for which it was once famous. No complete list of Thoreau MacDonald's bookplates has been kept but the number seems to be between forty and fifty. The earliest design shown is dated 1912 and the latest about 1967.

Three examples of typical linocuts, two used for his own Christmas cards and one designed as a Woodchuck Press device but not used for that purpose, are included, as are six decorated initials, part of a series for each chapter of H.D. Thoreau's *Walden*.

No posters were available for reproduction although some are known to exist. One, in particular, which has eluded me, was designed for the Jeu de Paume exhibition in Paris, 1927.

In the appendix there is a list of references to Thoreau MacDonald in print and a list of exhibitions in which he has participated.

A · Artist and Writer

1922

A1
MacDonald, Thoreau. *Early Canadian Woodcuts (lately discovered).* [Privately printed 1922]
[8] leaves
8 woodcuts plus cover woodcut; no text
Only 4 copies known

1927

A2
MacDonald, Thoreau. *The Canadian Forum Reproductions.* Toronto, J.M. Dent & Sons, 1927.
[12] leaves
12 drawings, loose in portfolio, label on portfolio

1932

A3
MacDonald, Thoreau. *A Landmark Lost; 1856-1932.* [Thornhill, privately printed, 1932] 3 p folder
Edition limited to 200 copies
2 drawings (1 vignette)
'Some travellers on Yonge Street will be sorry to see the historic little church at Willowdale now so sadly altered. It bore the date 1856, but was possibly much older and its neat and severe design made it the most interesting church south of Thornhill. To the regret of its many admirers it was remodelled and its spire heartlessly destroyed in July, 1932.'

A3

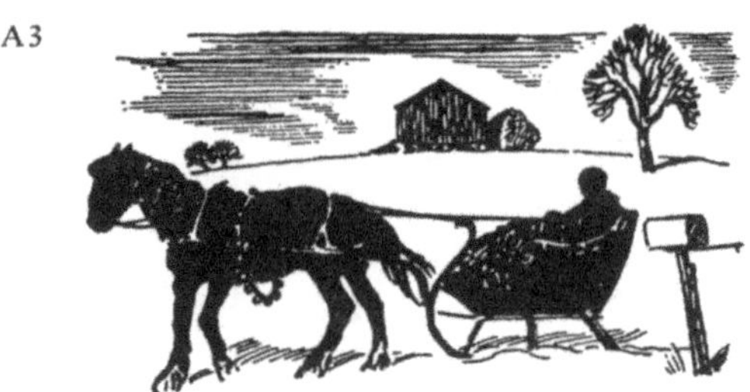

A1

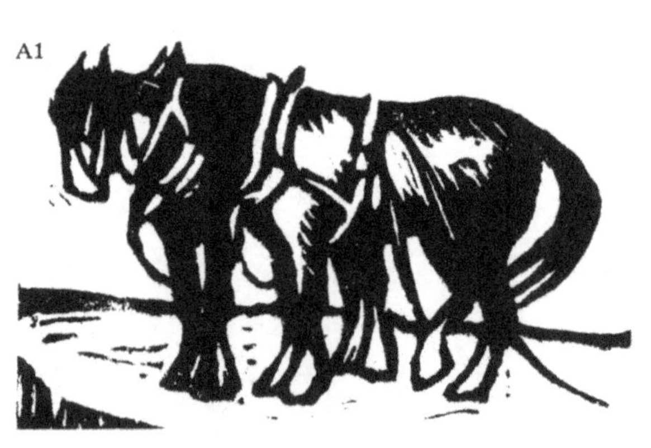

A3

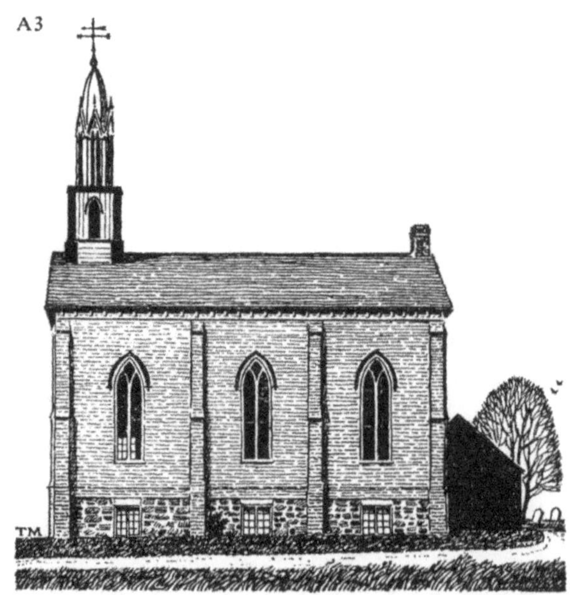

1933

A4

MacDonald, Thoreau. *A Few of the Old Gates at Thornhill and some Nearby Farms.* [Thornhill] Woodchuck Press [1933] [17] p
Cover title
Edition limited to about 200 copies
15 drawings (8 vignettes)
Woodchuck Press device on cover

'The village gates are fast disappearing now as the villagers pull down their fences in imitation of the city fashion. In old days, when cows roamed the roads, every house had its white fence and the gates were a form of village art, the crowning ornament of a well built fence. The ironwork came from the village blacksmith shop and most of it shows little or no sign of rust after sixty or ninety Canadian winters. To some these old gates may seem simple and crude, but they represent well the honest workmanship and love of home in Old Ontario.'

A4

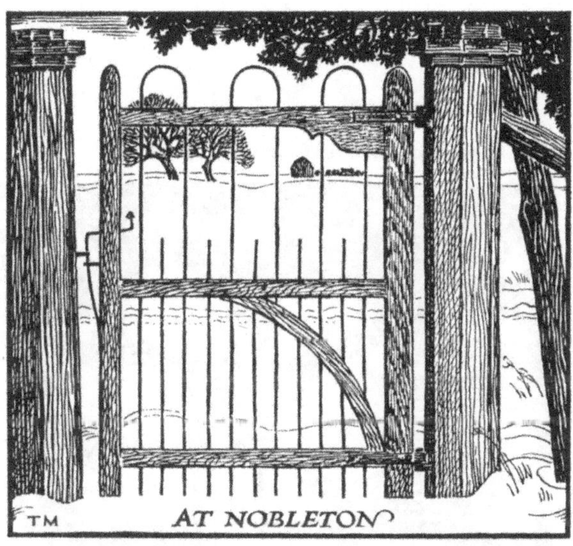

A4

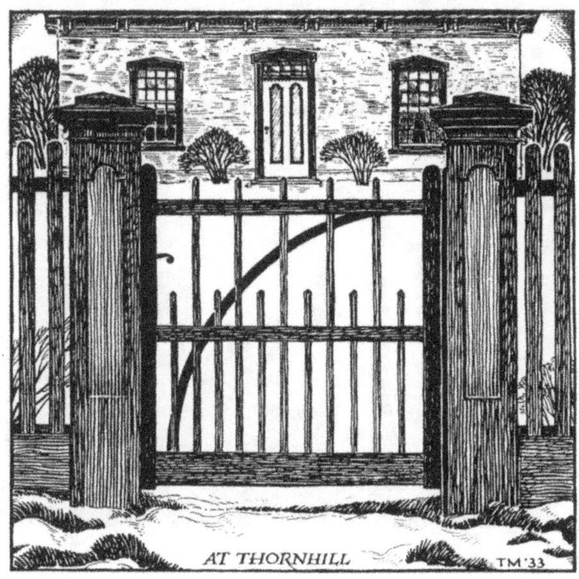

A4

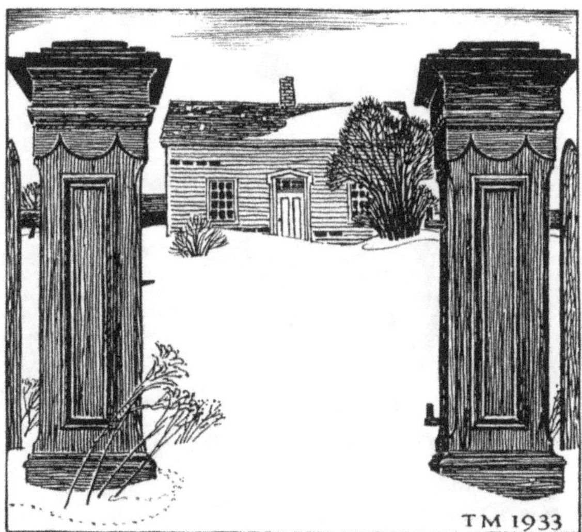

1934

A5

MacDonald, Thoreau. *A Year on the Farm; or, The Woodchuck's Almanac.* [Thornhill] Woodchuck Press, 1934. [19] p

Cover title

Edition limited to about 200 copies

17 drawings (2 vignettes)

Woodchuck Press device on cover

'Sayings like these are seldom used now as pioneer ways are left behind. Not long ago some old folks had a saying for any occasion. There may be others more picturesque but these are some often heard, in one form or another, on the farms of Old Ontario.'

A6

[MacDonald, Thoreau] *Some Proverbs from Russia.* Printed for the Russian Church Bazaar [1934]

9 leaves

Cover title

Privately printed

9 lino-cuts, cover design

A5 May: When Swallows fly low a Storm will soon blow

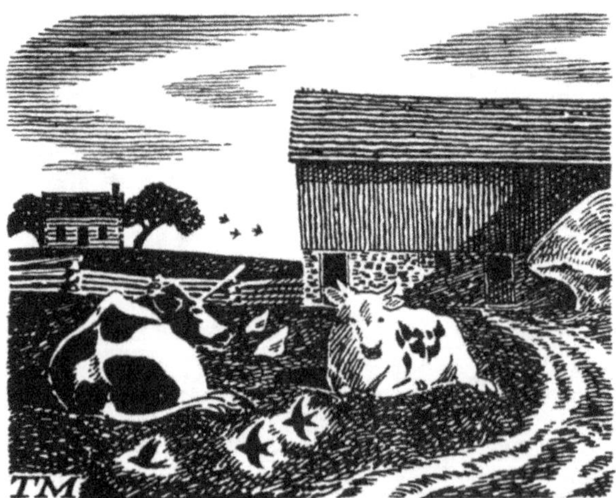

A5 November: Saw wood in an Indian Summer

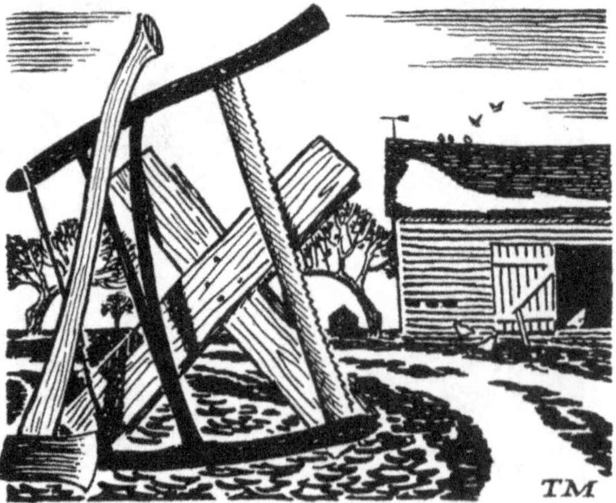

A6 Apples don't fall far from the Apple Tree

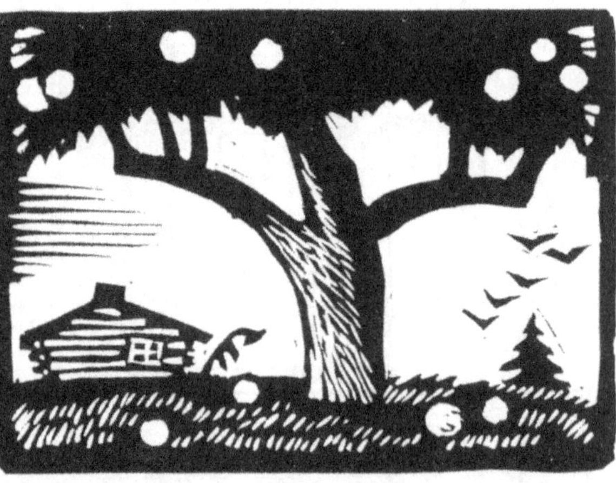

A6 Don't Spit in the Well, you might be thirsty

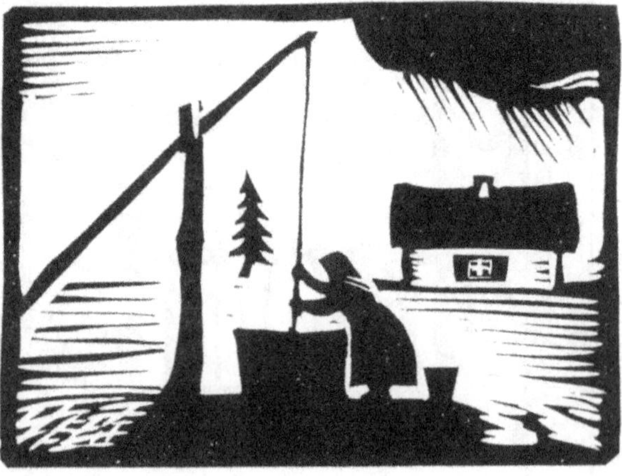

1936

A7

MacDonald, Thoreau. *Some Tools of the Pioneers.* [Thornhill] Woodchuck Press, 1936 [13] p
Cover title
10 full pages of drawings, cover design, and 3 vignettes

'In many an old Ontario barn and driving-shed or overgrown fence corner, the broken and rusty remains of the pioneers' tools may be found. All tools are interesting but especially these, for they were not bought "out of the catalogue" but made at home or in the nearest blacksmith shop. People had not then reversed the principle, "Never buy anything you can make." The first tool was the axe of course. The old country type seemed to change slightly after its arrival here as constant use developed a more compact head and evolved the fine lines of the handles. These usually vary a little on different farms according to the pattern cut by the old folks many years ago. The principal building tools were the axe, broadaxe, adze, froe, drawknife, and various saws, planes, and augers. Ironwork and tool making were often done at home and many good chisels, plane irons, and knives were made from old files or other scraps of steel. Grain was cut with scythe, sickle or cradle and threshed with a flail. It was handled with wooden forks, rakes, and scoops and these were sometimes made and sold by Indians. The old tools are being forgotten and there are not many who understand their uses but with the help of farmer friends and neighbors these drawings were made from the actual objects and try to record some of the noble implements of old times.'

A7

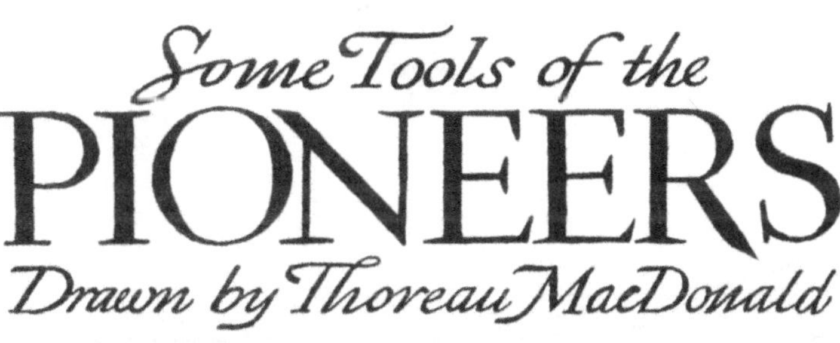

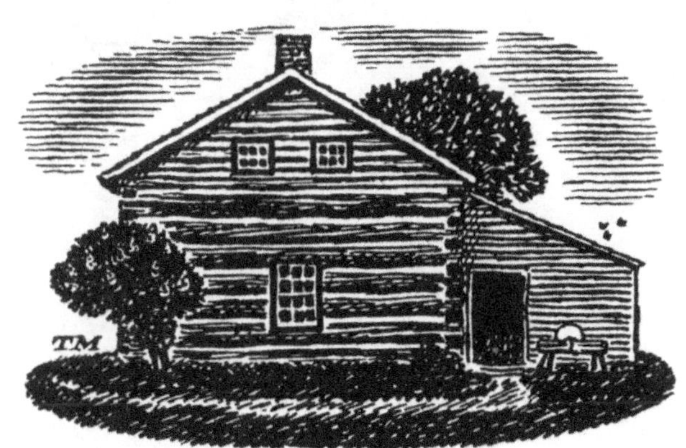

A7

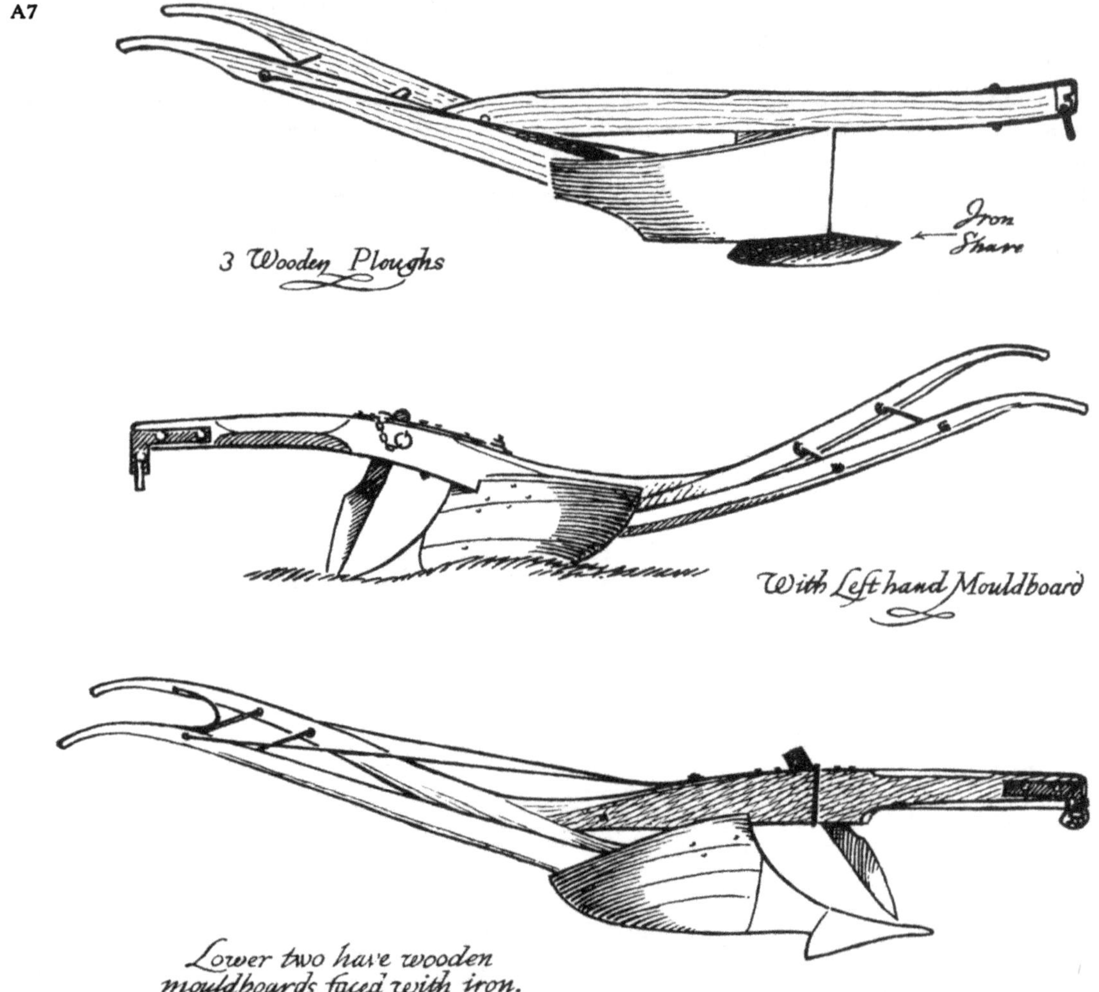
Iron
Share
3 Wooden Ploughs
With Left hand Mouldboard
Lower two have wooden
mouldboards faced with iron.
These ploughs are very well made but who made them & when is forgotten now.

A7

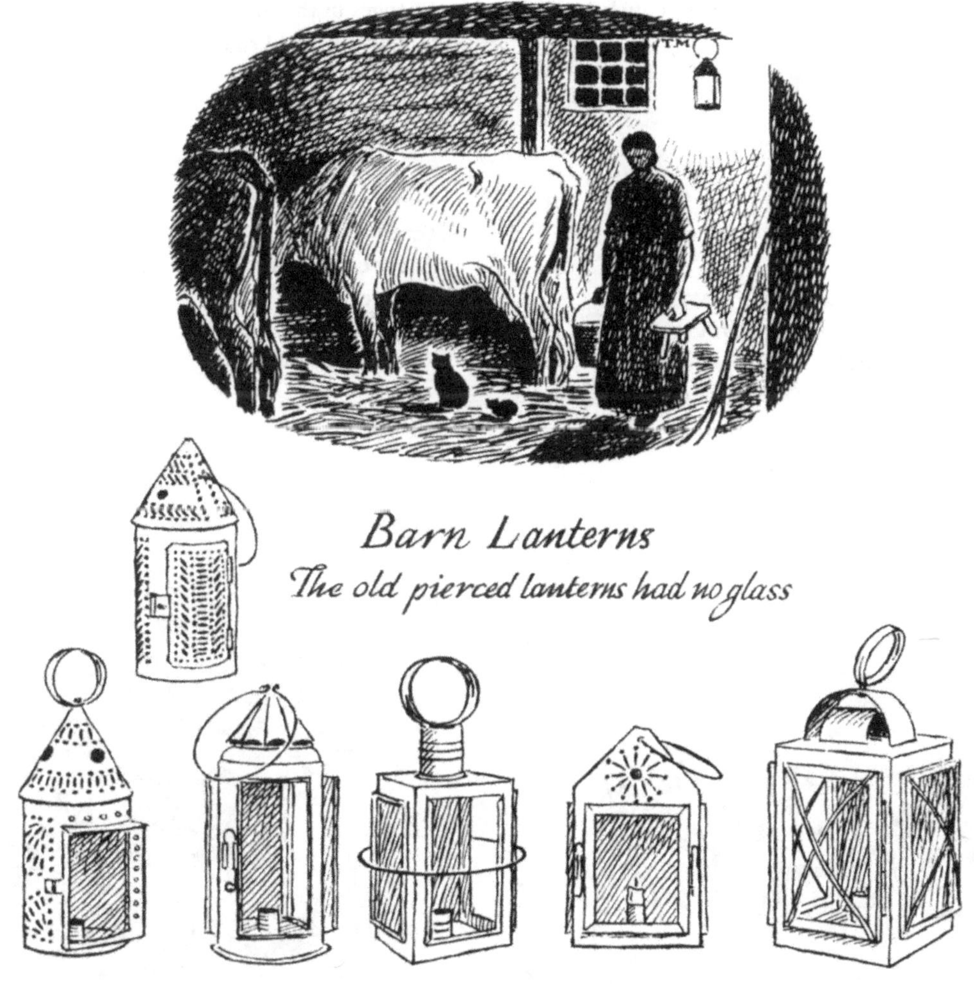

1938

A8

[MacDonald, Thoreau] *The Industrious Bear, from Krylov's Fables.* [Printed for the Russian Church Bazaar. Thornhill, Woodchuck Press, 1938]
[6] leaves
Cover title
Edition limited to about 500 copies
5 drawings, title page, cover, and Woodchuck Press device

1944

A9

MacDonald, Thoreau. *The Group of Seven.* Toronto, Ryerson Press (The Canadian Art Series) [1944]
34 p
Published in rust cloth and yellow wrappers
30 illustrations (1 coloured) of Group of Seven paintings and drawings
Series colophon device, cover design of paperback issue

- Second edition 1945
  Same as preceding except the coloured frontispiece changed from 'Country North of Lake Superior' by Lawren Harris to 'The Beaver Dam' by J.E.H. MacDonald.
- Third edition 1952. 29 p
  Issued only in buff wrappers
  2 vignettes, and cover design
  Series colophon device changed
  Changes in the illustrations
- Fourth edition 1962
- Fifth edition 1966
- Sixth edition 1967
- Seventh edition 1968
- Eighth edition 1969
- Ninth edition 1970
- Tenth edition 1972
  These editions issued in variously coloured wrappers

A8

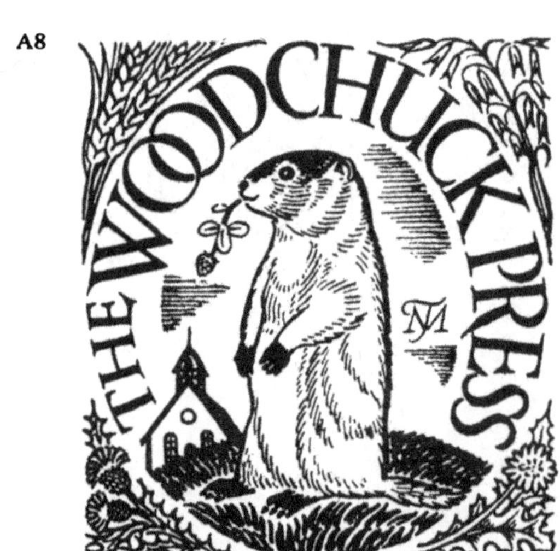

A8

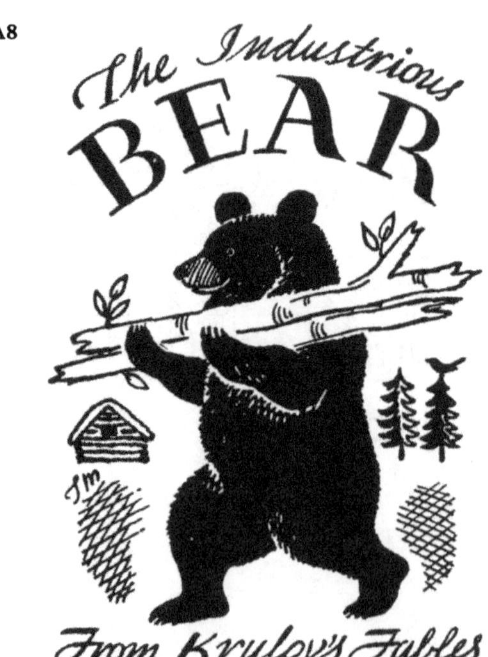

A9 *Thoreau MacDonald*

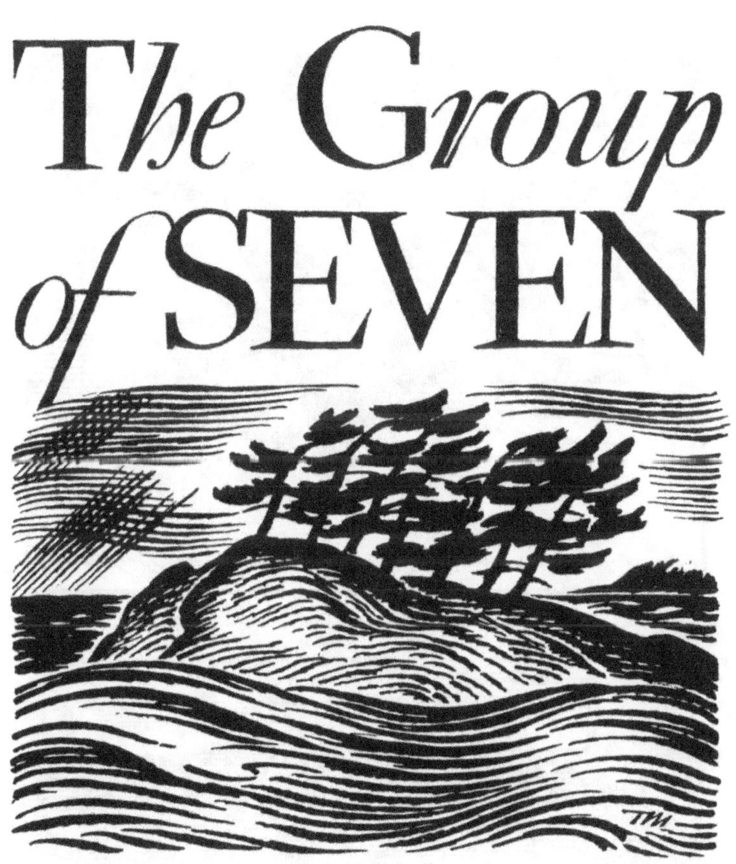

The Canadian Art Series

1946

A10
MacDonald, Thoreau. *A Specimen Book of Cuts used by the Woodchuck Press.* Toronto, Ryerson Press [1946] [21] p
Edition limited to about 500 copies
40 drawings, title page, and Woodchuck Press device on cover

A11
MacDonald, Thoreau. *Talks with a Hunter.* [Thornhill, Woodchuck Press, 1946] [10] p
Written by TM for the *Liberal*, Richmond Hill, and reprinted by him
Cover title, 27 drawings, cover design, and Woodchuck Press device

A10

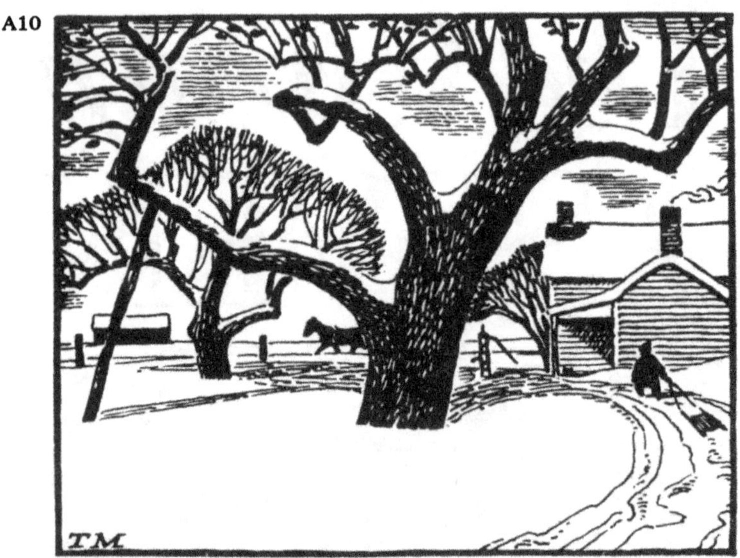

A10

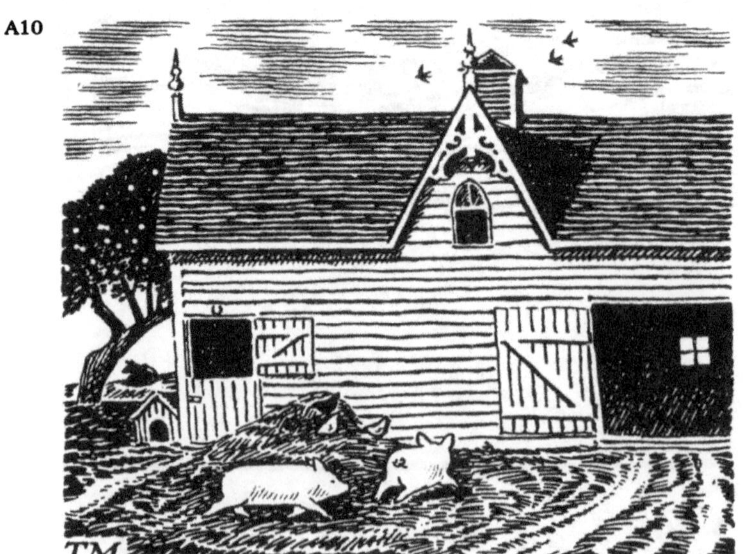

1951

A12.
MacDonald, Thoreau. *Woods and Fields.* Toronto, Ryerson Press [1951] 45 p
Edition limited to about 500 copies
70 drawings (4 vignettes), title page and cover
Envelope, reproducing cover design, included
'These drawings have no significance apart from the subject. They are only a reminder of the immediate past, remnants of what might be called the Dan Patch, Maud S., Lou Dillon era. They are all line drawings, not because the writer likes this wiry and difficult medium, but because it's cheaper to print than any other. The draftsman can only hope his meaning is clear and try for some of the style and finish we like to see in all good work, whether ploughing, carpentry, or a well built woodpile. Only 3 of the drawings have been previously printed.'

A12

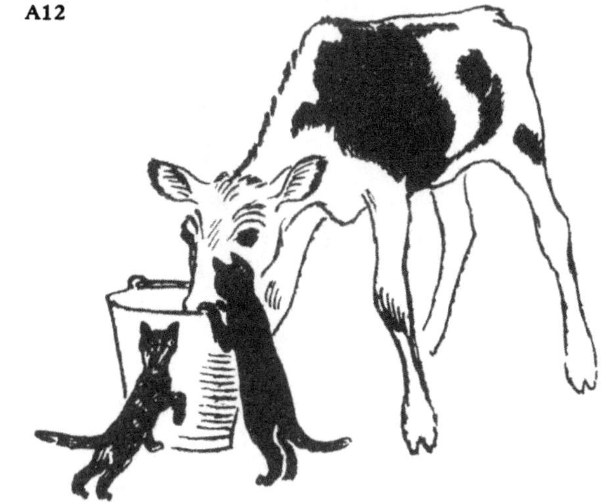

A12

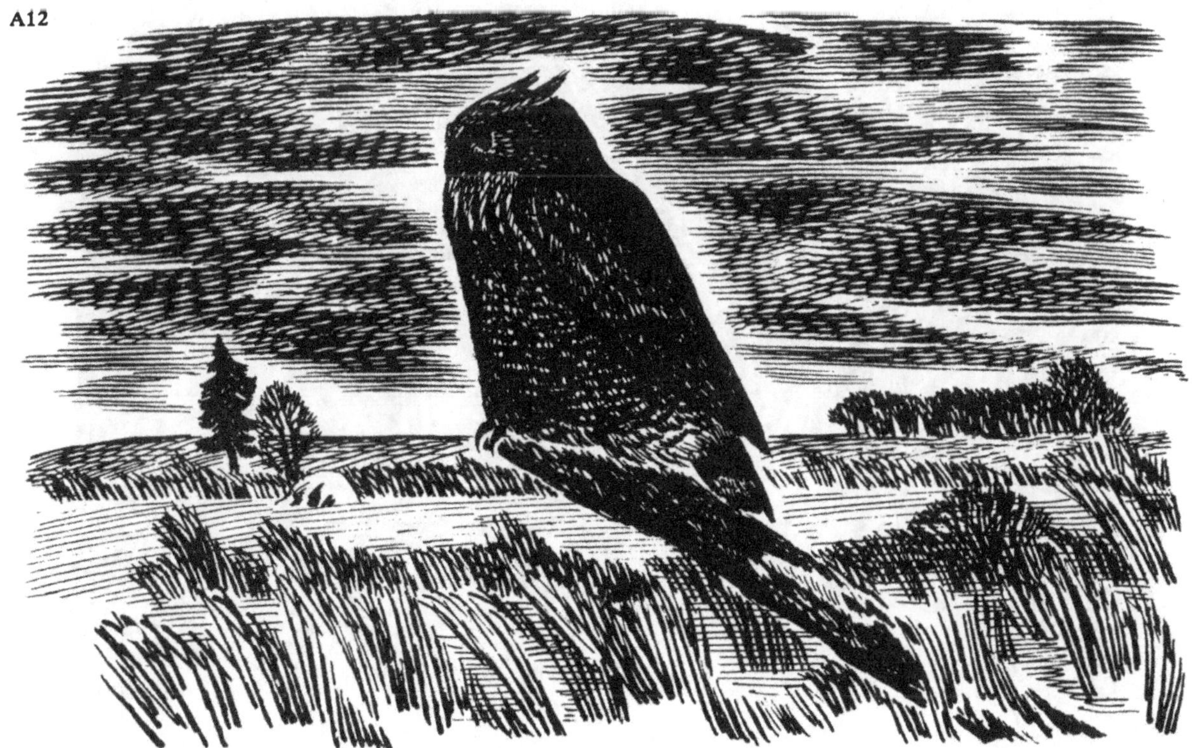

A12

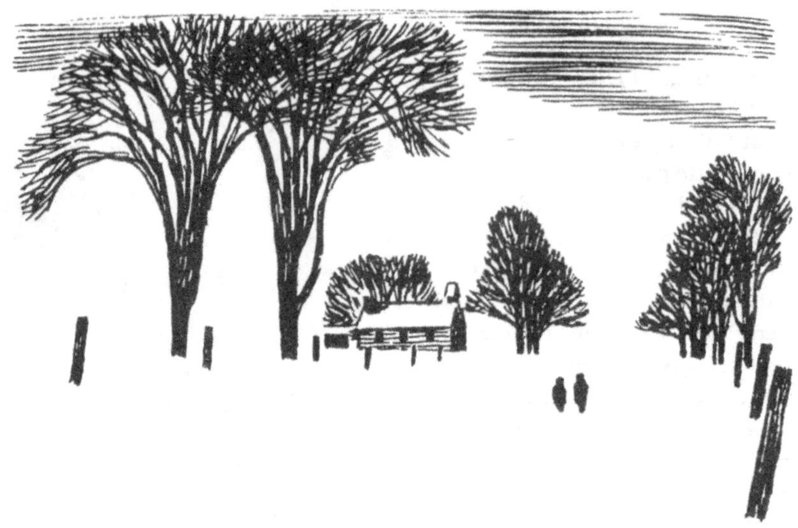

A12

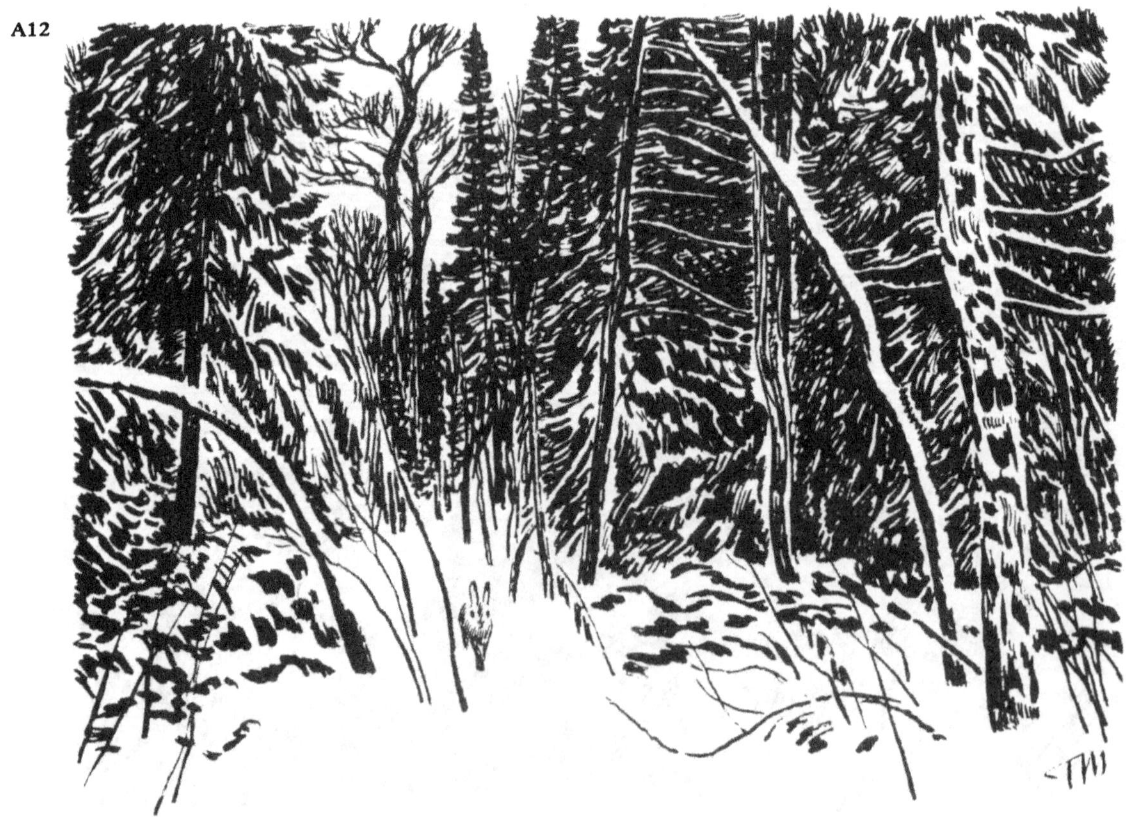

A12

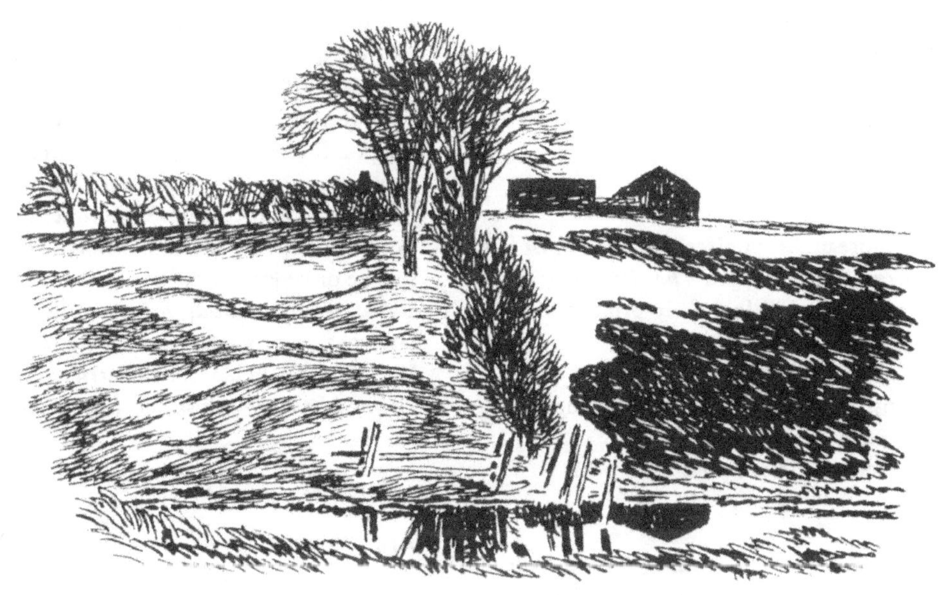

A12

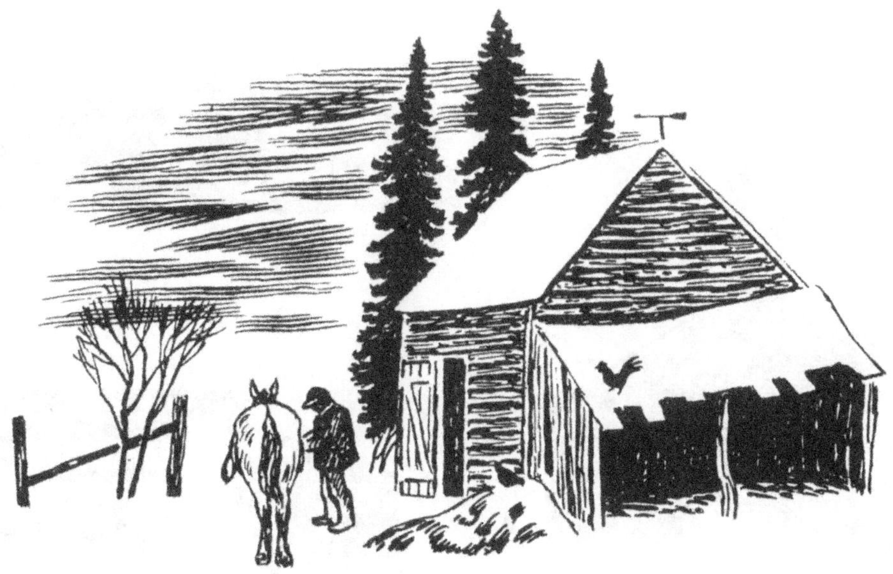

1952

A13
MacDonald, Thoreau. Line drawing, in London Public Library and Art Museum, *Thoreau MacDonald* [catalogue] London, Ont. [1952] 4 p folder
Exhibition, February 1952
Introduction

1964

A14
MacDonald, Thoreau. 'Reminiscences,' in FitzGerald, Doris M. *Thornhill, 1793-1963: The History of an Ontario Village.* Thornhill [privately printed] 1964. 131 p
Edition limited to 1500 copies
TM's chapter pp 52-7. Layout and 14 drawings (2 maps, title page vignette)
Errata slip, lettered by TM, tipped in at p 11

A15
MacDonald, Thoreau. *54 Old Houses, mostly from Farms in the Thornhill Area.* [Thornhill, privately printed] 1964. 23 p
Edition limited to about 200 copies
66 photographs 'made during the 1929 depression'
2 drawings, title page, and cover vignettes

1965

A16
MacDonald, Thoreau. *House and Barn.* [Thornhill, privately printed, 1965] 39 p
Edition limited to 200 copies
88 drawings (1 vignette), covers (2 vignettes)
Reprinted (500 copies)
'Now that the small farm is declared obsolete and a drag on the economy we may soon see the last of those groups of weathered buildings that meant home to so many of us. Sometimes near big fountain formed elms, or farther north with a horizon of spruce or cedar swamp.
The dark barn broods, lofty and wide
Over the crops within, and by its side
The banded silo leans, and cattle shove
To feed beneath the strawstack's hollowed cove.'

A16

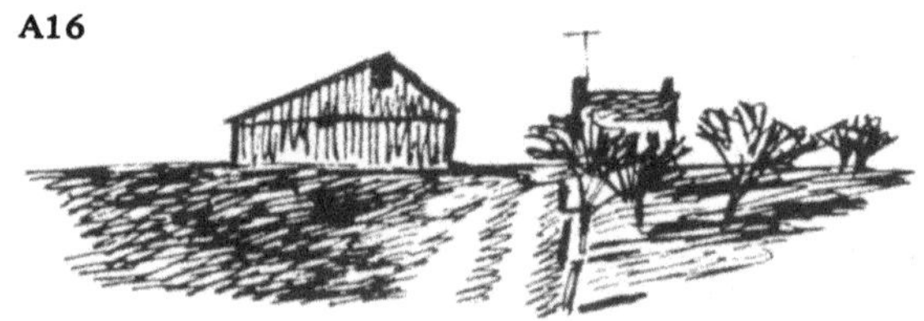

A16

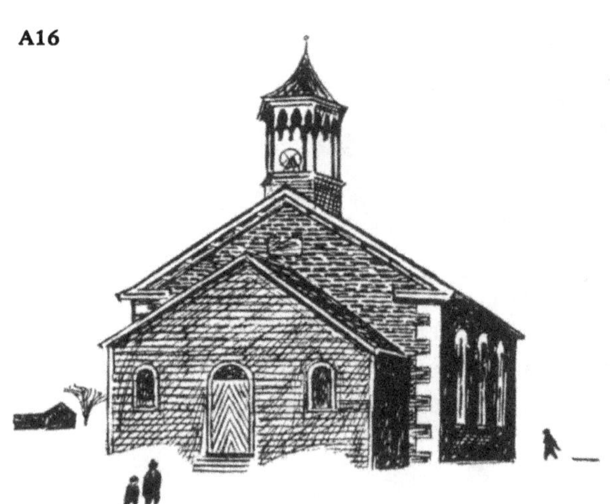

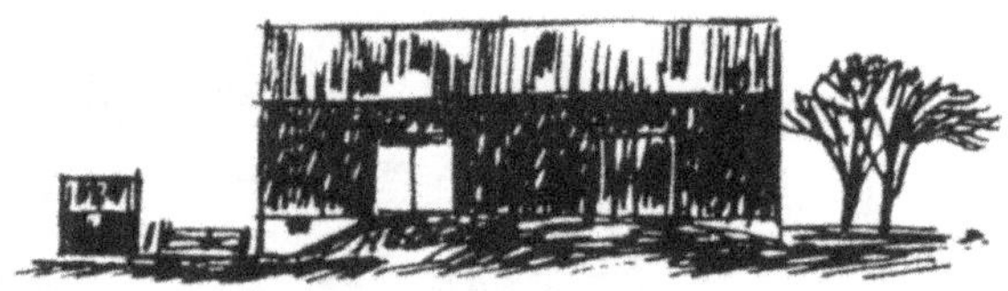

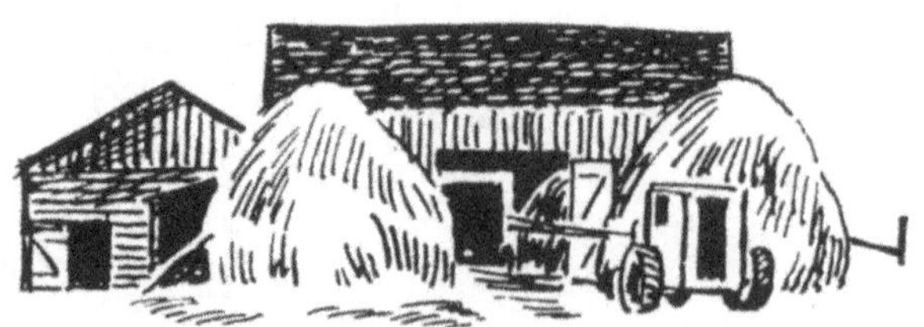

A16

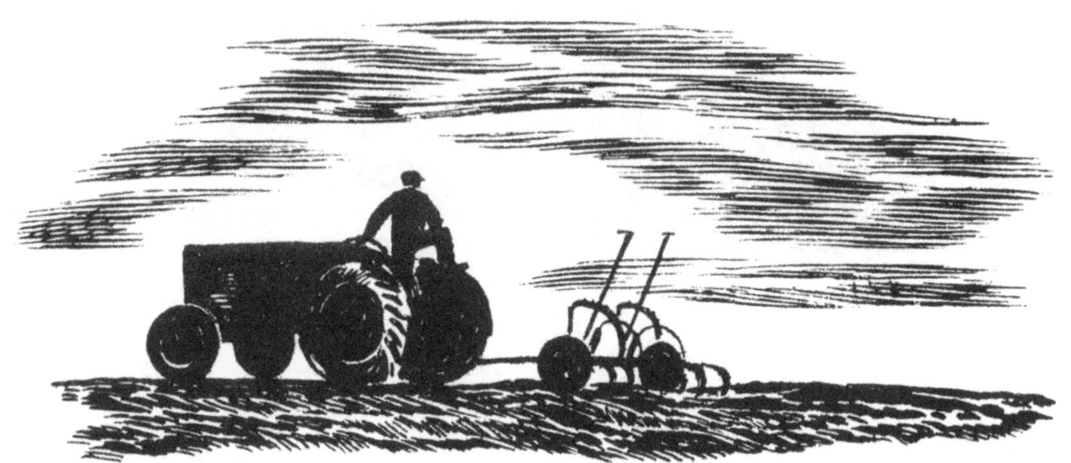

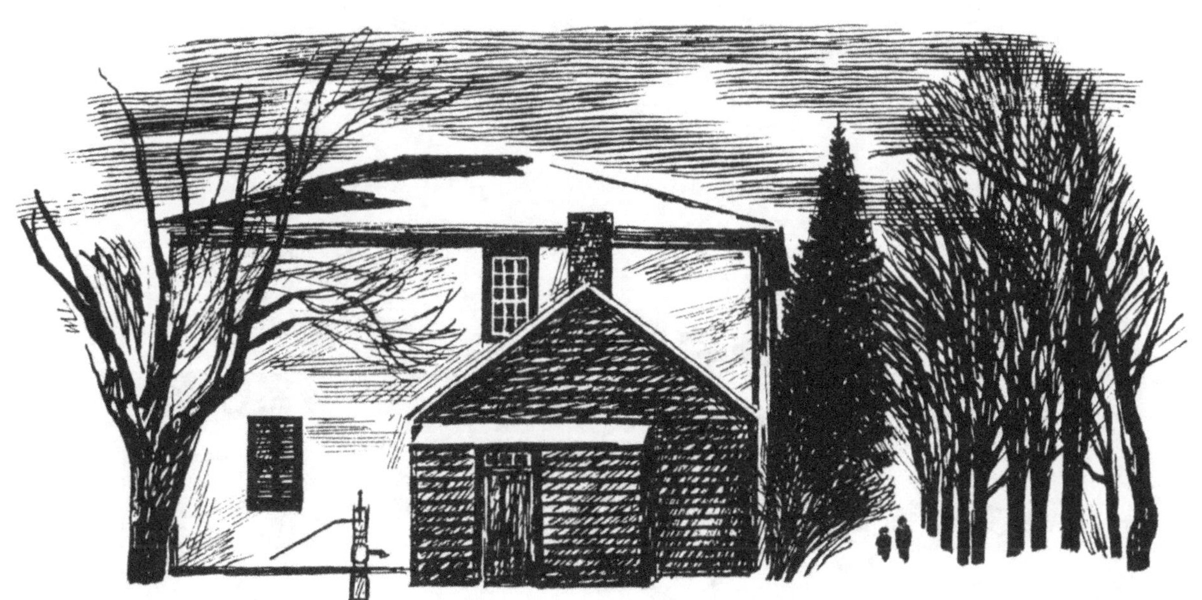

A16

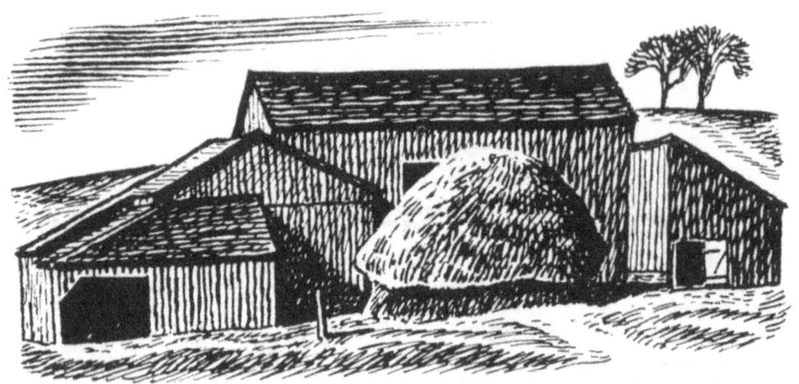

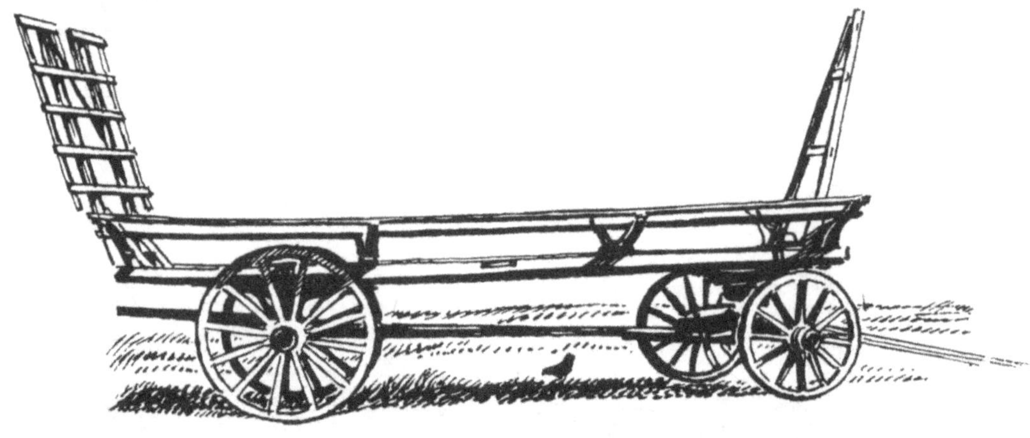

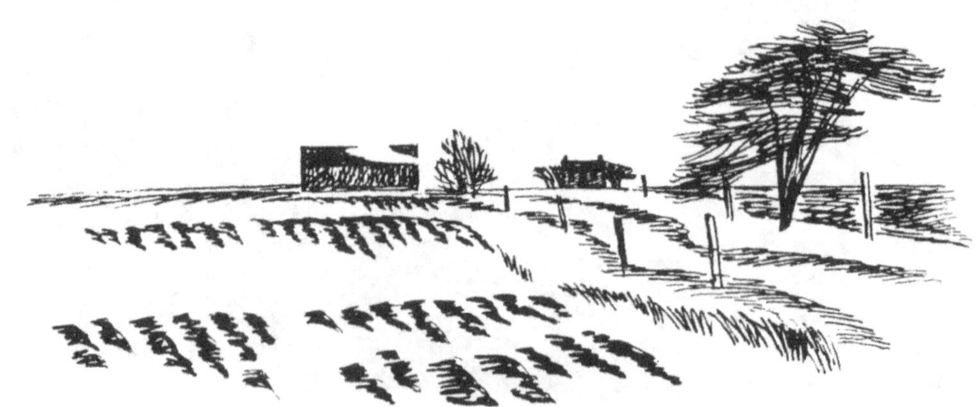

A16

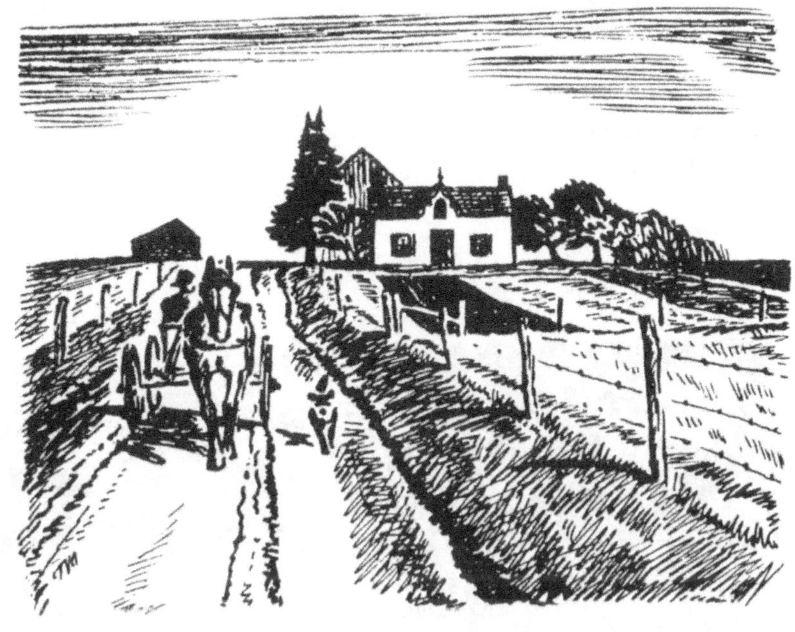

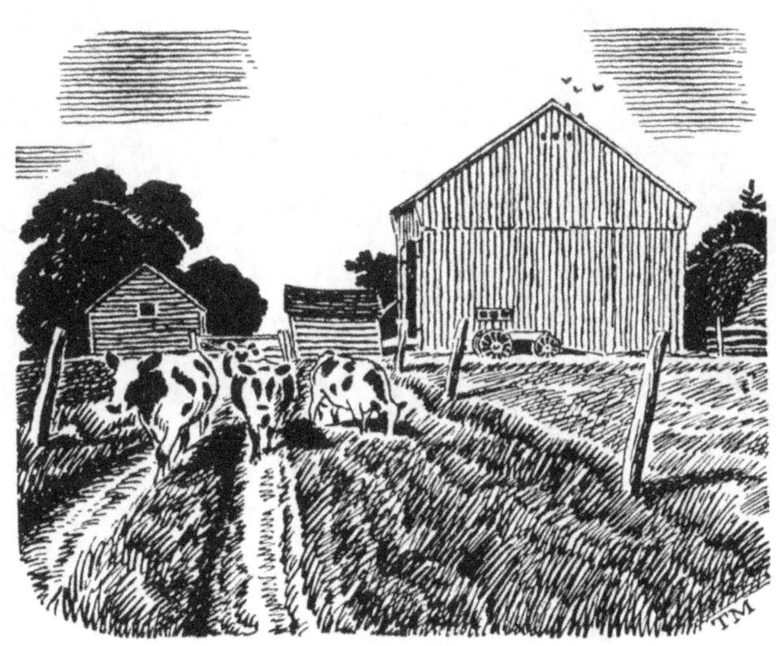

1968

A17
MacDonald, Thoreau. *Birds & Animals.* [Thornhill, privately printed, 1968] 27 p
Cover title
Edition limited to 200 copies
53 drawings (2 vignettes), cover design
Reprinted 1970 (100 copies)

'It's a thrill to see any wild animal tending his affairs in his home environment. These drawings are a kind of record of meetings with animals. They are not the work of a naturalist, nor an artist, just a fond observer.'

A17

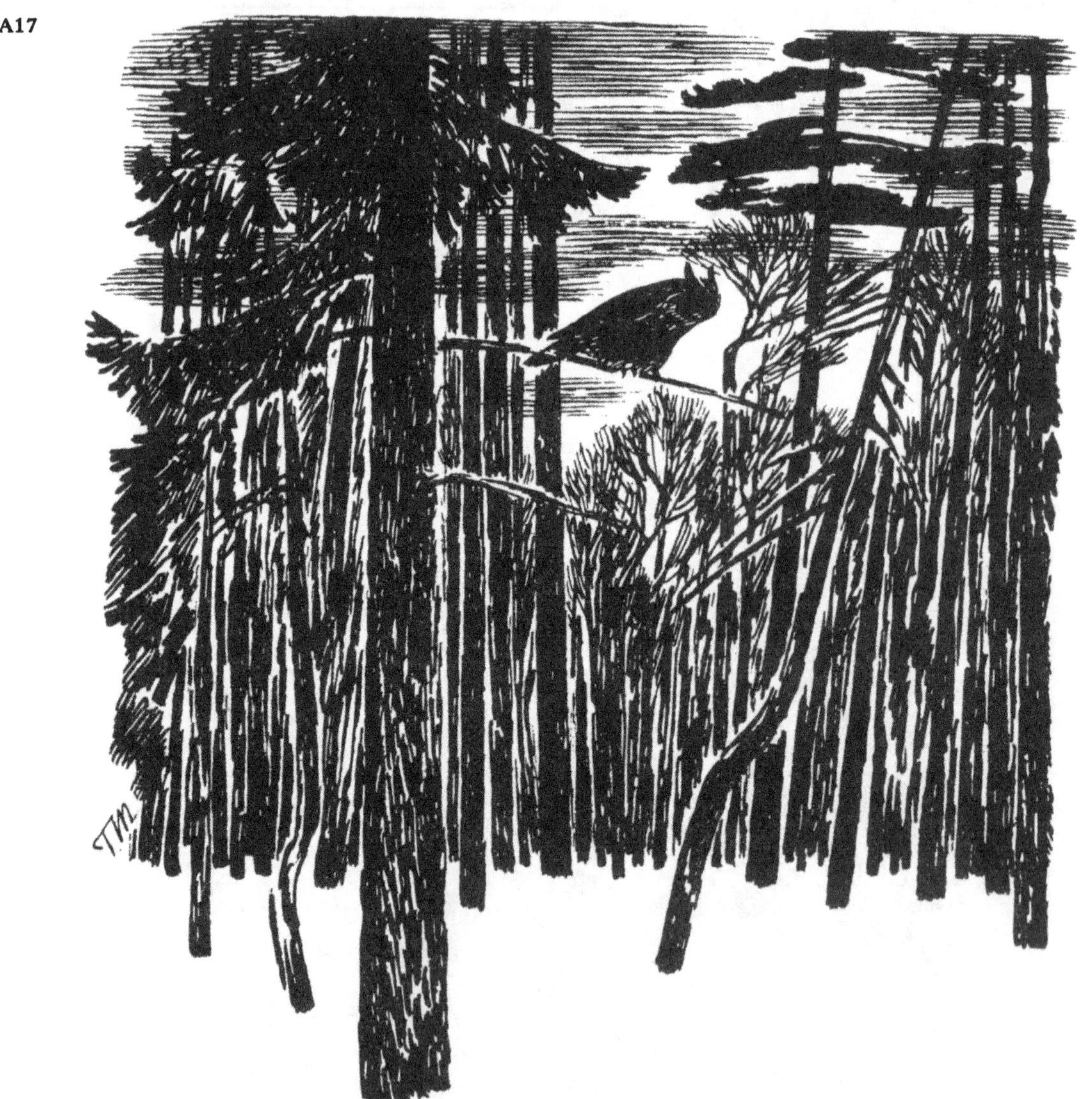

A17

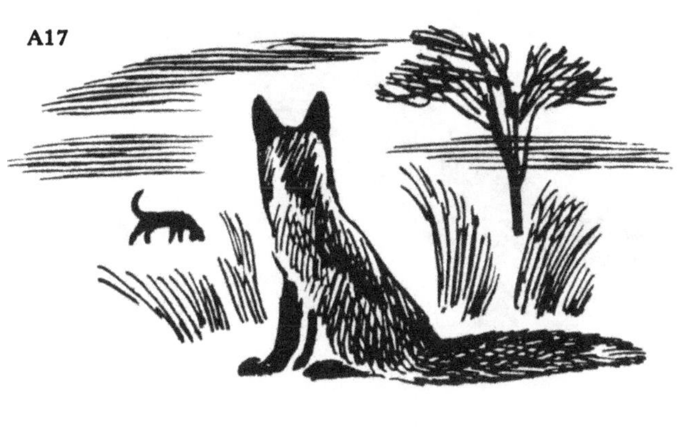

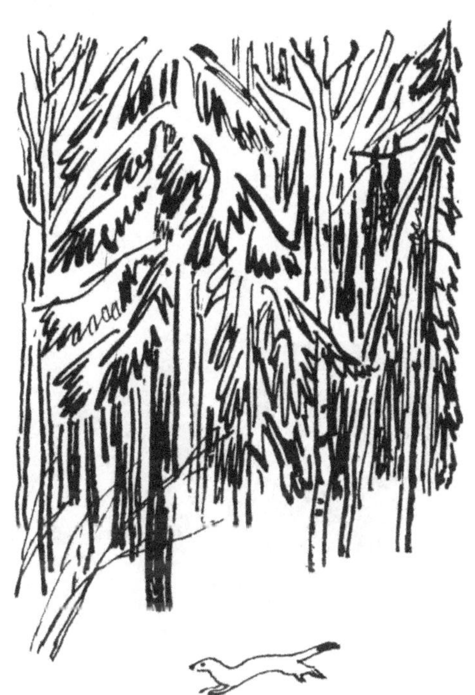

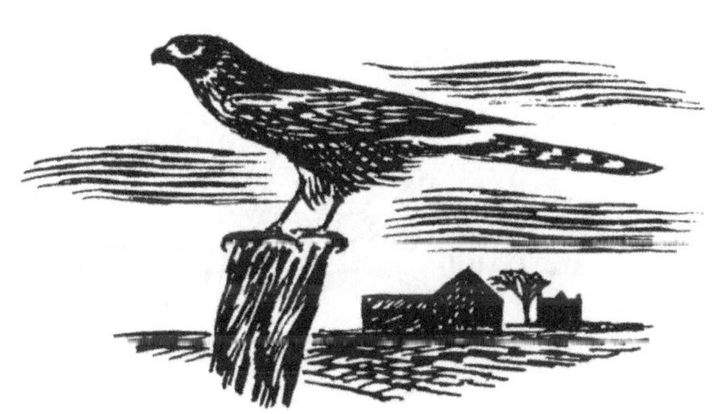

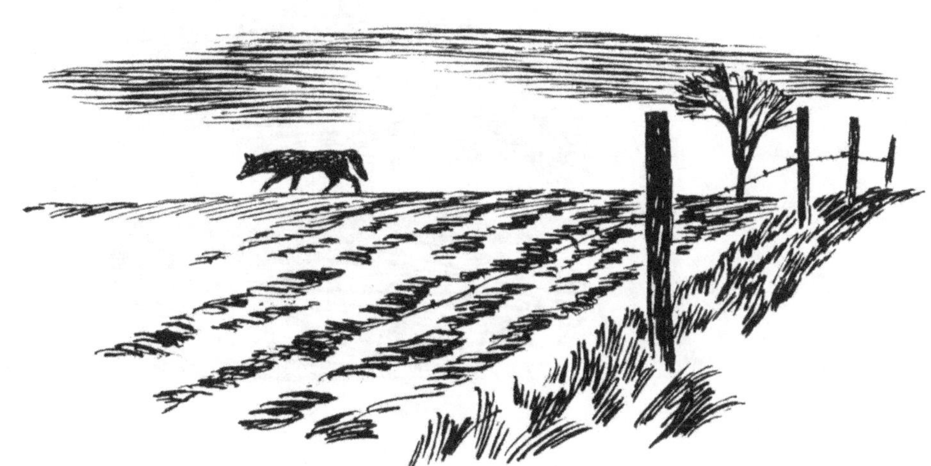

A17

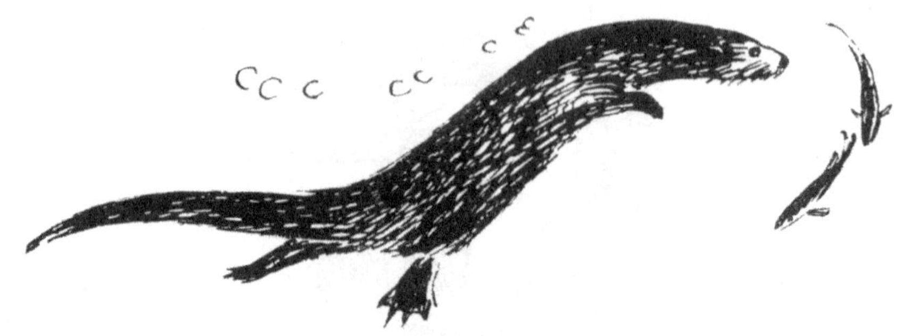

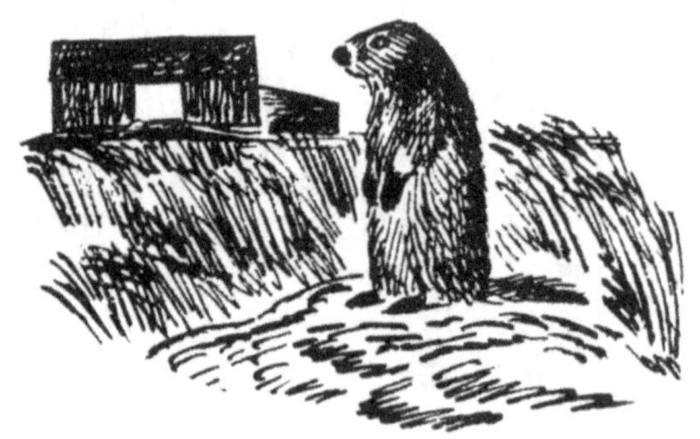

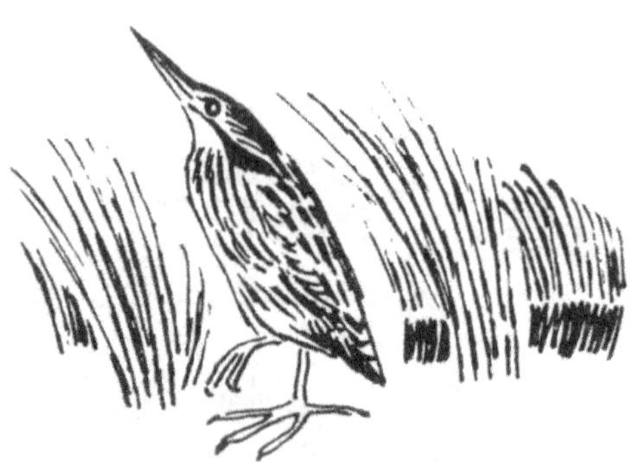

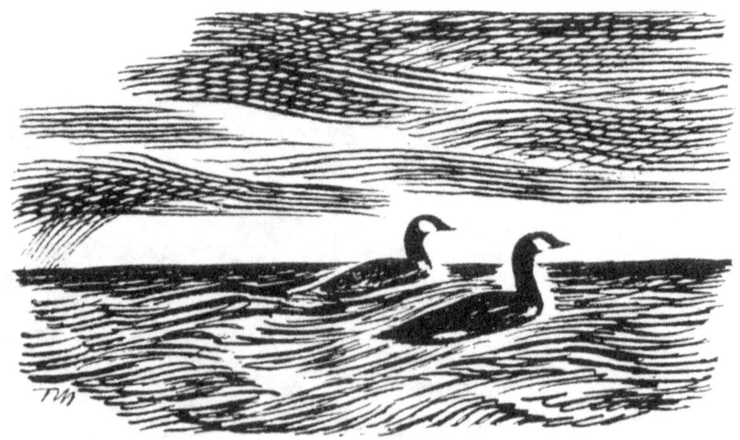

A17

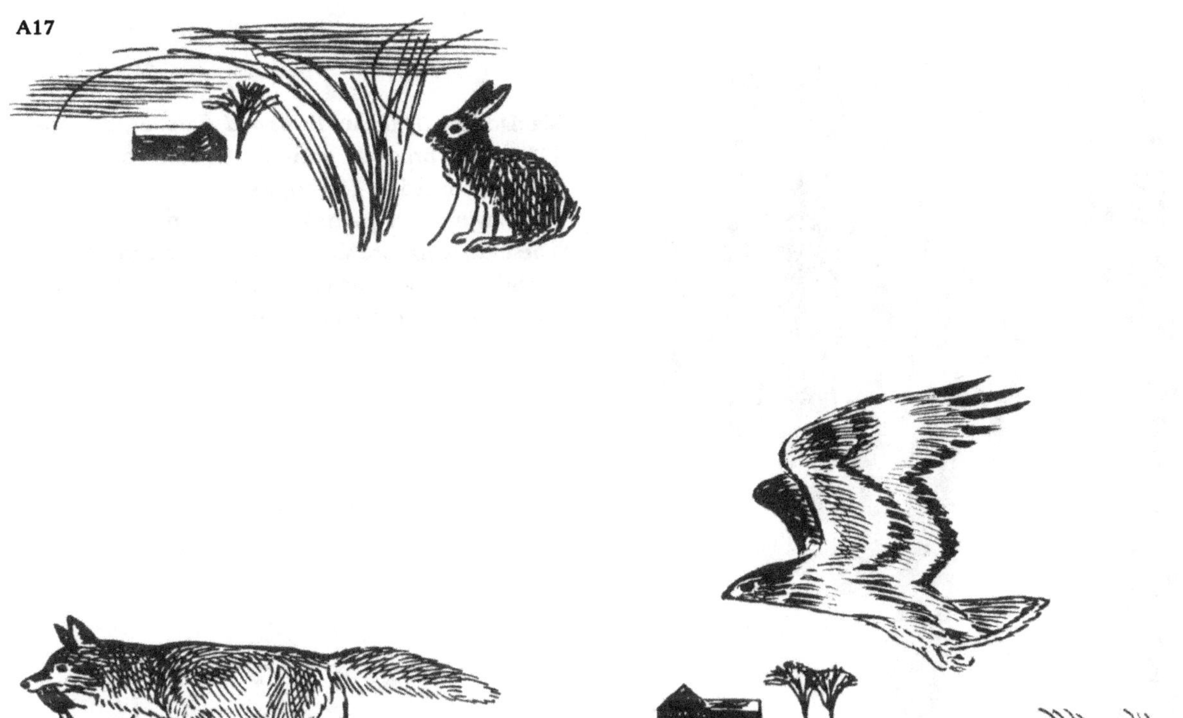

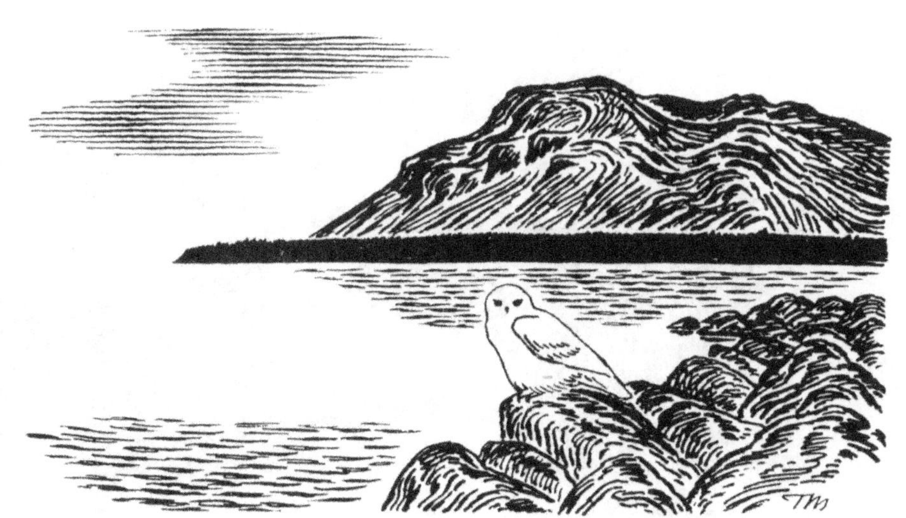

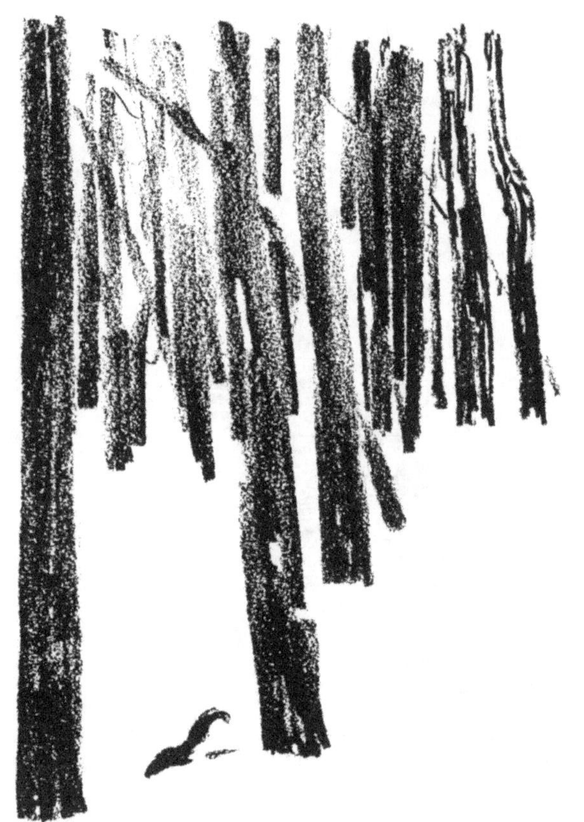

1971

A18
MacDonald, Thoreau. *Birds and Animals, 2d series.*
[Thornhill, privately printed, 1971] 34 p
Edition limited to 150 copies
57 drawings (1 vignette), cover design
'These drawings are similar to the first series and nothing new need be said about them. A few line cuts and stencils are included.'

A18

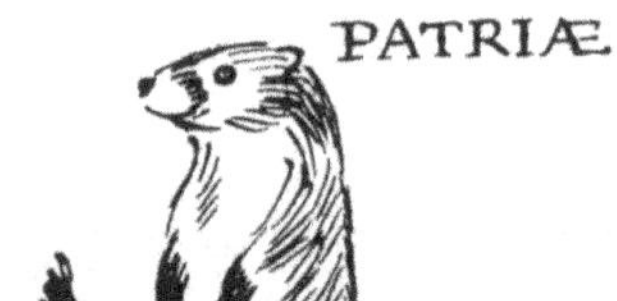

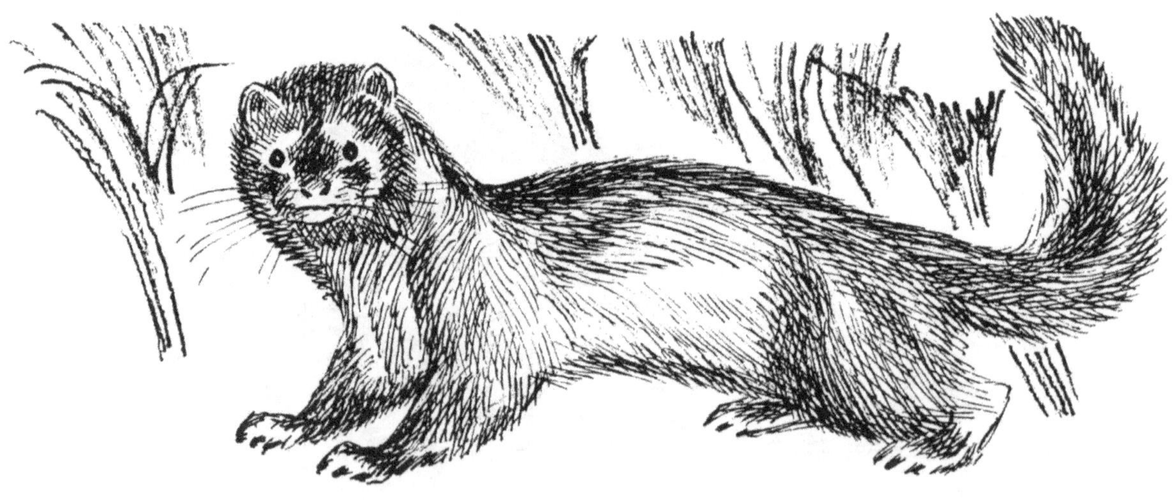

A18

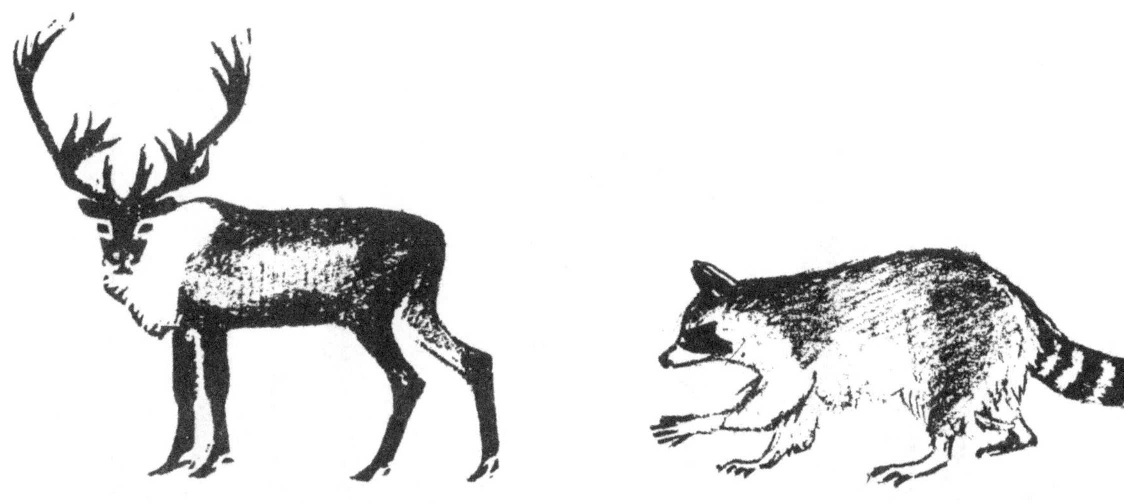

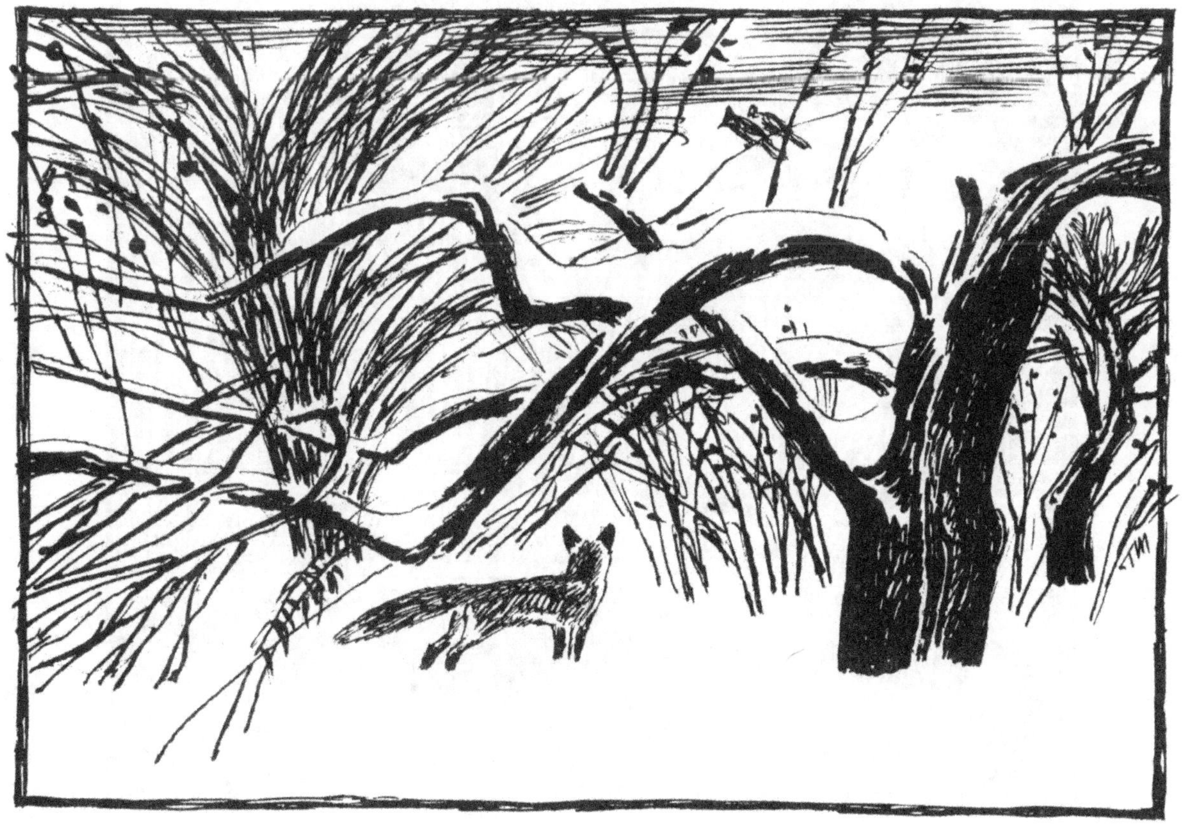

A18

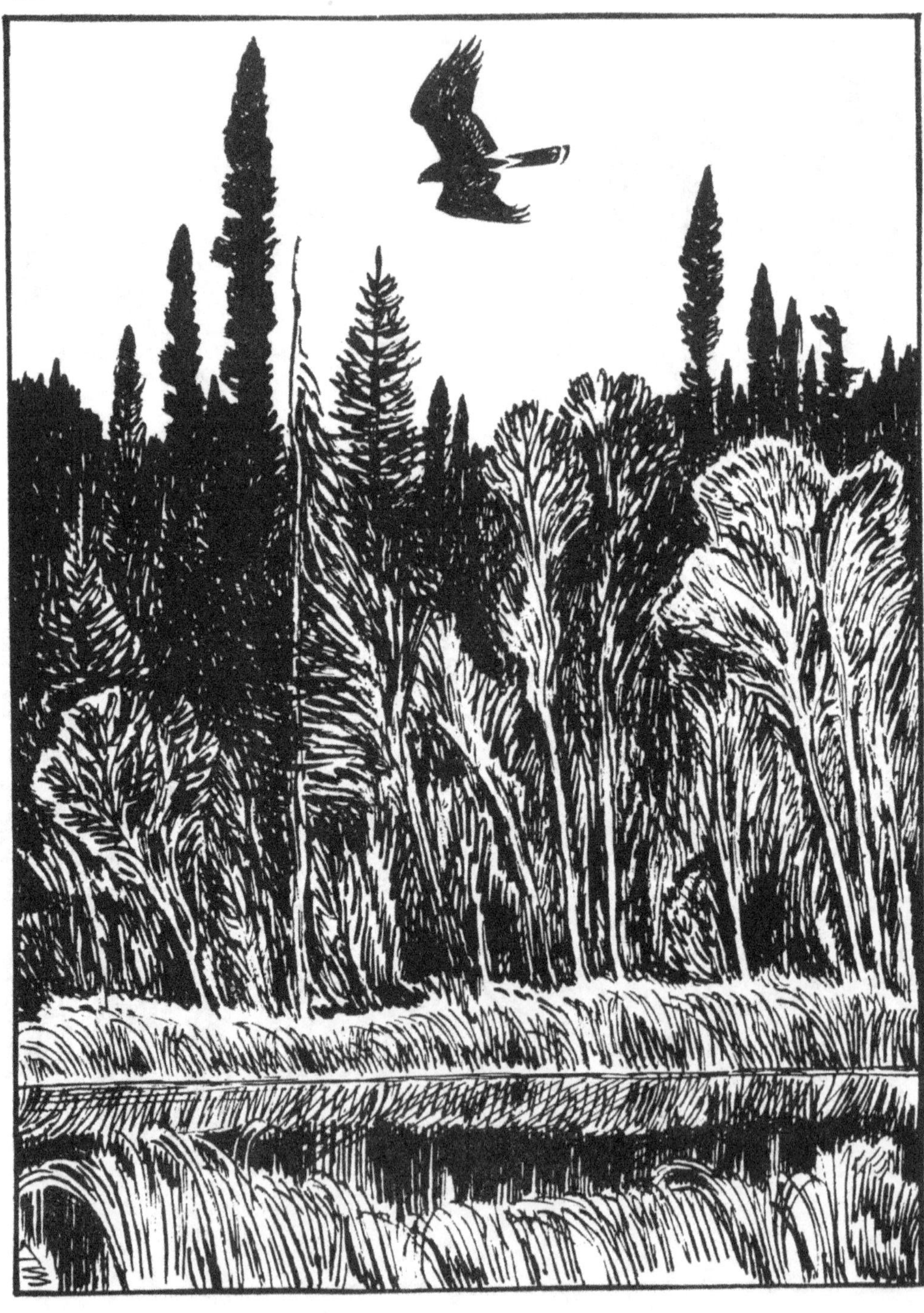

A19
MacDonald, Thoreau. *Farm Drawings.* [Thornhill, privately printed, 1971] 39 p
Cover title
Edition limited to 150 copies
72 drawings (3 vignettes), cover design

'Ill fares the land, to hastening ills a prey
*Where factories multiply and farms decay.'**

'These are mostly old drawings, remnants from a happier time.'

*paraphrase of Goldsmith's *The Deserted Village*

A19

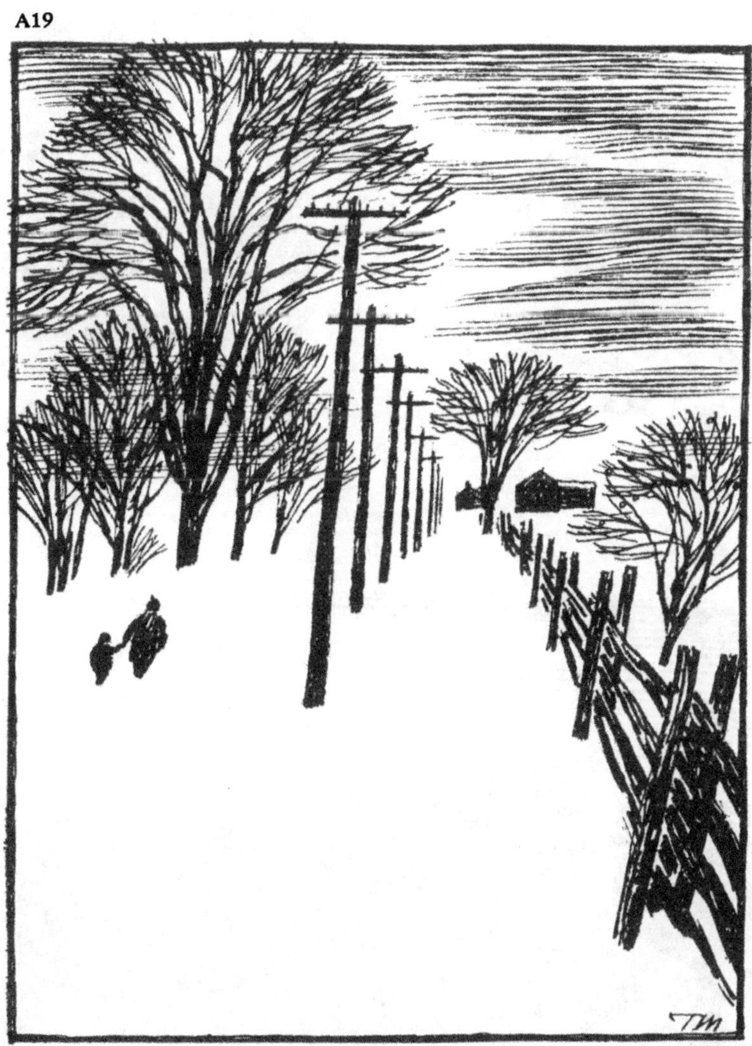

A19

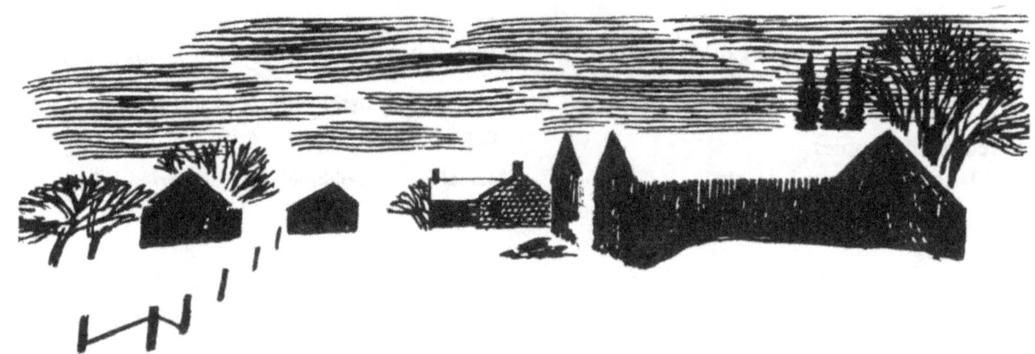

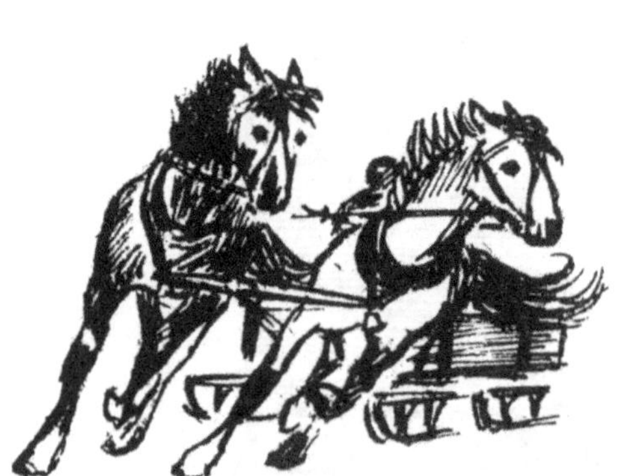

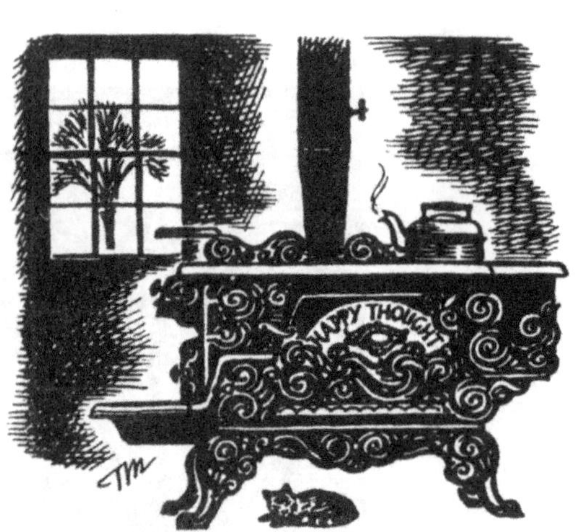

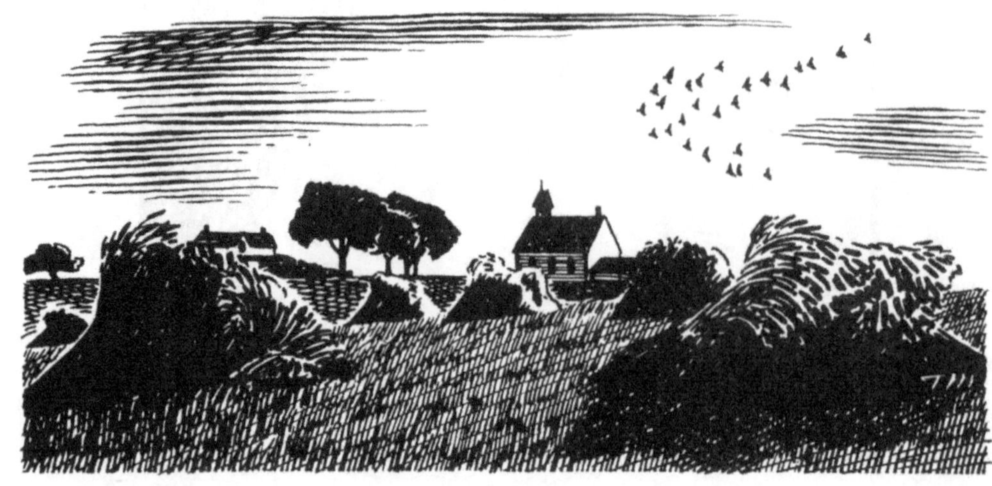

B · Books wholly Illustrated and Catalogue Designs

1925

B1
Victorin, Brother Marie. *The Chopping Bee and other Laurentian Stories.* [Toronto] Musson Book Co. [1925] 255 p
Translated by James Ferres
Title page, cover, jacket, and end papers
11 drawings, including title page

B2
Dunlap, David A. *Shahwandahgooze Days.* [Toronto] privately published [1925] 76p
Edition limited to 175 copies
21 drawings (11 vignettes), title page and cover designs

1926

B3
Catalogue of the Exhibitions of the Group of Seven and Painting, Sculpture and Wood Carving of French Canada, May 7th to May 31st, 1926. Toronto, Art Gallery of Toronto, 1926. 12 p
Cover design

B1

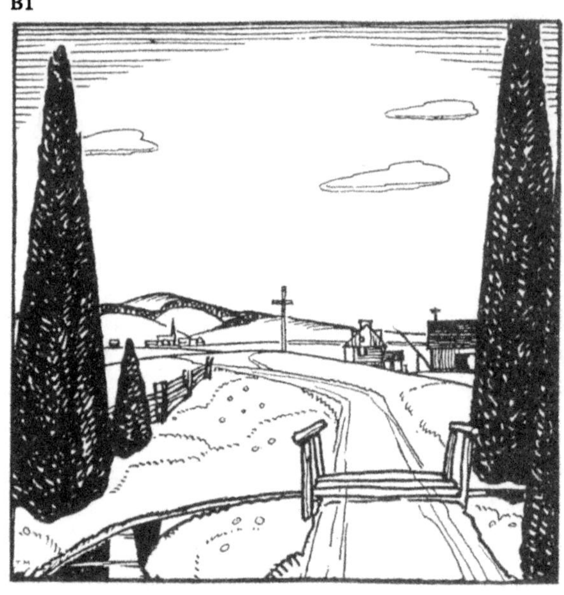

B1

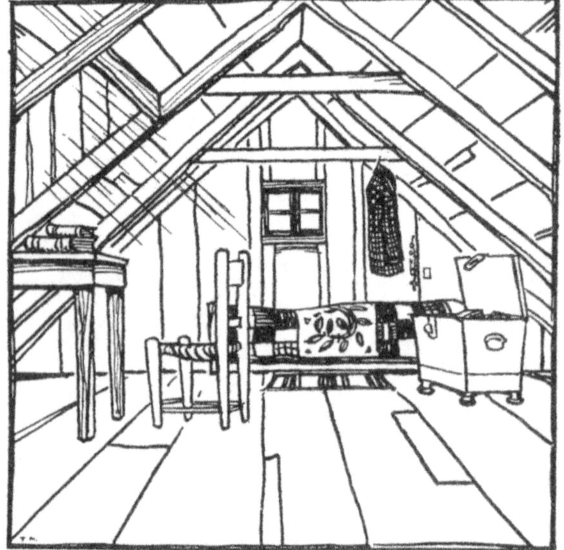

B2

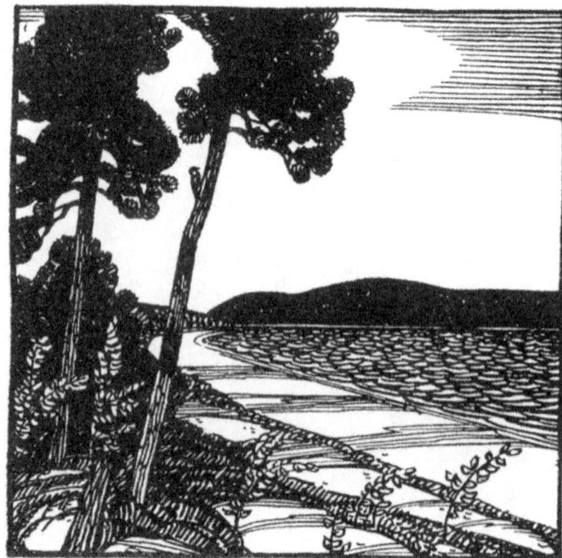

B3 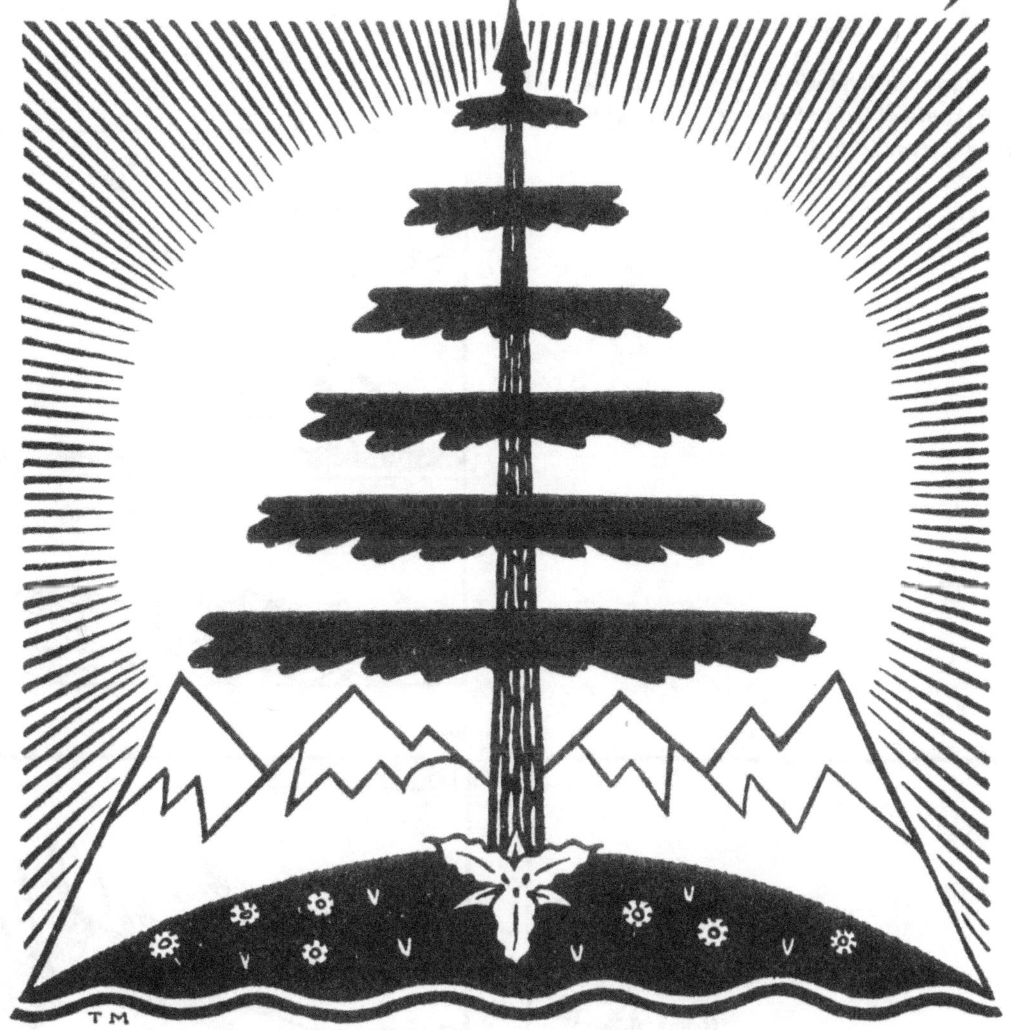
EXHIBITIONS
OF THE GROUP OF 7
TM
& ART IN FRENCH
CANADA MAY 7th.
—31st. 1926

B4
Shaw, Marlow A. *The Happy Islands: Stories and Sketches of the Georgian Bay.* Toronto, McClelland & Stewart [1926] 254 p
7 drawings (1 map); cover and jacket design.

1927

B5
Canadian National Exhibition. *Catalogue of Fine, Graphic & Applied Arts & Salon of Photography, Aug. 27th to Sept. 10th, 1927.* unpaged
Cover title
Cover design

B4

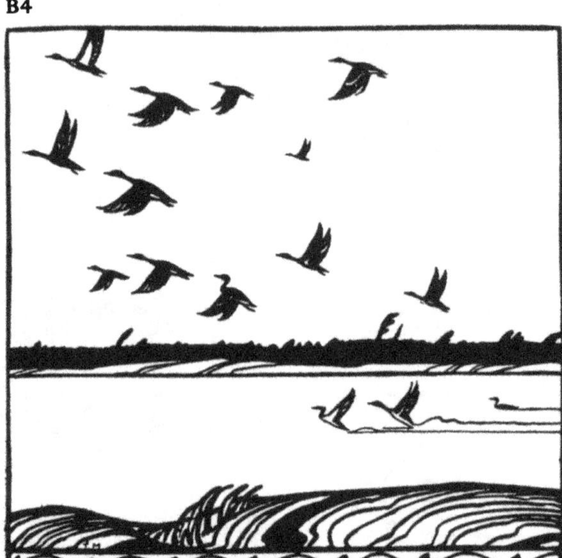

B4

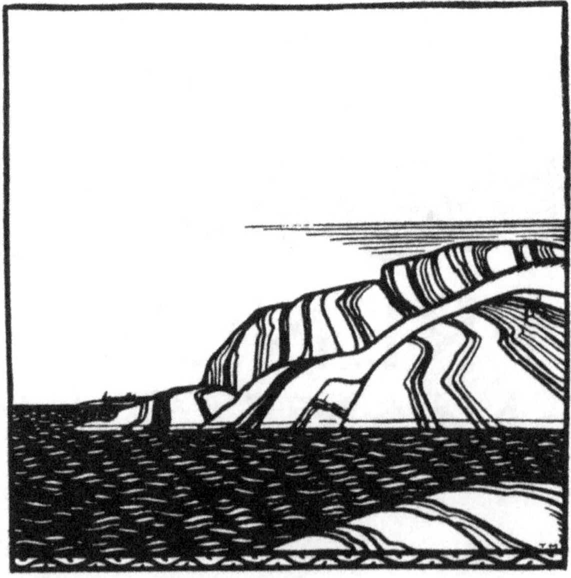

B4

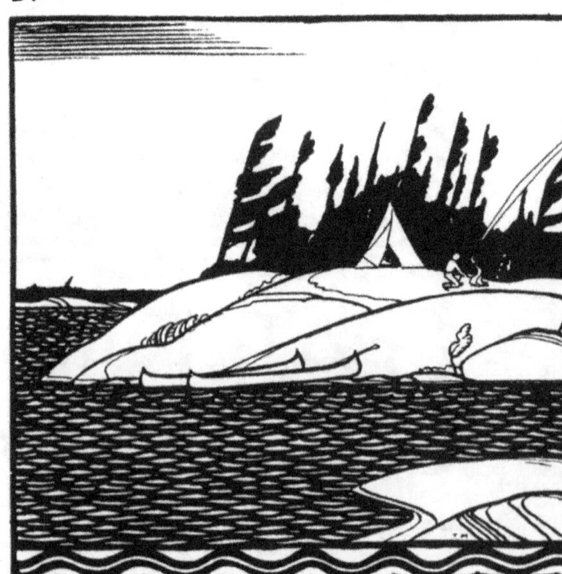

B6
MacDonald, Wilson. *An Ode on the Diamond Jubilee of Confederation.* [Toronto] published by Wilson MacDonald [1927] 15 leaves
Edition limited to 495 copies
11 initials and decorative head-line, cover, spine lettering, and jacket design

B6

AN ODE
ON THE DIAMOND
JUBILEE OF
CONFEDERATION
by Wilson MacDonald

PUBLISHED BY
WILSON MACDONALD

B7

Pratt, Edwin J. *The Iron Door (An Ode).* Toronto, Macmillan of Canada, 1927. 30 p
Edition limited to 1000 copies (100 copies on handmade paper, numbered, and signed by the author)
7 drawings (2 vignettes), title page
Jacket design by Eric Arthur

1930

B8

Canadian National Exhibition. *Catalogue of the Fine, Graphic and Applied Arts, and Salon of Photography, August 22nd to September 6th, 1930.* 110 p
Cover title
Cover design

B7

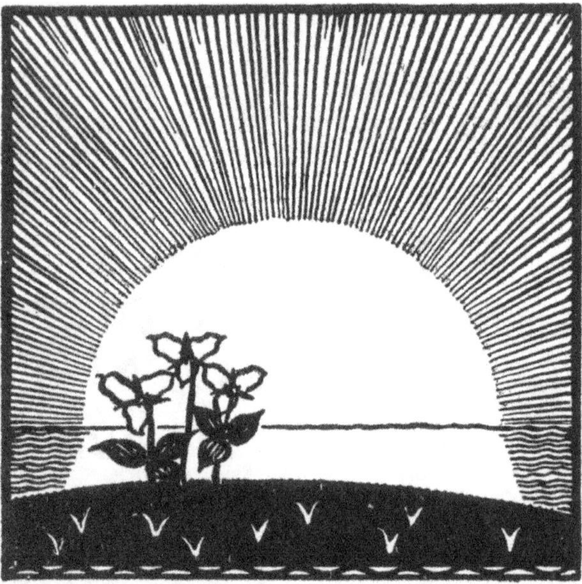

B7

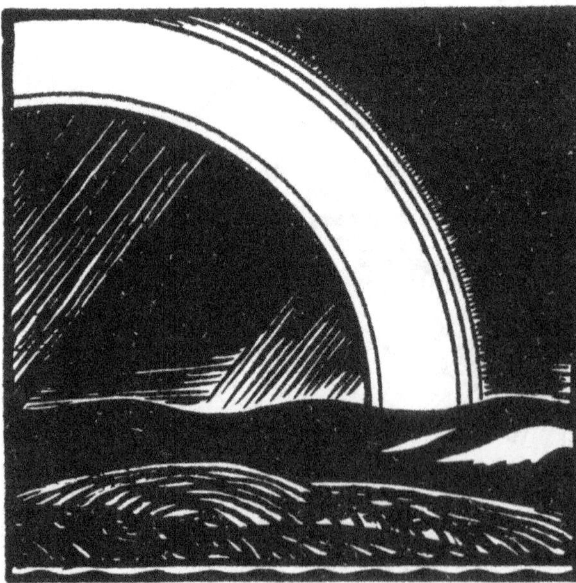

B7

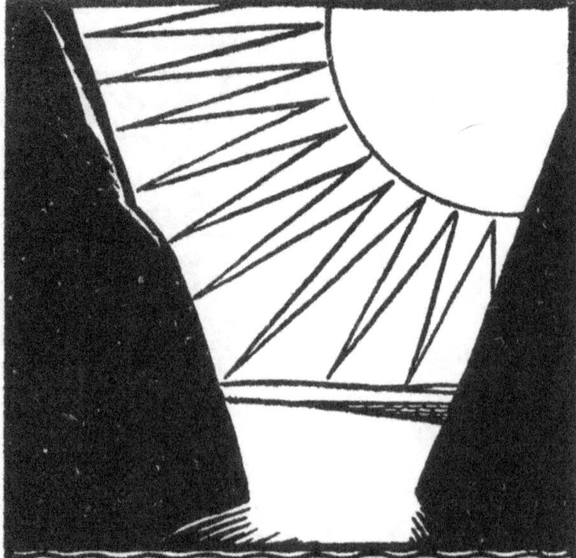

B8

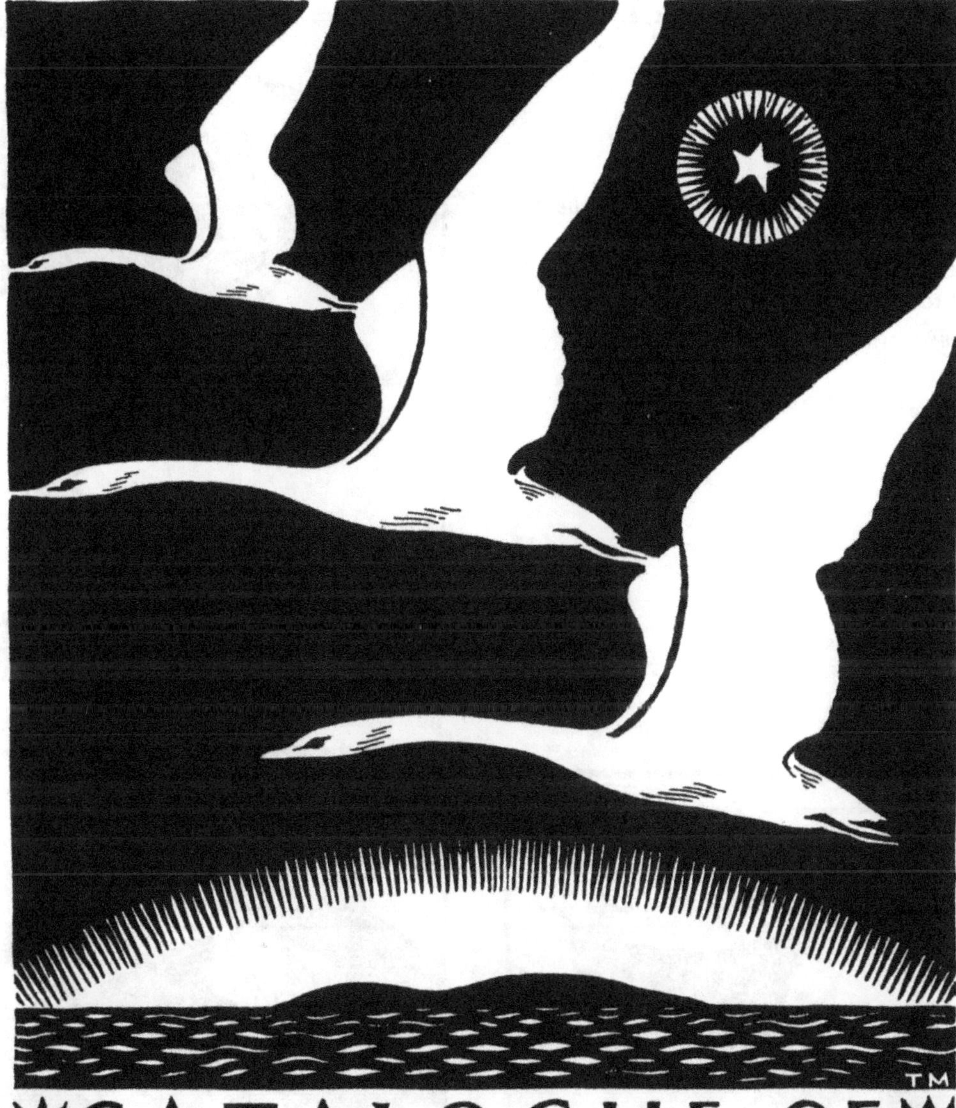
TM
CATALOGUE OF
FINE, GRAPHIC, AND
APPLIED ARTS, AND
SALON of PHOTOGRAPHY
Canadian National Exhibition
August 22nd to September 6th 1930

B9
Mackay, Isabel Ecclestone. *Indian Nights.* Toronto, McClelland & Stewart [1930] 198 p
11 drawings, title page vignette, jacket, and end papers

1931

B10
Canadian National Exhibition. *Catalogue of the Arts, 1931.* 190 p
Cover title
28 August to 12 September 1931
Cover design

B9

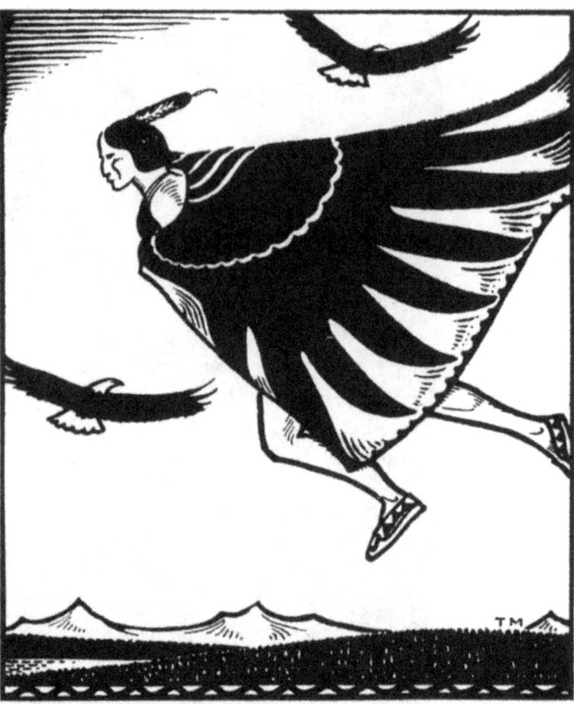

B9

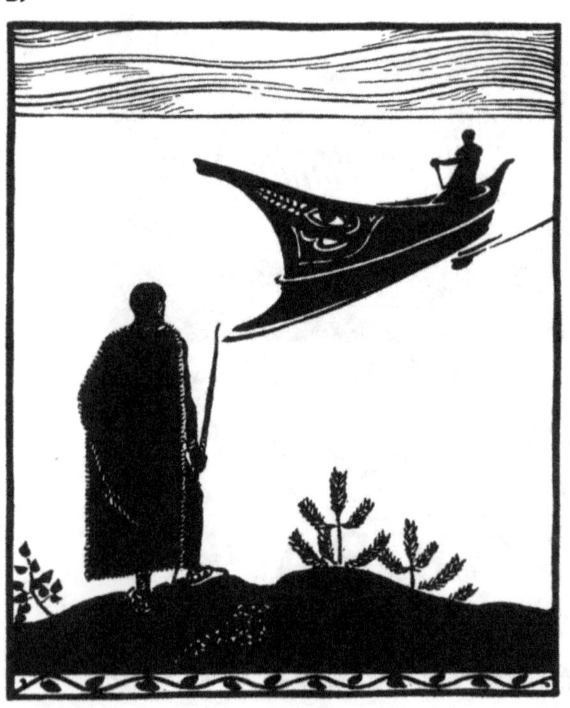

B9

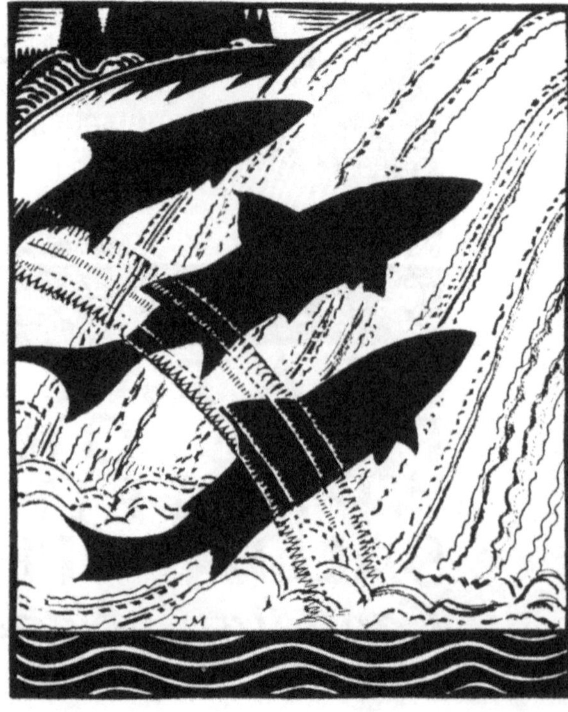

B11
Gordon, Ronald K. *A Canadian Child's* ABC, *Verses.*
Toronto, Dent [1931] [57] p
26 drawings (1 map), title page design
Binding variants

B11

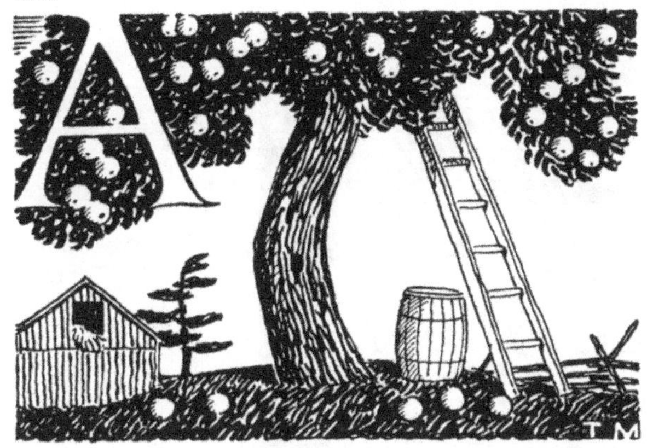

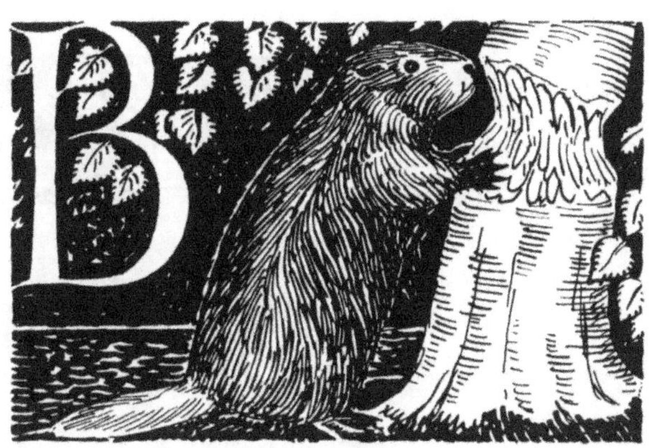

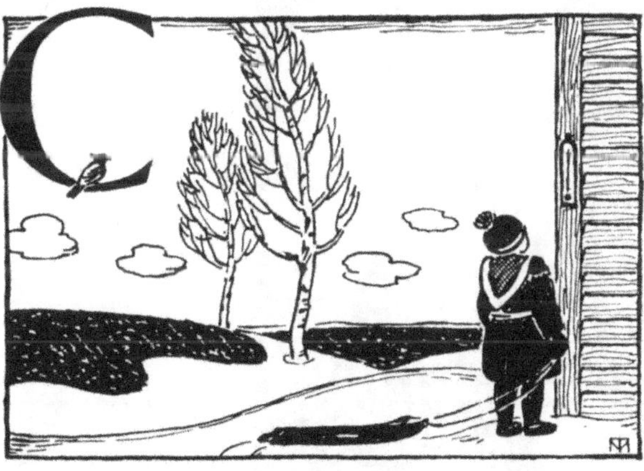

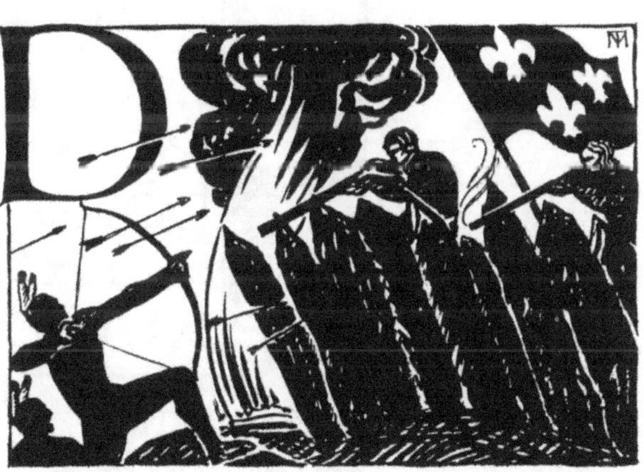

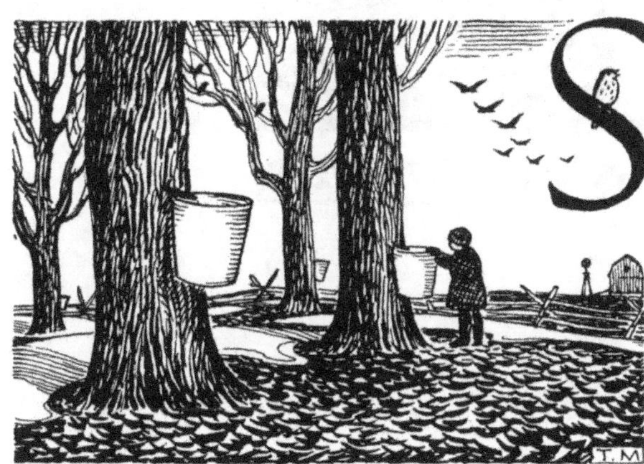

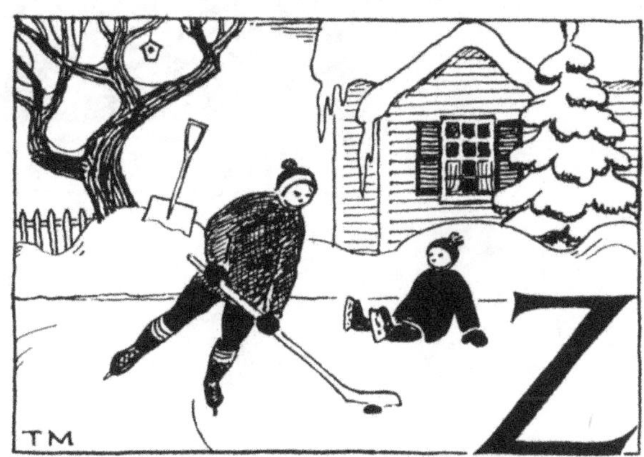

B11

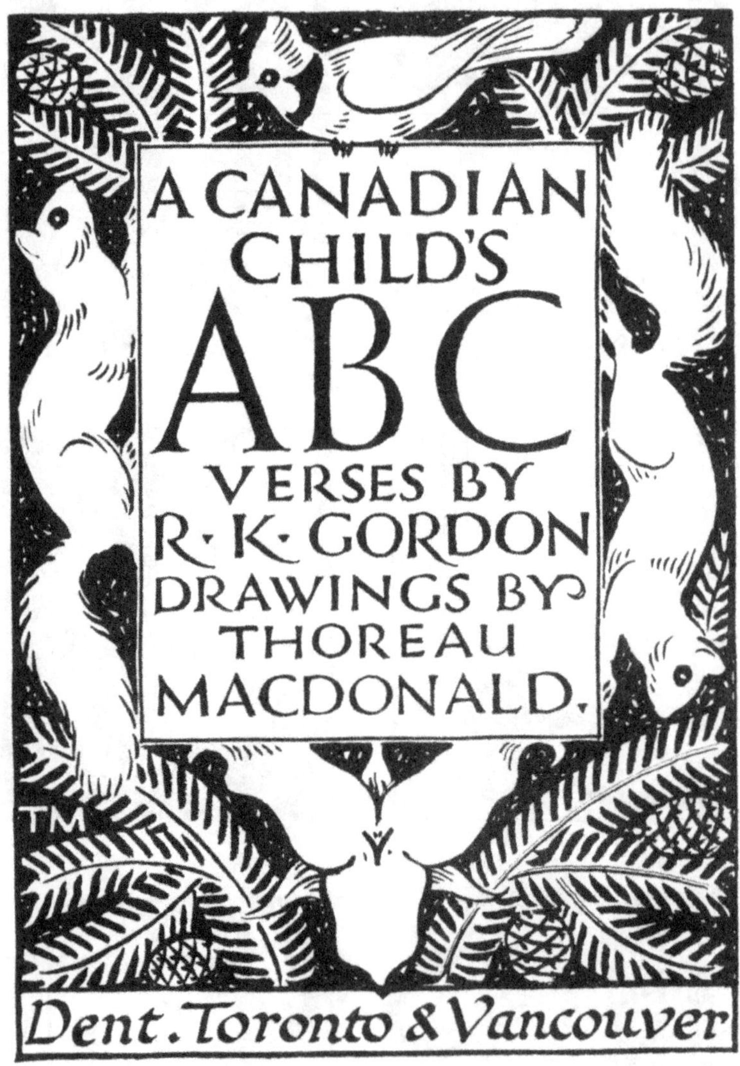
A CANADIAN
CHILD'S
ABC
VERSES BY
R·K·GORDON
DRAWINGS BY
THOREAU
MACDONALD.
TM
Dent. Toronto & Vancouver

B12
Davies, Blodwen. *Storied York: Toronto Old and New.* Toronto, Ryerson Press [1931] 127 p
17 drawings and jacket drawing
Also issued in wrappers

1932

B13
Canadian National Exhibition. *Catalogue of the Arts, 1932.* 134 p
Cover title
26 August to 10 September 1932
Cover design

B12

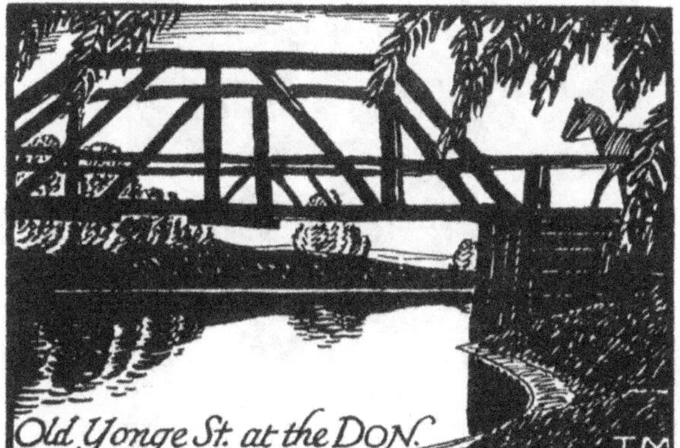

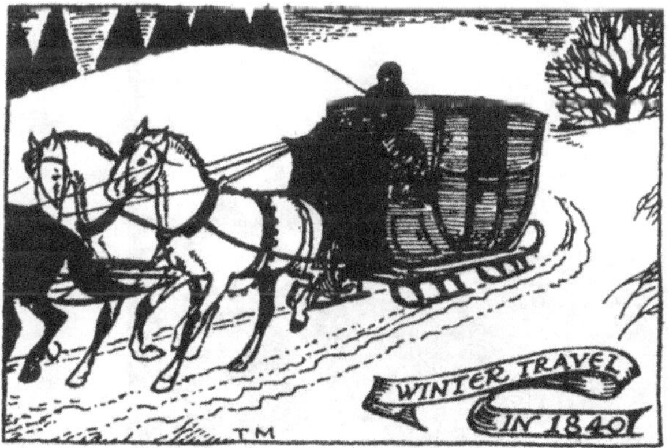

B12

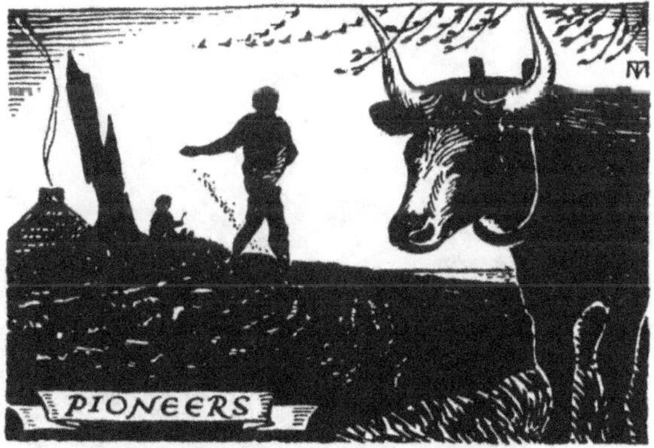

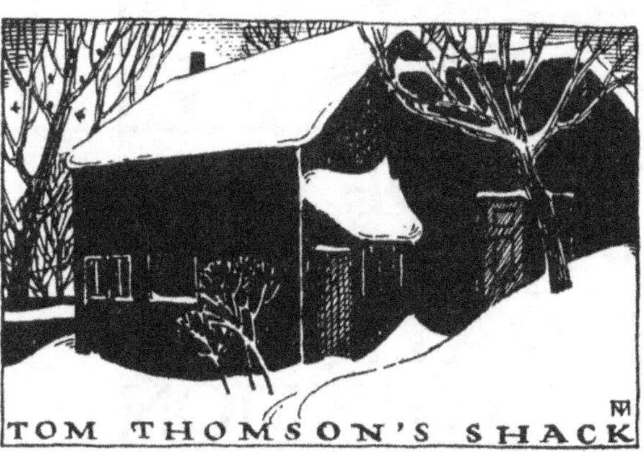

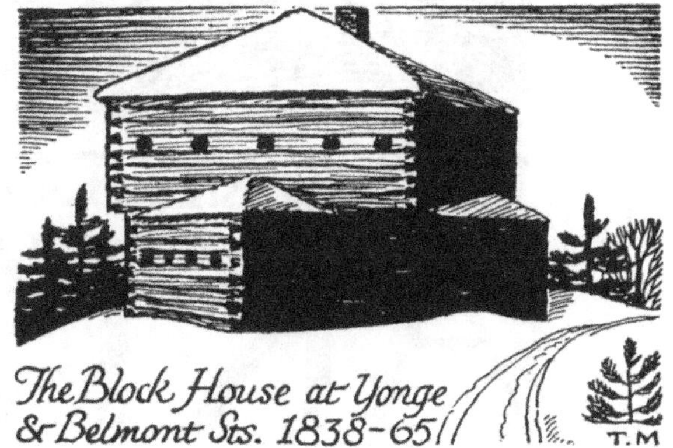

B14

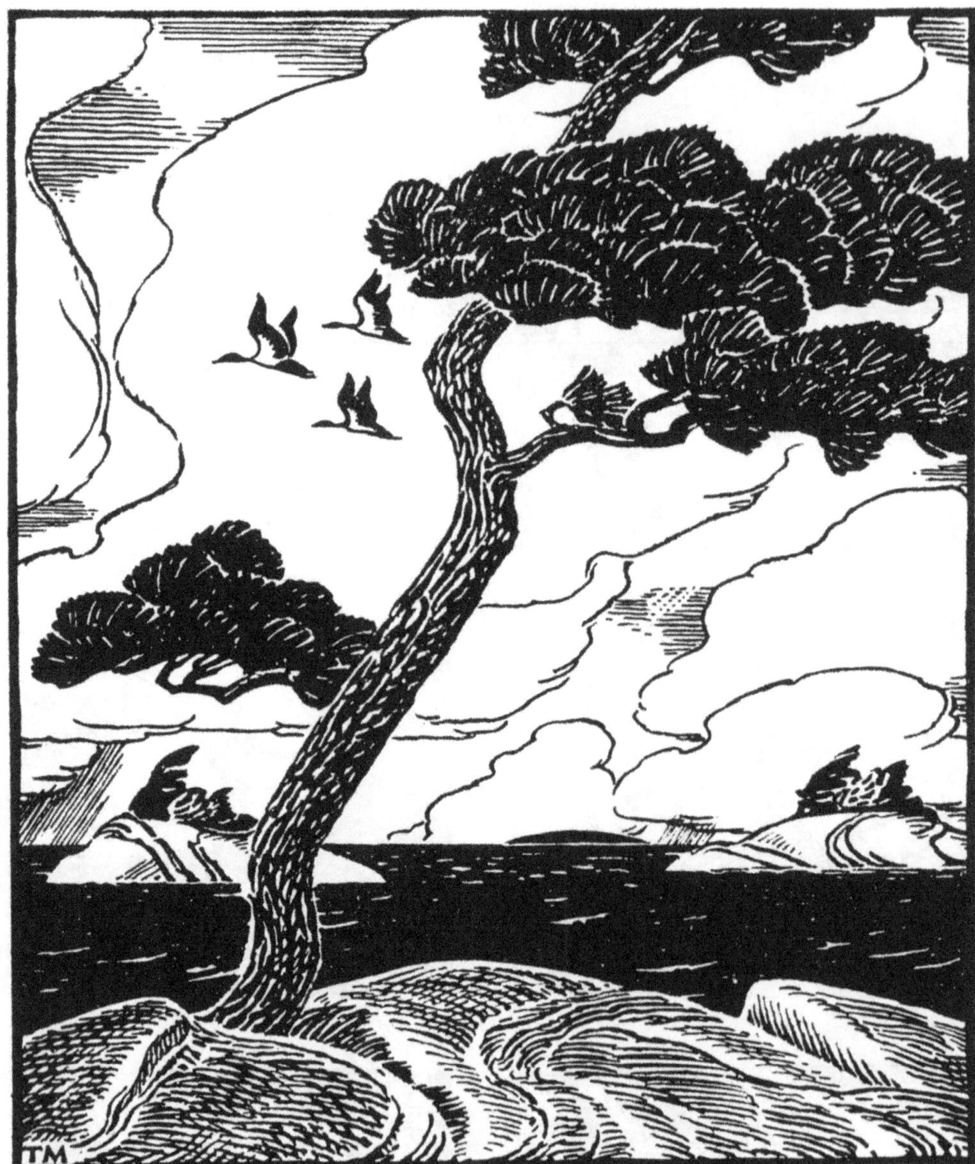

1933 CATALOGUE OF THE ARTS CANADIAN NATIONAL EXHIBITION

1933

B14
Canadian National Exhibition. *Catalogue of the Arts, 1933.* 111 p
Cover title
25 August to 9 September 1933
Cover design

B15
MacDonald, James E.H. *Village and Fields: a few Country Poems.* Thornhill [Woodchuck Press, 1933]
[17] p
Cover title
Edition limited to about 200 copies
3 drawings (2 vignettes), Woodchuck Press device

B15

VILLAGE
& FIELDS
A Few Country Poems by
J. E. H. MACDONALD

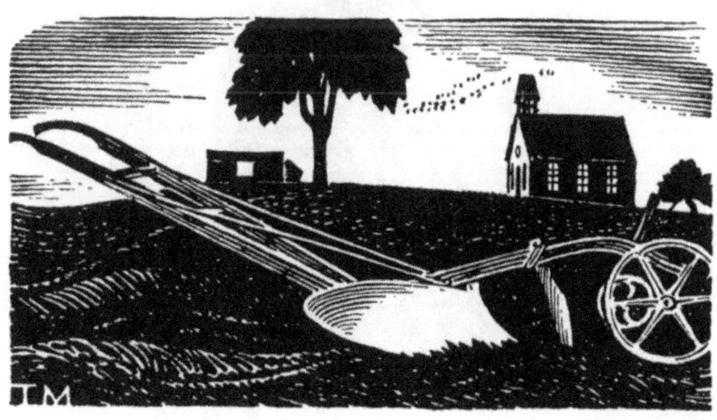

B16
MacDonald, James E.H. *West by East, and other Poems.* Toronto, Ryerson Press, 1933. 37 p
Edition limited to 500 copies, of which 250 were for sale
20 drawings, design, jacket, spine lettering, and title page vignette
Boxed

1934

B17
Canadian National Exhibition. *Catalogue of the Arts, 1934.* 154 p
Cover title
24 August to 8 September 1934
Cover design

B16

WEST *BY* EAST
AND OTHER POEMS BY
J. E.H. MACDONALD

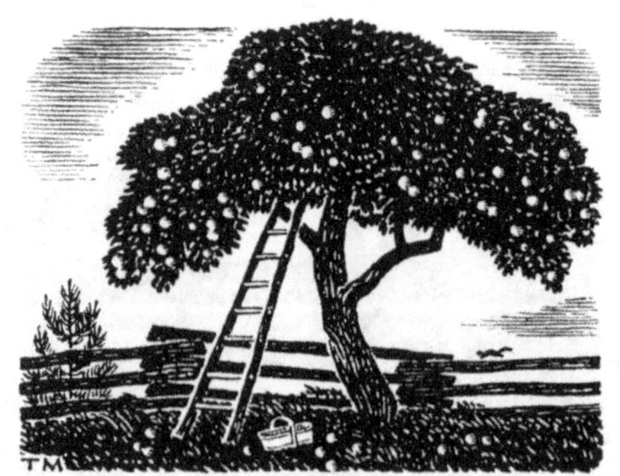

With Drawings by Thoreau MacDonald
TORONTO, The RYERSON PRESS, 1933

B16

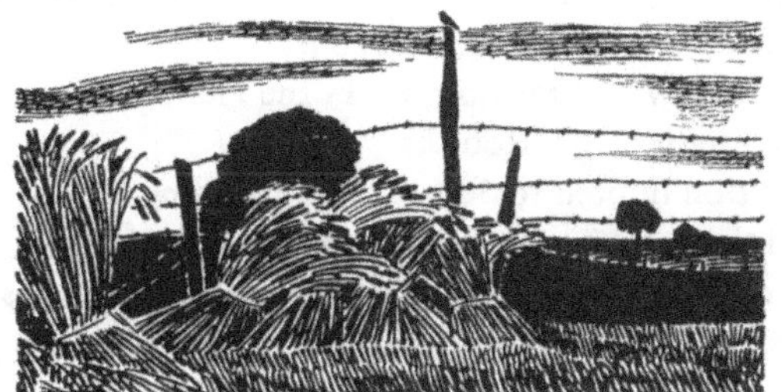

B16

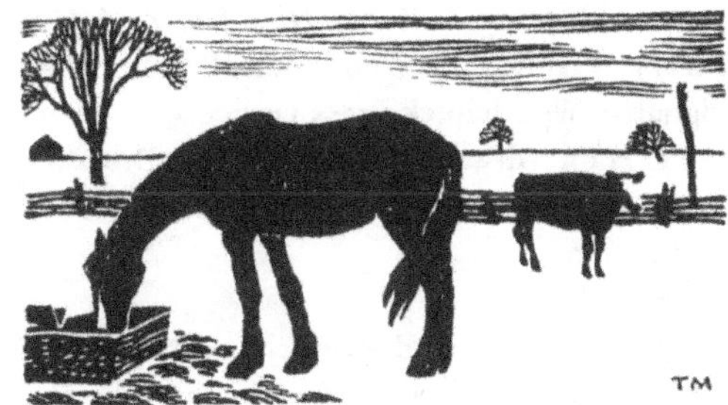

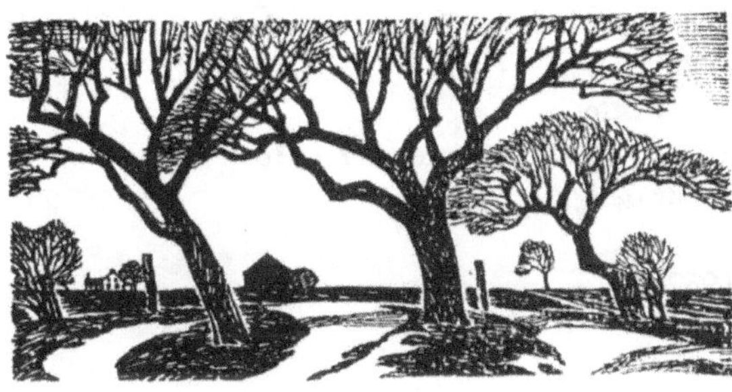

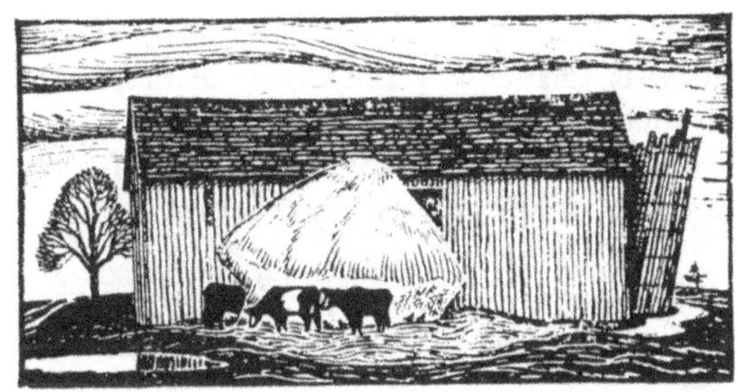

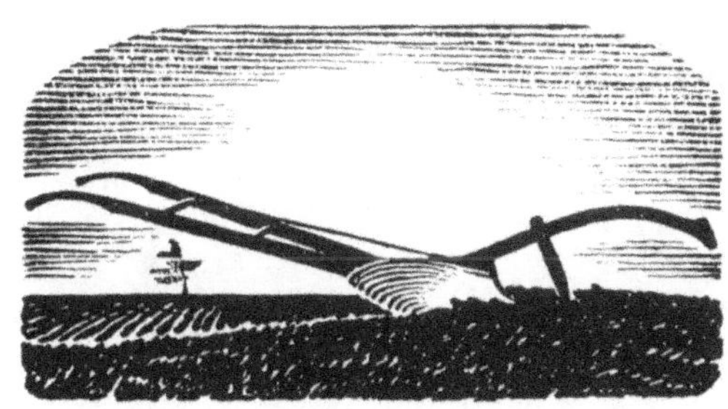

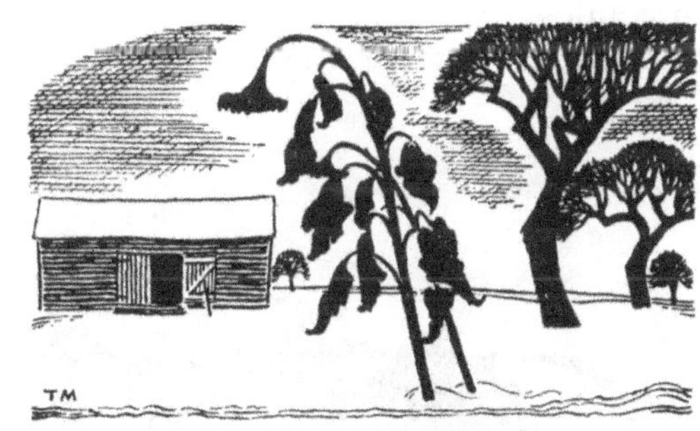

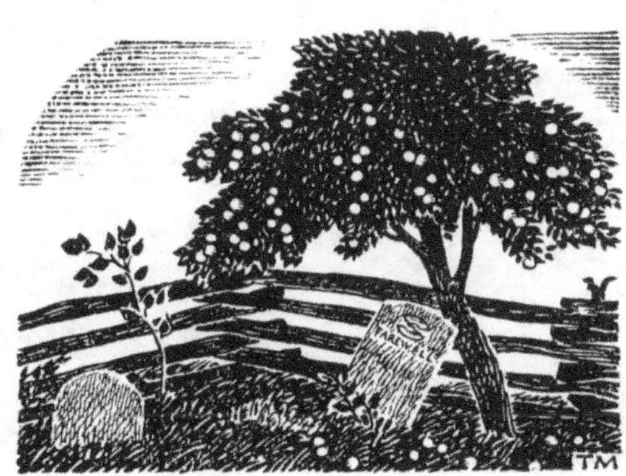

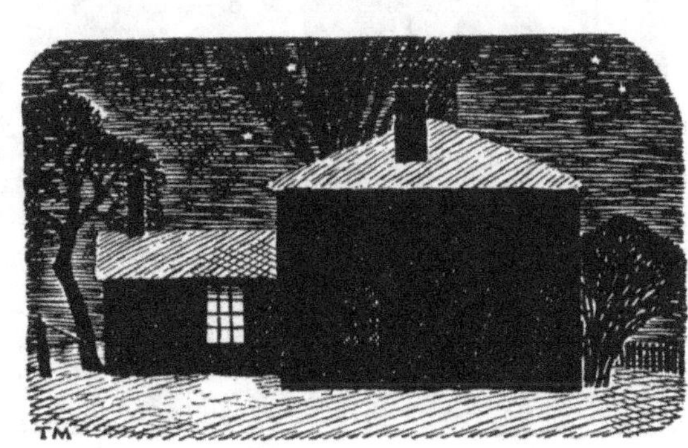

B18
MacDonald, James E.H. *My High Horse: A Mountain Memory.* [Thornhill] Woodchuck Press, 1934. [9] p
1 vignette, Woodchuck Press Device
'Lake O'Hara' (drawing) by J.E.H. MacDonald
- another edition. [Thornhill, Woodchuck Press, 1934] 7 p
Cover title
1 vignette, cover, and Woodchuck Press device
This edition, in a smaller format than the preceding, does not contain the drawing by J.E.H. MacDonald.

B19
Roberts, Charles G.D. *The Iceberg, and other Poems.* Toronto, Ryerson Press, 1934. 31 p
Edition limited to 500 copies; 100 copies for sale
6 vignettes, title page design, and cover

1935

B20
Canadian National Exhibition. *Catalogue of the Arts, 1935.* 158 p
Cover title
23 August to 7 September 1935
Cover design

B21
Sherman, Francis. *The Complete Poems.* Toronto, Ryerson Press, 1935. ix, 178 p
Edited, with a memoir, by Lorne Pierce, foreword by Charles G.D. Roberts
Edition limited to 500 copies (including special edition of 25 copies on handmade paper)
7 drawings (2 repeated), incorrectly described as woodcuts, title page, and cover design

1936

B22
Canadian National Exhibition. *Catalogue of the Arts, 1936.* 150 p
Cover title
28 August to 12 September 1936
Cover design

1937

B23
Canadian National Exhibition. *Catalogue of the Arts, 1937.* 141 p
Cover title
27 August to 11 September 1937
Cover design

B18

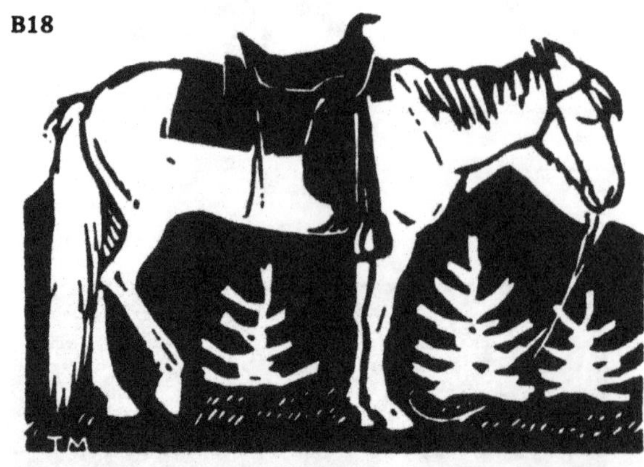

B21

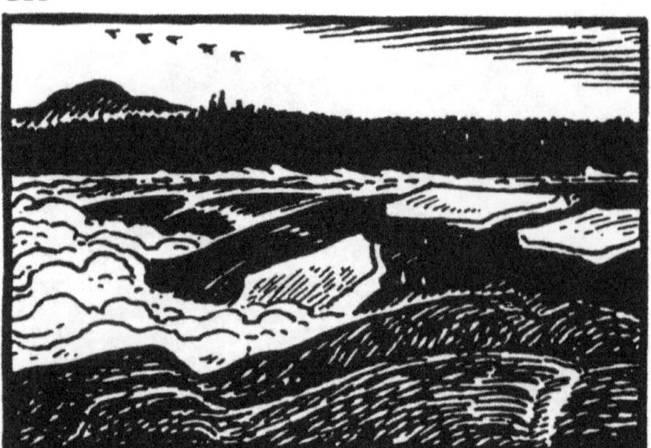

B20

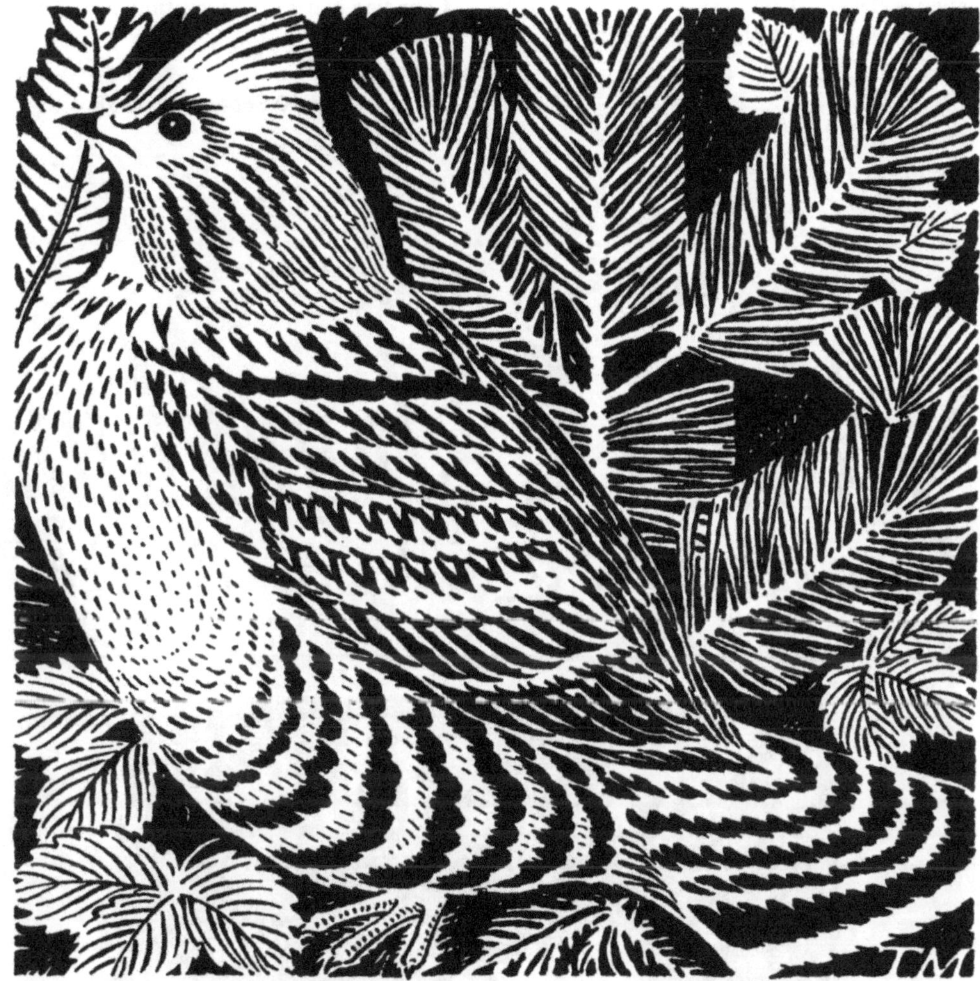

1935 CANADIAN NATIONAL EXHIBITION

CATALOGUE of the ARTS

B24
Catalogue; a Loan Exhibition of the Work of J.E.H. MacDonald, R.C.A., *November, 1937.* Toronto, Mellors Galleries, 1937. 11 p
Exhibition, 30 October – 13 November 1937
Cover design

1938

B25
Canadian National Exhibition. *Arts Catalogue, 1938.* 164 p
Cover title
26 August to 10 September 1938
Cover design

B26

LOUIS HÉMON'S
Maria Chapdelaine
Translated by W. H. BLAKE

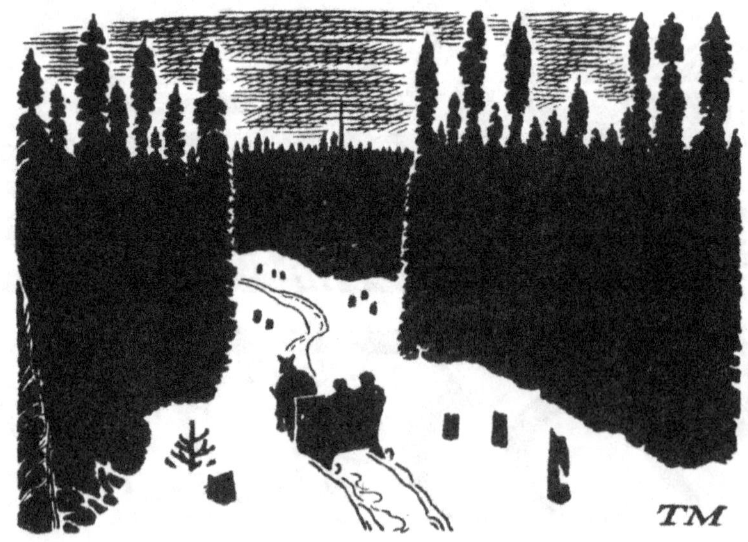

With a Historical Introduction by Hugh Eayrs
Illustrated by Thoreau MacDonald

B26

Hémon, Louis. *Maria Chapdelaine*. Toronto, Macmillan of Canada, 1938. 174 p

Translated by W.H. Blake, with introduction by Hugh Eayrs

45 drawings (14 vignettes), title page, cover, and jacket

This edition was the first to be illustrated by TM. (The book was first issued by Macmillan in 1921.) The drawing on p 68 ('Wendigo pursuing the trespassing hunter') was exhibited at the American Institute of Graphic Arts show, International Book Illustration, 1935-1945 (New York, Pierpont Morgan Library, September–October 1946) catalogue issued.

- another edition. Toronto, Macmillan of Canada, 1965. xiii, 161 p
  Translated, and with an introduction by W.H. Blake
  42 drawings (12 vignettes), title page vignette, and jacket illustration
  This edition entirely reset and reissued in cloth and paper

B26

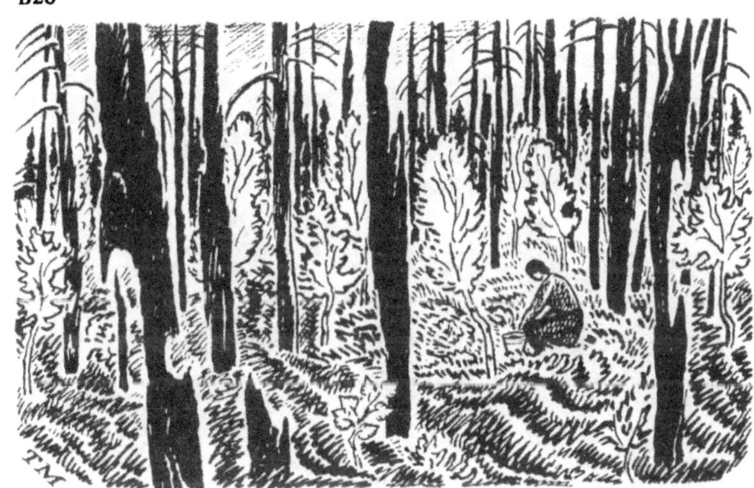

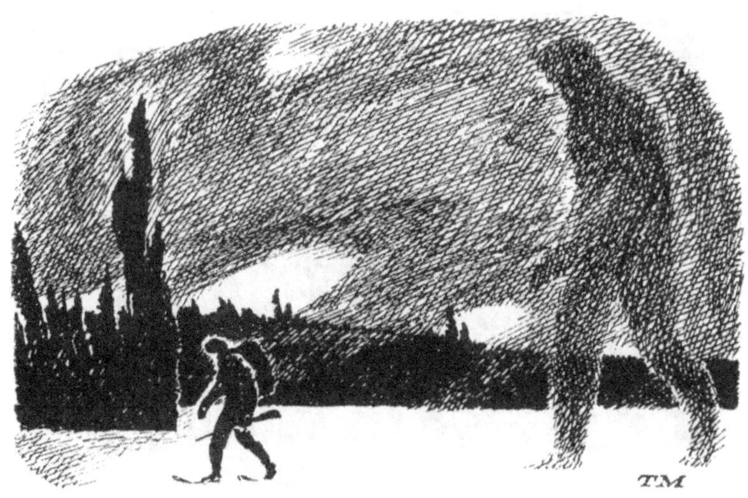

B26

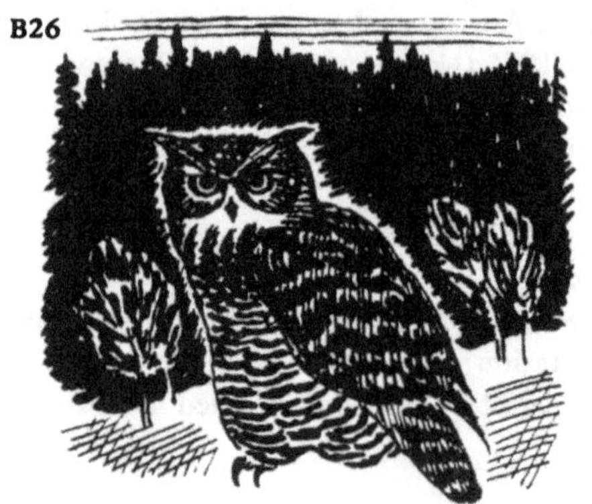

1939

B27
Canadian National Exhibition. *Catalogue of the Arts, 1939*. 107 p
Cover title
25 August to 9 September 1939
Cover design

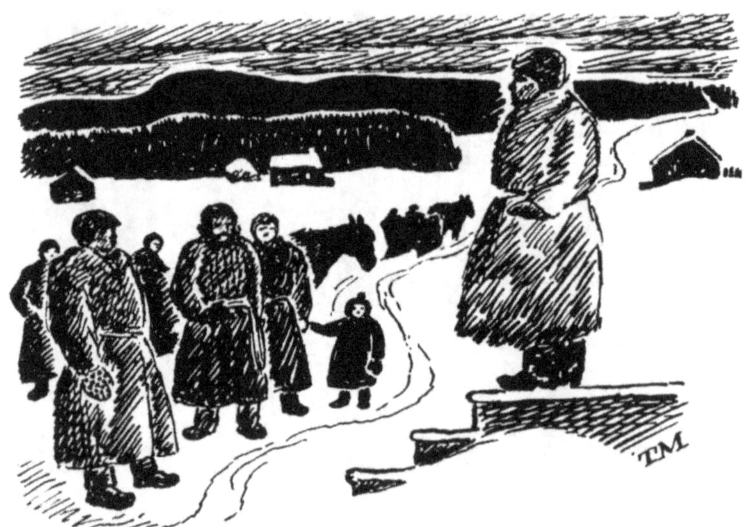

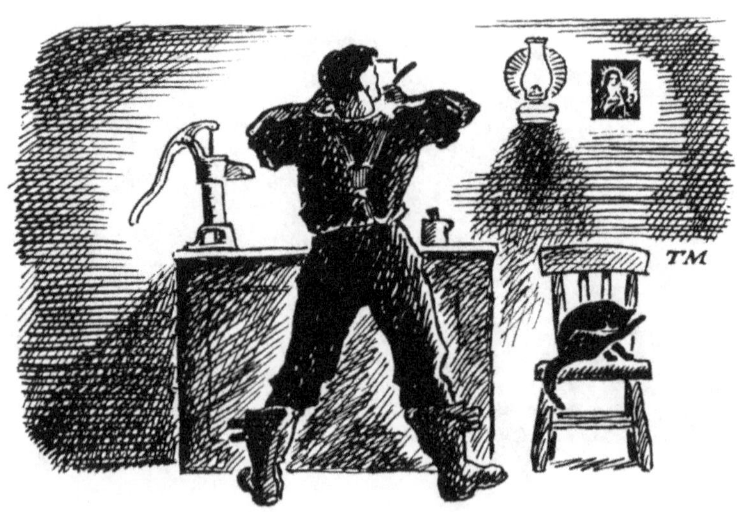

B27

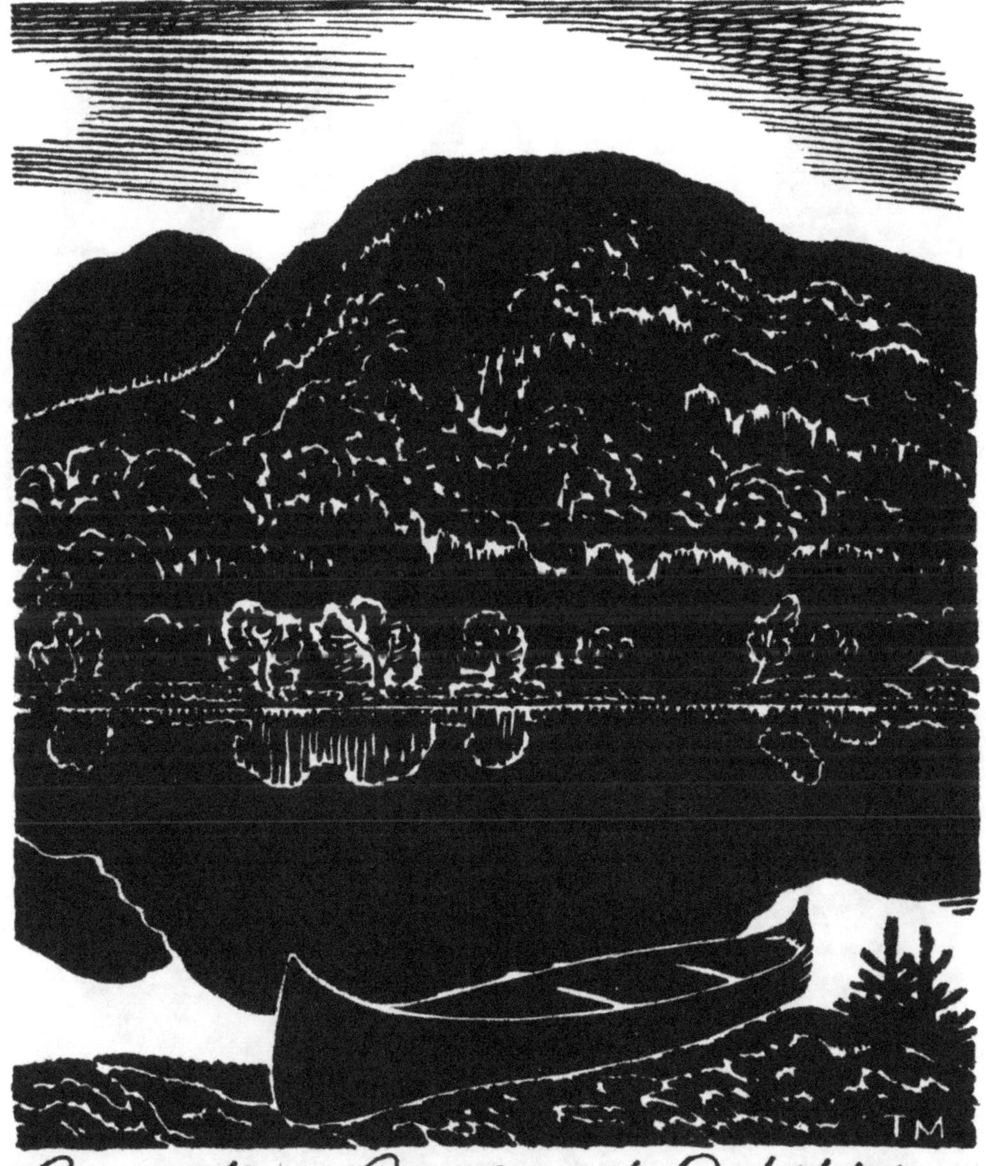

Canadian National Exhibition
Catalogue of the ARTS 1939

B28

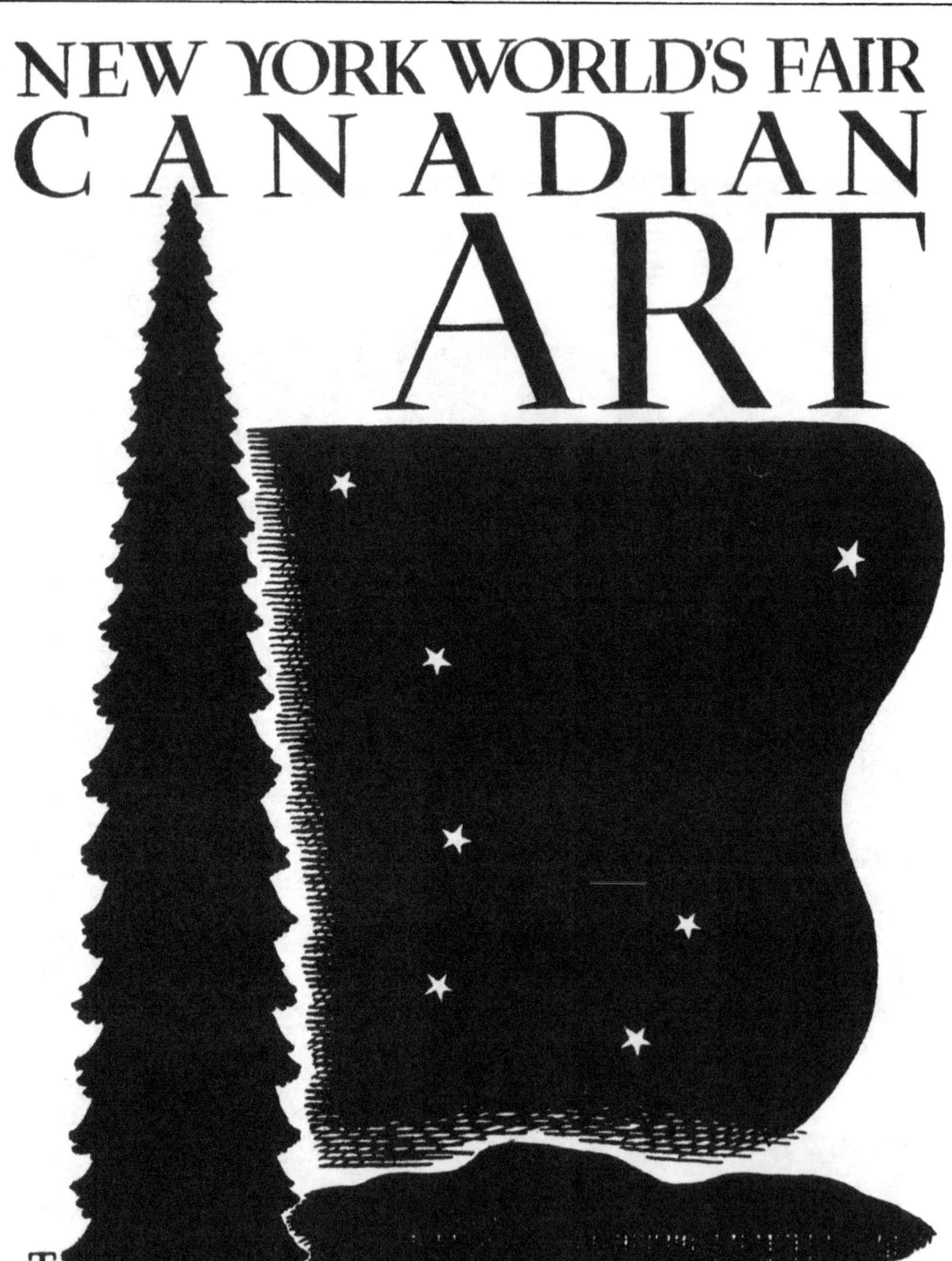

B28
Exhibition of Canadian Art. New York World's Fair, 1939. Ottawa, The National Gallery of Canada [1939] 21 p
Cover title: New York World's Fair; Canadian Art. 'The Canadian Society of Painters in Watercolour; The Sculptors' Society of Canada, June 19–July 31, 1939'
Cover design
A variant cover design, reading 'Canadian Art,' was also issued.

B29
Exhibition of the Work of Tom Thomson and J.E.H. MacDonald, February 1st to 18th, 1939. Toronto, Mellors Galleries, 1939. [3] p folder.
Design and preface

1942

B30
Canadian Group of Painters 1942 Travelling Exhibition. Ottawa, The National Gallery of Canada [1942] 8 p
Cover design

B31
Clarence Gagnon, 1881-1942; Memorial Exhibition. Ottawa, The National Gallery of Canada [1942] 24 p
Cover design

1944

B32
Barbeau, Marius. *Mountain Cloud.* Caldwell, Idaho, Caxton Printers; Toronto, Macmillan of Canada, 1944. 300 p
32 drawings
Reproduction of painting on jacket
Title page design by A.Y. Jackson
End papers by Naomi, Geneva, and Constance Jackson

B32

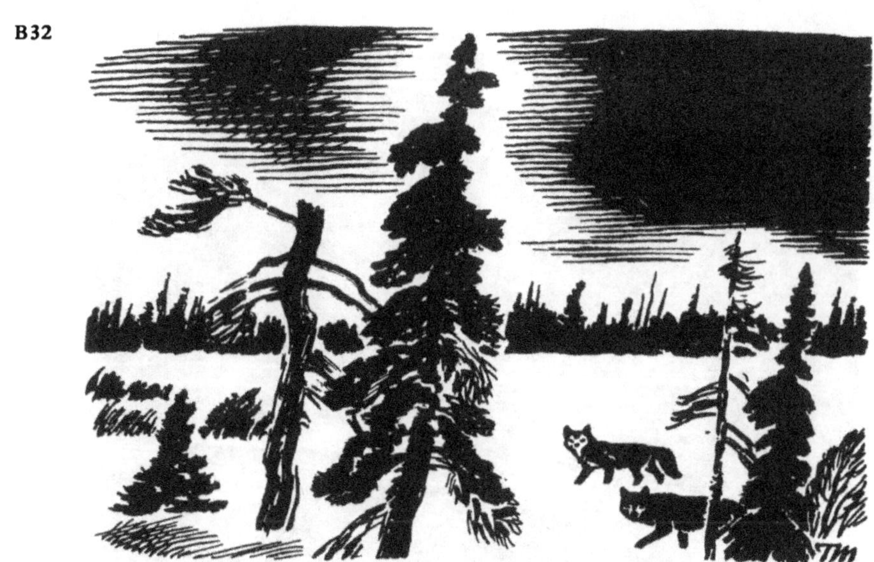

B32

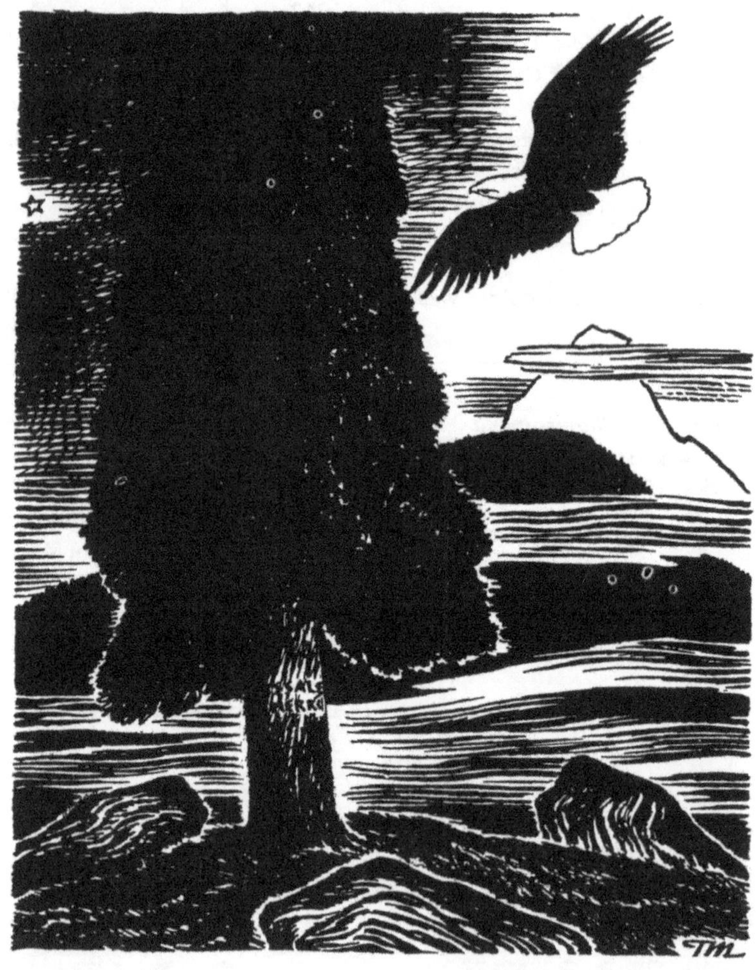

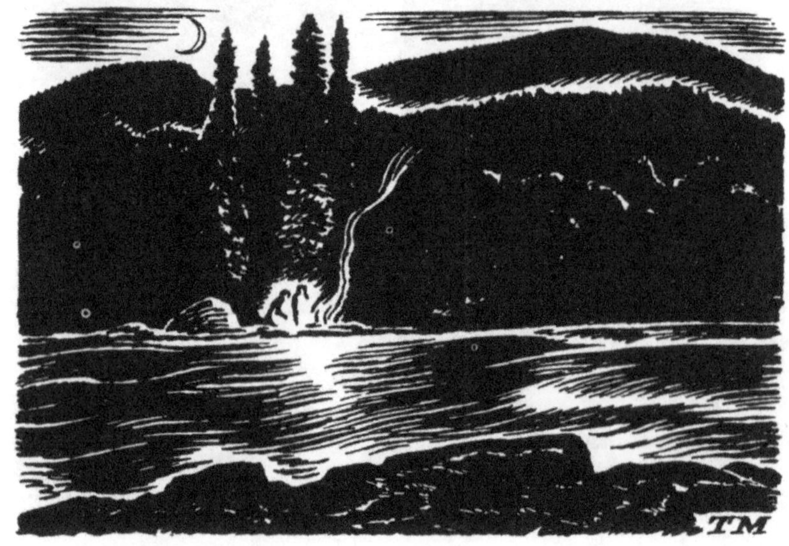

B33
RCAF Exhibition of Painting & Drawings, April, 1944. [Ottawa, National Gallery of Canada, 1944] 28 p
Cover design

B35

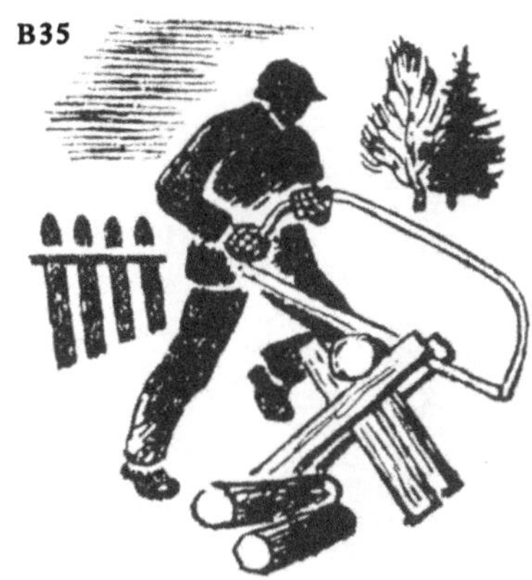

1945

B34
Kiriline, Louise de. *The Loghouse Nest.* [Toronto] S.J. Reginald Saunders [1945] 173 p
28 drawings (14 vignettes, including repeats) jacket drawing, and spine lettering
End paper designs by the author

B35
Scott, Duncan Campbell. *In the Village of Viger.* Toronto, Ryerson Press [1945] 114 p
22 drawings (12 vignettes, including repeats), jacket design

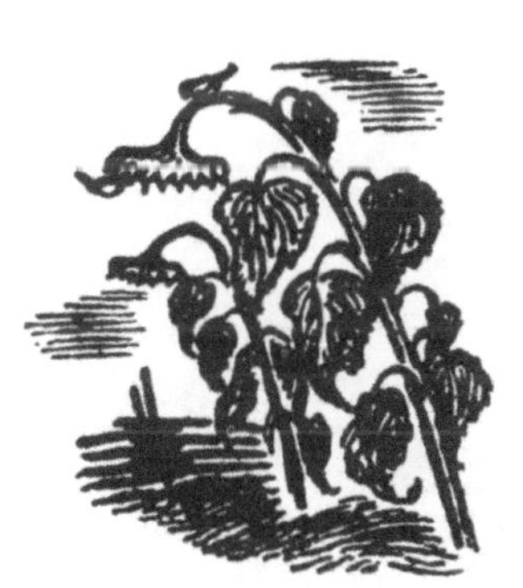

B35

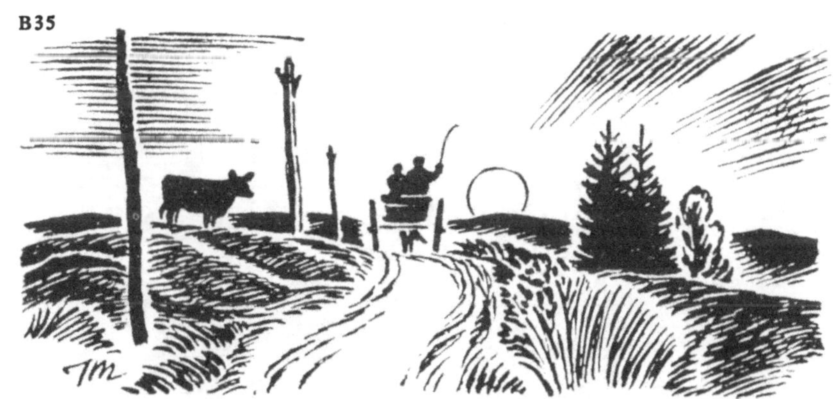

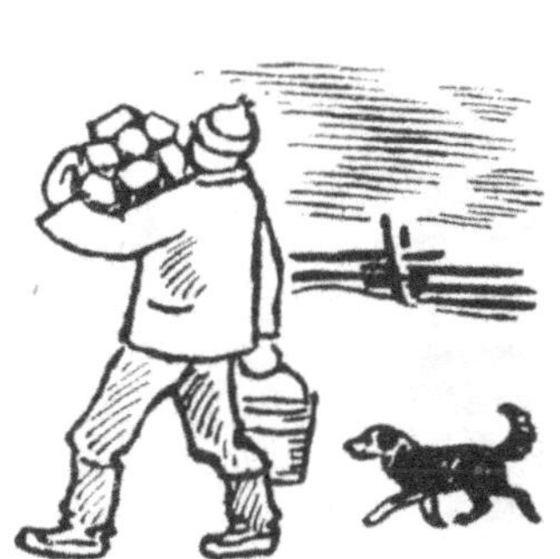

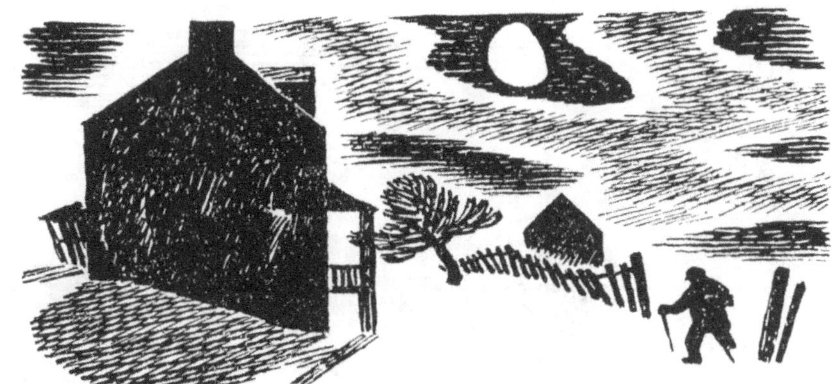

1947

B36
Canadian National Exhibition. *Catalogue of the Arts, 1947.* 40 p
Cover title
22 August to 6 September 1947
Cover design

B37
Middleton, Clara J. and Middleton, Jesse Edgar. *Green Fields Afar: Memories of Alberta Days.*
Toronto, Ryerson Press [1947] 61 p
10 drawings, title page drawing

B37

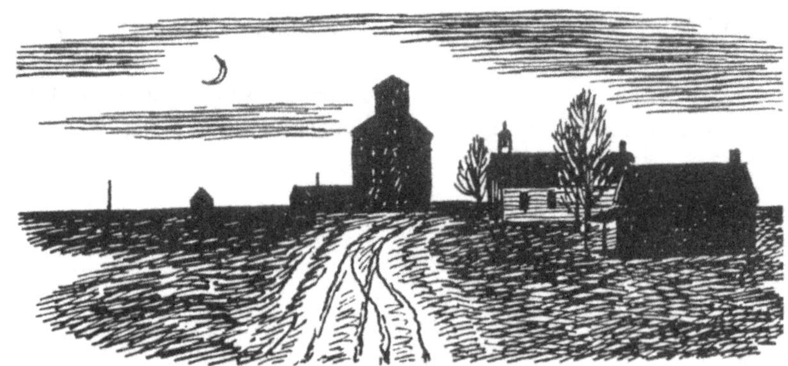

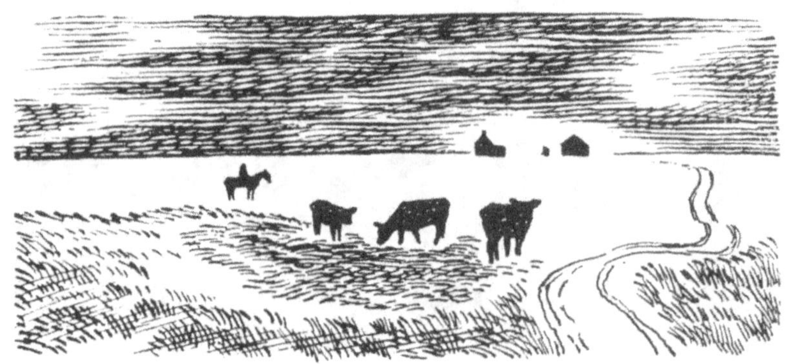

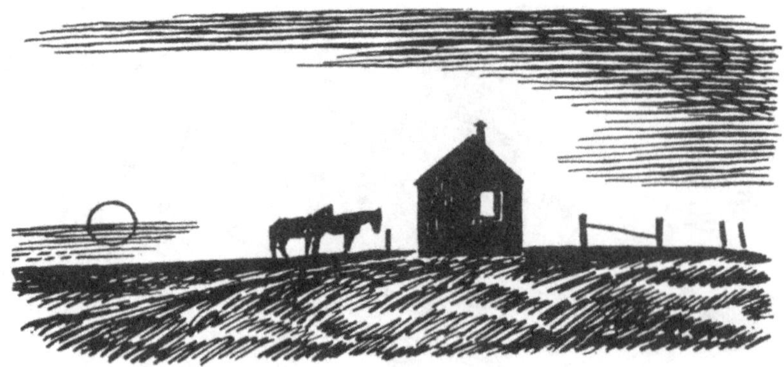

B38
Scott, Duncan Campbell. *The Circle of Affection and Other Pieces in Prose and Verse.* Toronto, McClelland and Stewart [1947] xiv, 237 p
10 vignettes, jacket design

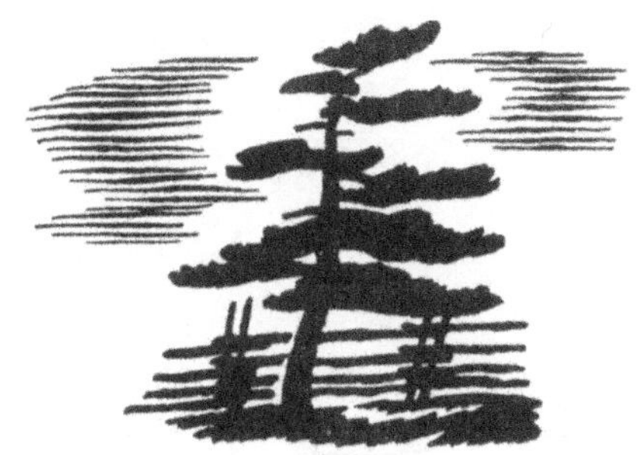

B38

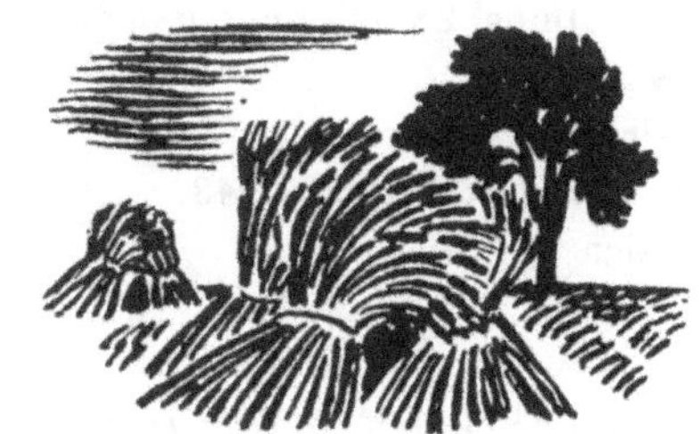

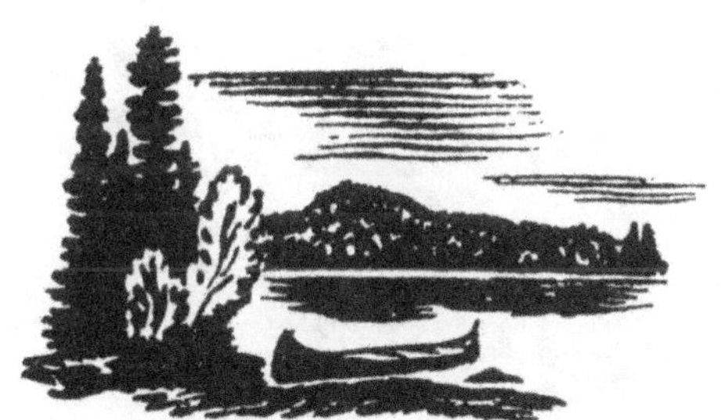

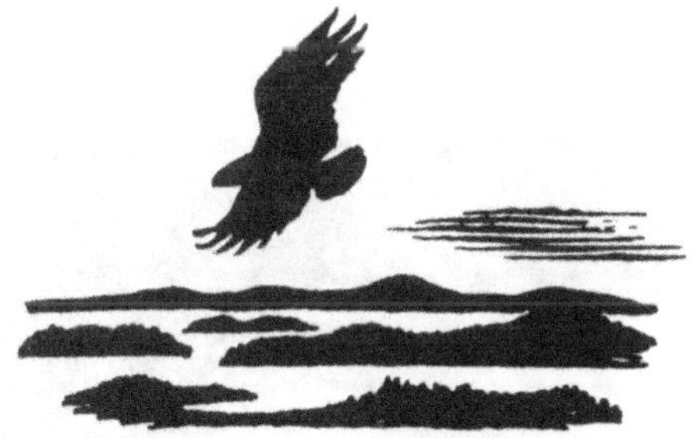

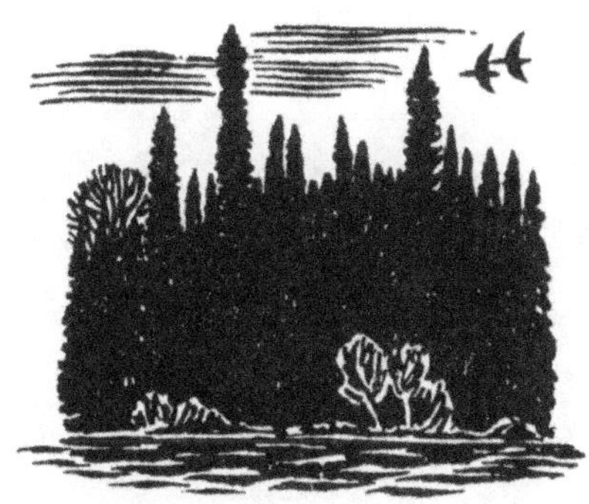

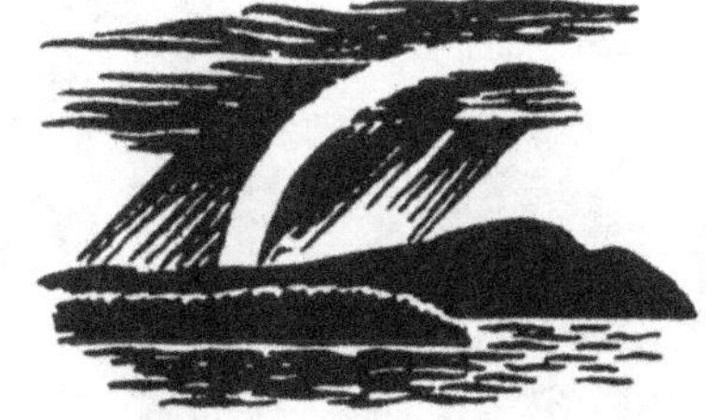

1948

B39
Beston, Henry. *Northern Farm: A Chronicle of Maine.* New York, Rinehart & Co. [1948] viii, 246 p
47 drawings, title page drawing and jacket design
Jacket exhibited at Second Annual Exhibition, Book Jacket Designers Guild (New York, 9 May–30 June 1949); catalogue issued

B40
Canadian National Exhibition, *Catalogue of the Arts, 1948.* 24 p
Cover title
27 August to 11 September 1948
Cover design

B41
Hambleton, Jack. *Forest Ranger.* Toronto, Longmans, Green and Co. [1948] 226 p
32 drawings (4 vignettes including repeats), title page vignette, and jacket illustration

B39

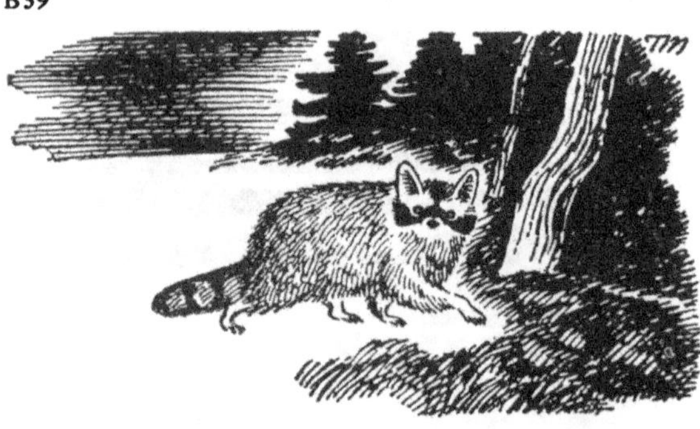

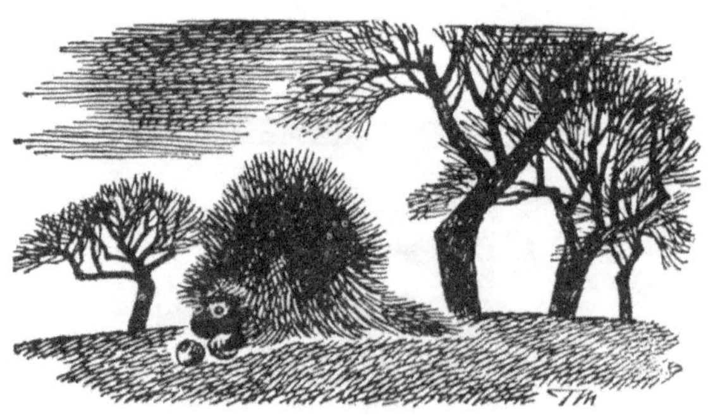

B42
Klein, Abraham Moses. *The Rocking Chair, and Other Poems.* Toronto, Ryerson Press [1948] 56 p
Design and cover lettering (no illustrations)
- another edition [1951]
  reprint, with 24 drawings, half-title, cover, and jacket lettering
- reprinted 1966 (same as preceeding)

B42

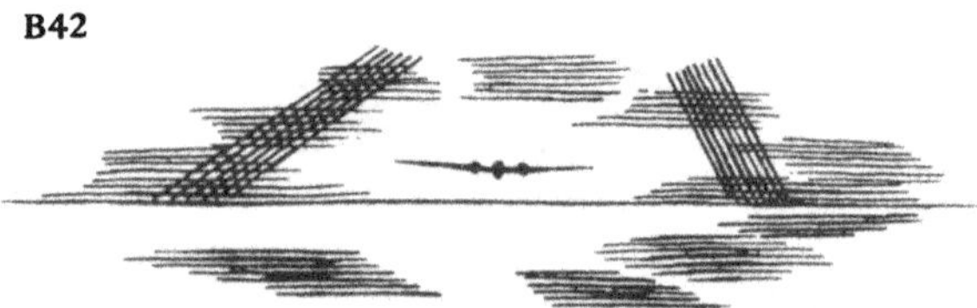

B39

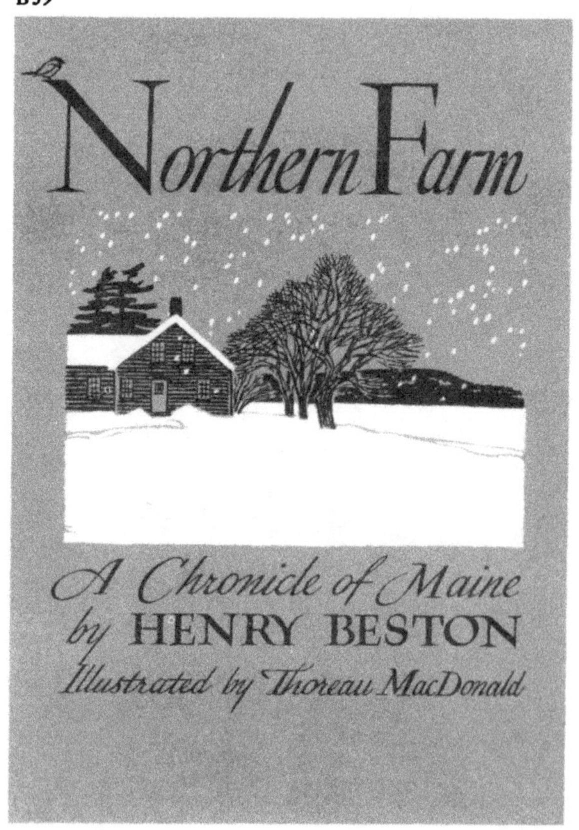

1949

B43
Canadian National Exhibition. *Catalogue of the Art Gallery, 1949.* 26 p
Cover title
26 August to 10 September 1949
Cover design

B44
Clarke, Andrew David. *Andy Clarke and his Neighbourly News.* Toronto, Ryerson Press [1949] xxv, 158 p
Introduction by Greg Clark
13 drawings (1 vignette), title page, and jacket design

B44

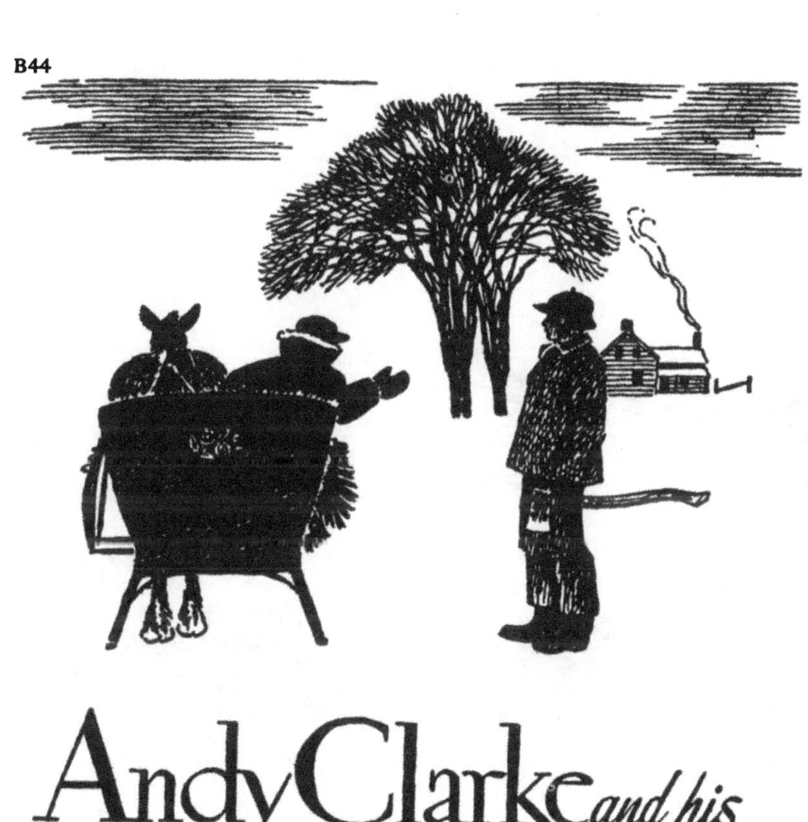

Andy Clarke and his Neighbourly News

With an Introduction by GREG CLARK

Toronto · The Ryerson Press

B45
Hambleton, Jack. *Young Bush Pilot.* Toronto, Longmans, Green and Co. [1949] vi, 200 p
38 drawings (11 vignettes including repeats), title page vignette and jacket design

B46
Roberts, Leslie. *The Mackenzie.* New York, Rinehart & Co. [1949] xii, 276 p
14 drawings (4 double page), end papers, and jacket drawing
2 maps not by TM
(Rivers of America series, edited by Hervey Allen and Carl Carmer)

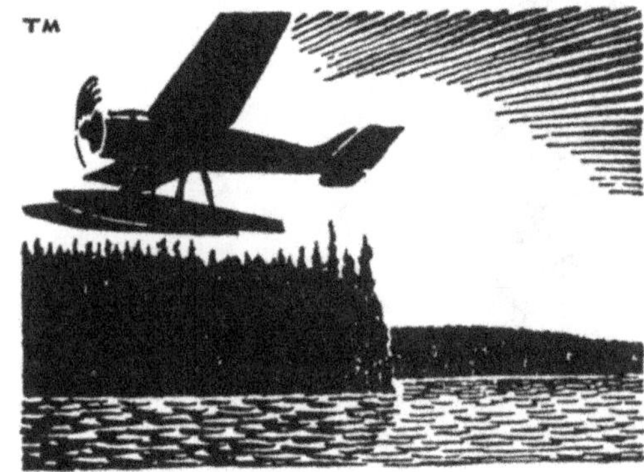

B45

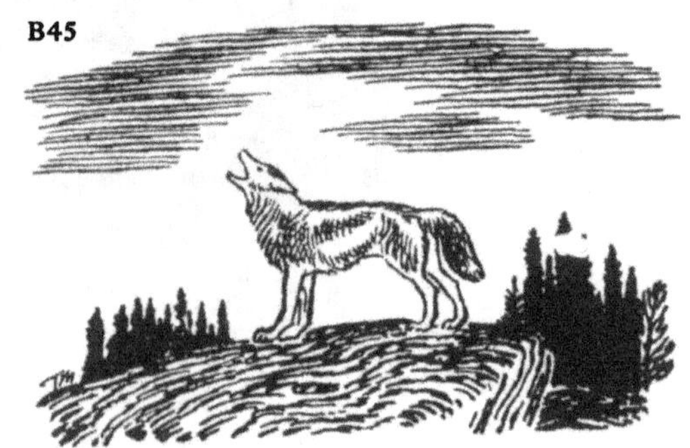

B46

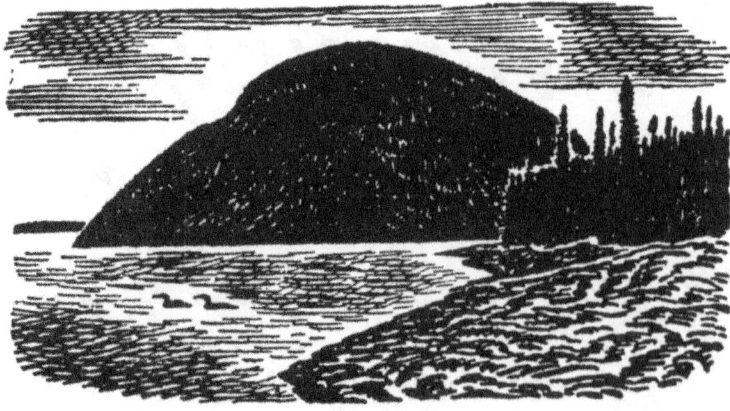

B46

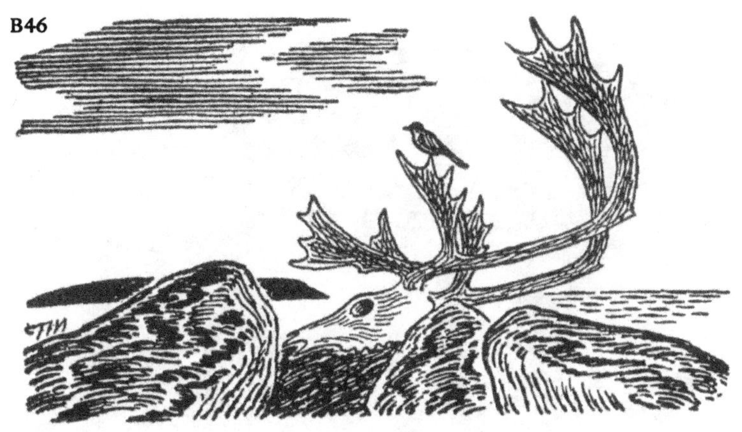

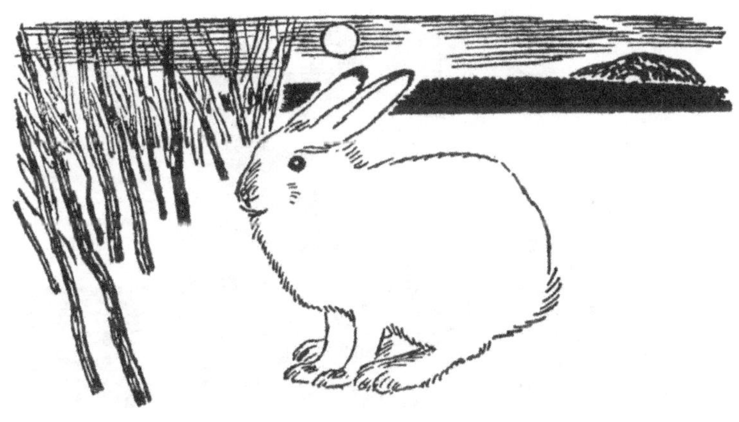

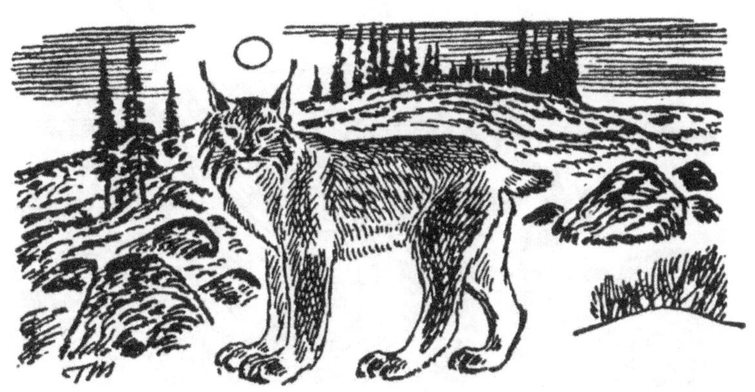

B46

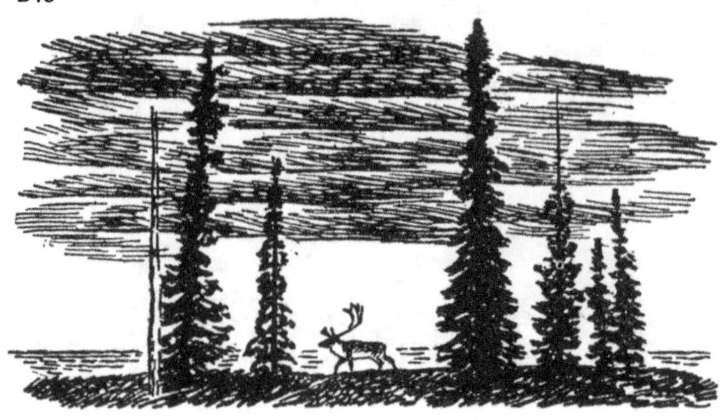

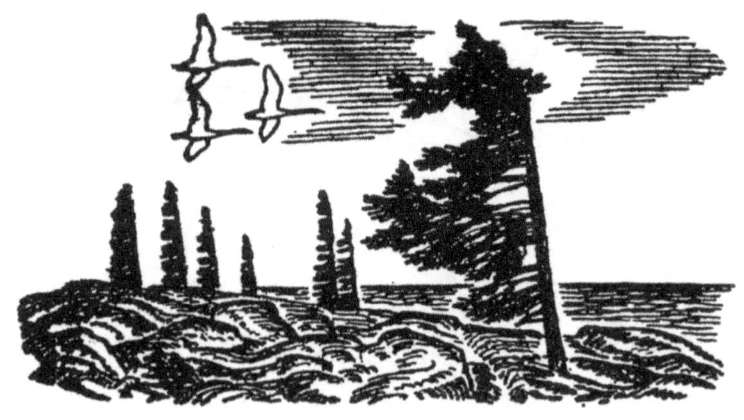

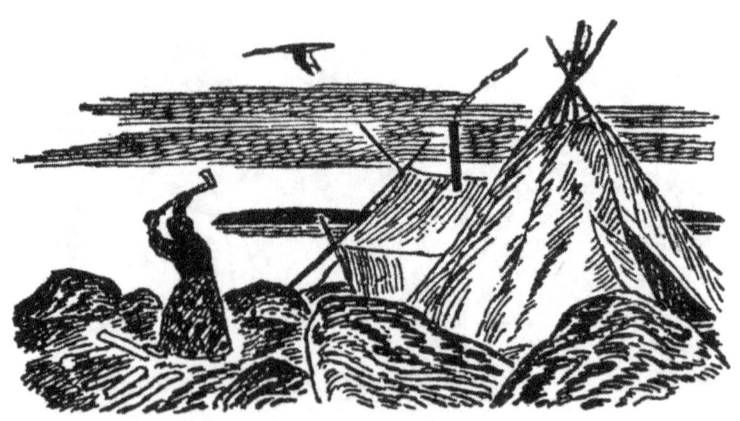

1950

B47
Canadian National Exhibition. *Catalogue of the Art Gallery, 1950.* 29 p
Cover title
25 August to 9 September 1950
Cover design

B48
Hambleton, Jack. *Abitibi Adventure.* Toronto, Longmans, Green and Co. [1950] vi, 173 p
32 drawings (11 vignettes), title page vignette, and jacket design

B49
MacDonald, Thoreau. *Thoreau MacDonald's Drawings for Dartmouth.* Lunenburg, Vt, North Country Press [1950] [15] p
Edition limited to 200 copies
5 drawings (mounted)
Cover headpiece
Printed by Roderick D. Stinehour at the Graphic Arts Workshop, Dartmouth College
The first North Country Press Book

B49

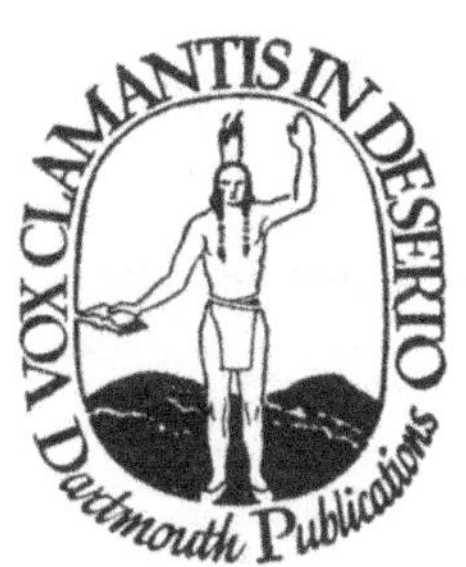

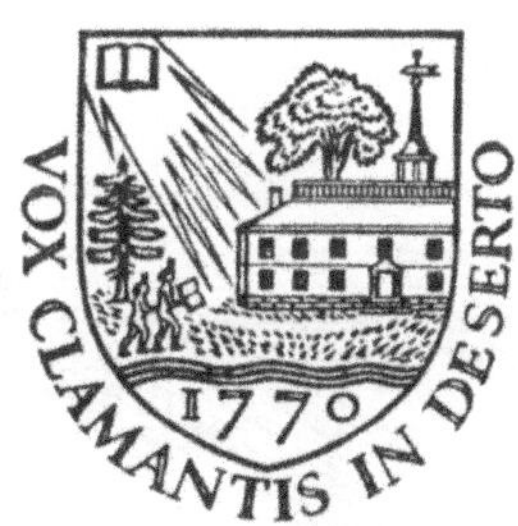

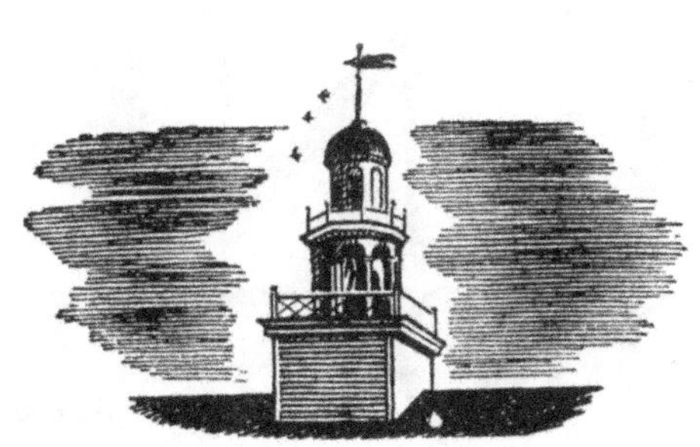

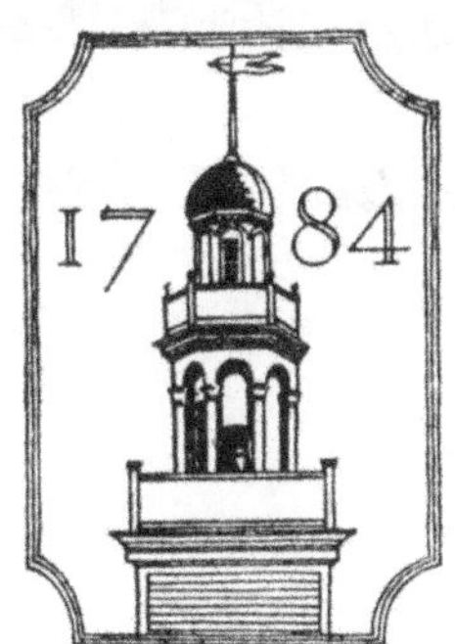

1951

B50
Canadian National Exhibition. *Catalogue of the Art Gallery, 1951.* 27 p
Cover title
24 August to 8 September 1951
Cover design

1952

B51
Canadian National Exhibition. *Catalogue of the Art Gallery, 1952.* 36 p
Cover title
22 August to 6 September 1952
Cover design

1953

B52
Canadian National Exhibition. *Catalogue of the Arts, 1953.* (Coronation Year, 75th Anniversary) 26 p
Cover title
28 August to 12 September 1953
Cover design

1954

B53
Canadian National Exhibition. *The Arts* [catalogue], 1954. 23 p
Cover title
27 August to 11 September 1954
Cover design

1955

B54
Canadian National Exhibition. *The Arts* [catalogue], 1955. 29 p
Cover title
26 August to 10 September 1955
Cover design

B51

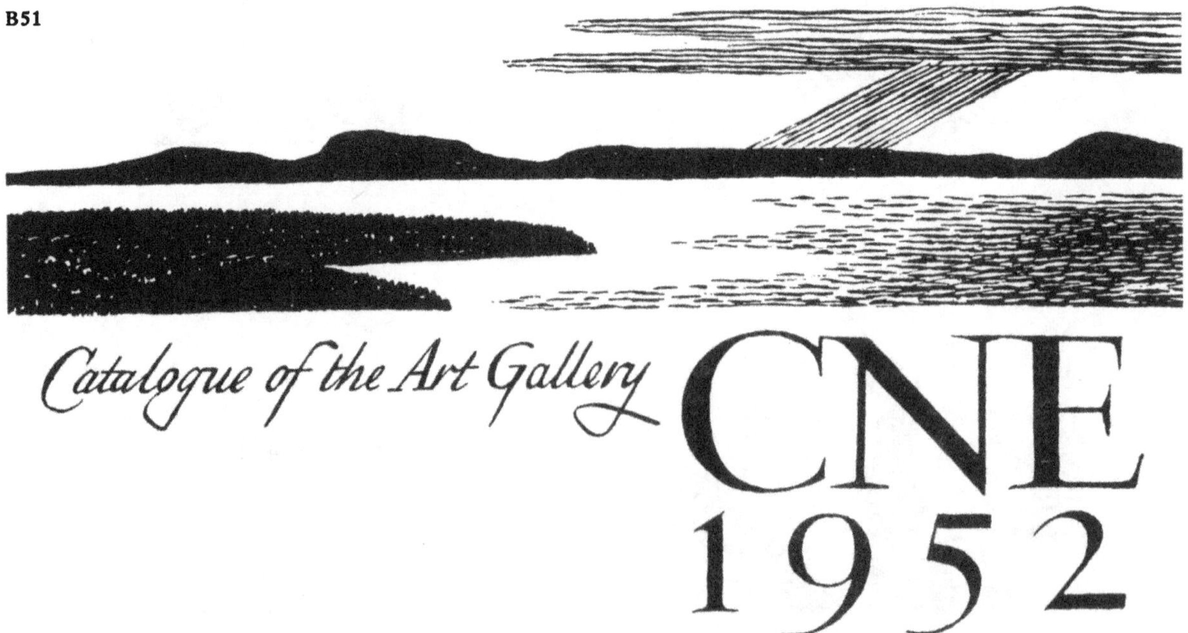

1956

B55
Canadian National Exhibition. *The Arts* [catalogue], 1956. 29 p
Cover title
24 August to 8 September 1956
Cover design

B56
Roberts, Leslie. *Noranda.* Toronto, Clarke, Irwin & Co. [1956] xiii, 223 p
12 drawings
Jacket reproduction of painting by A.J. Casson

B56

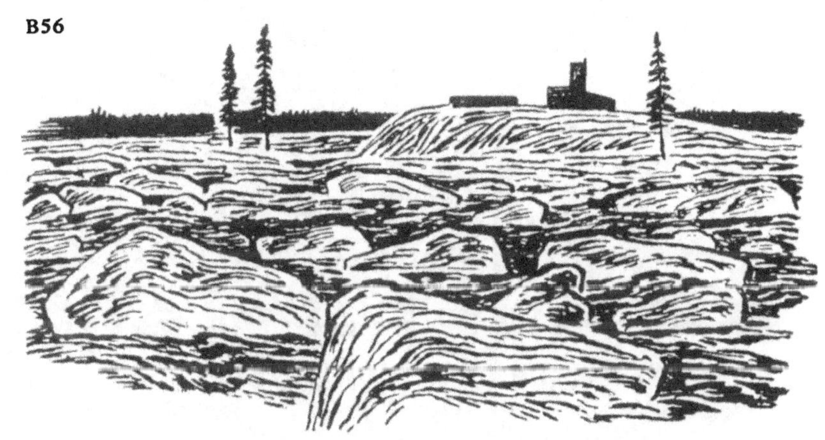

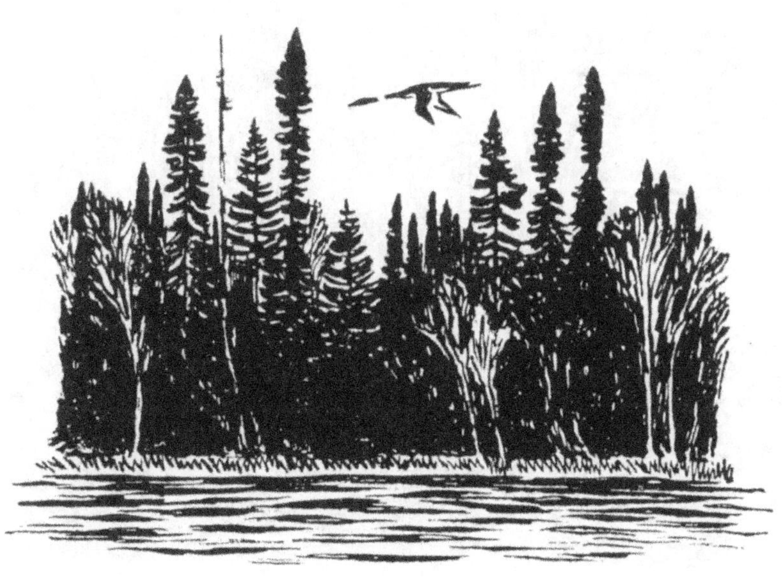

B57
Thoreau, Henry David. *The Succession of Forest Trees.* [Thornhill, privately printed] 1956. [32] p
Edition limited to about 500 copies.
'An address read to the Middlesex Agricultural Society in Concord, September 1860. Reprinted by T.M. 1956, courtesy of Thoreau's publishers, Houghton, Mifflin Co.'
Design, cover illustration, and 5 drawings
Reprinted 1968

B57

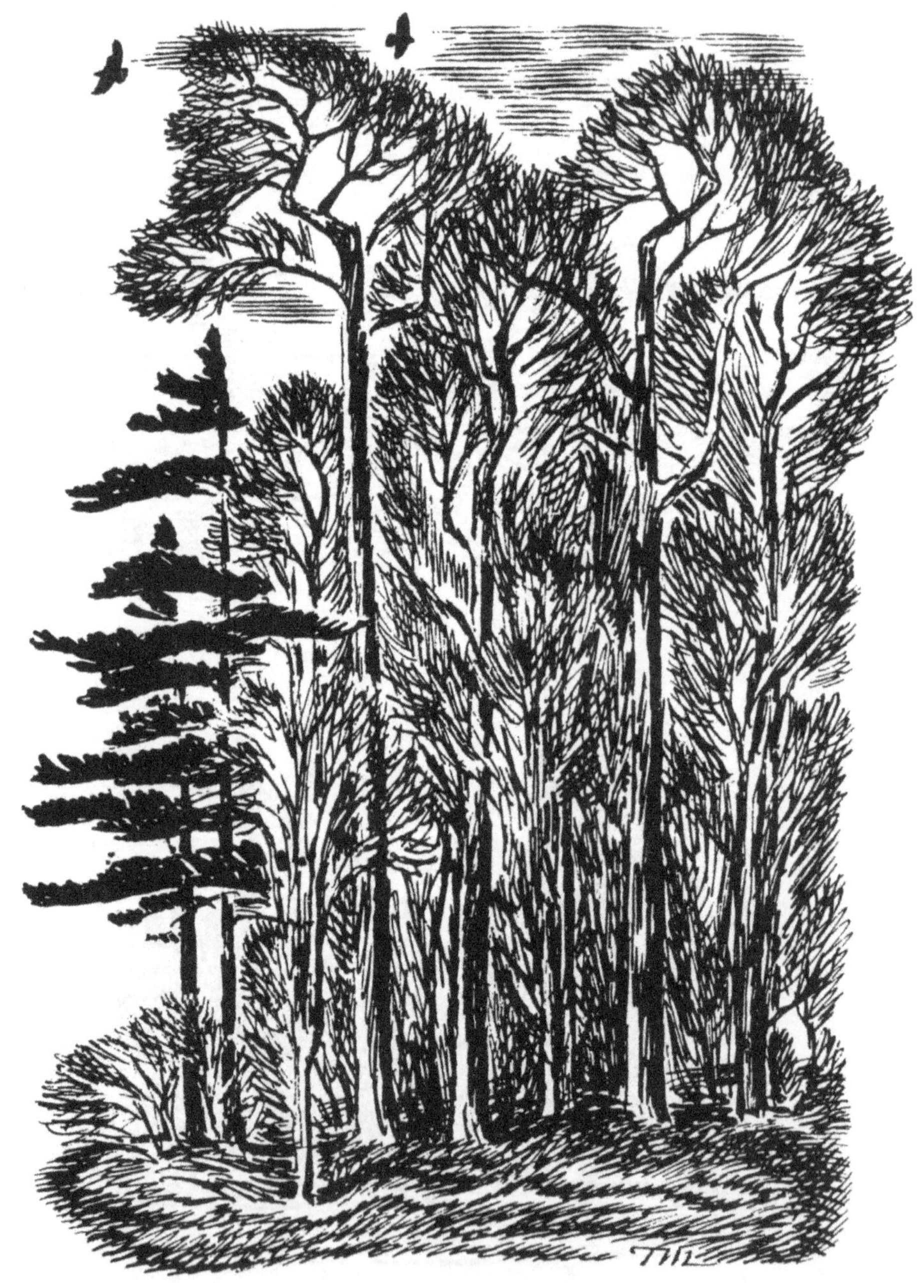

1957

B58
J.E.H. MacDonald, 1873-1932. The Art Gallery of Hamilton, March, 1957. [7] p
Design and 2 page introduction

1958

B59
Newton-White, E. *Hurt Not the Earth.* Toronto, Ryerson Press [1958] xvi, 188 p
35 drawings (6 vignettes), spine lettering, and jacket design

B59

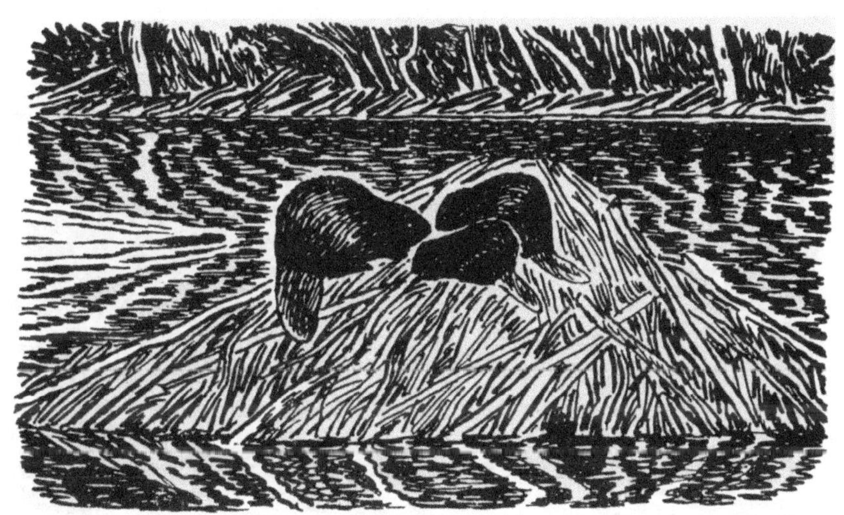

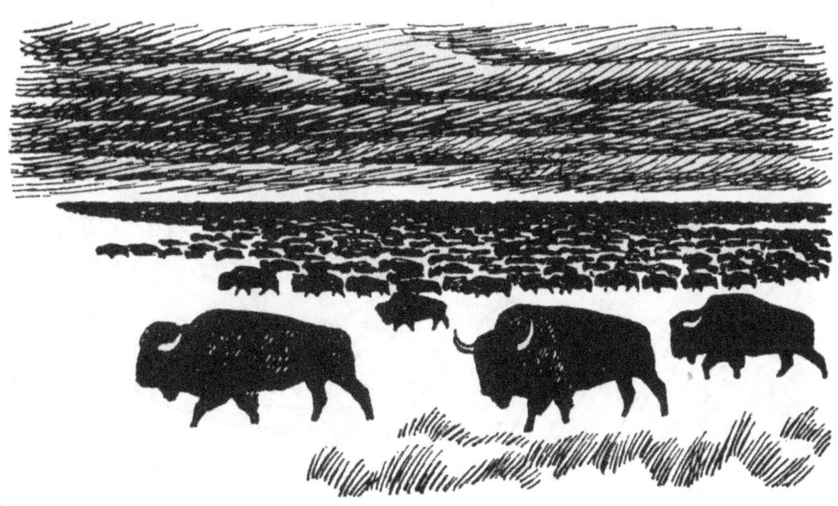

B59

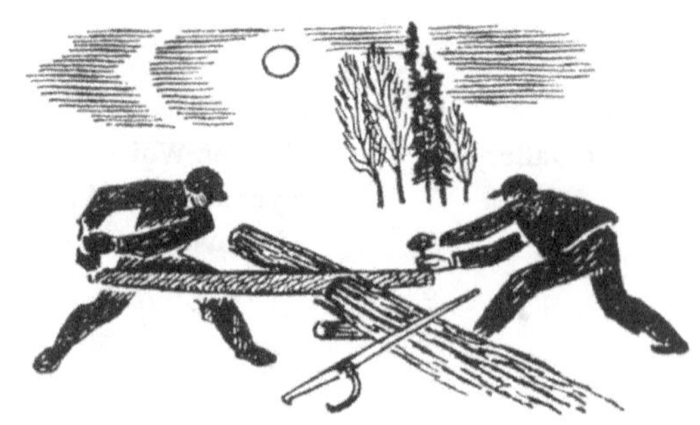

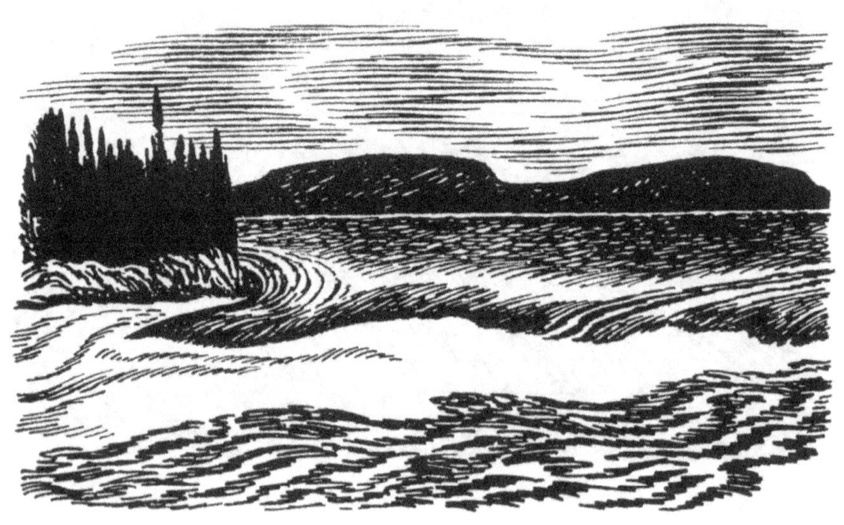

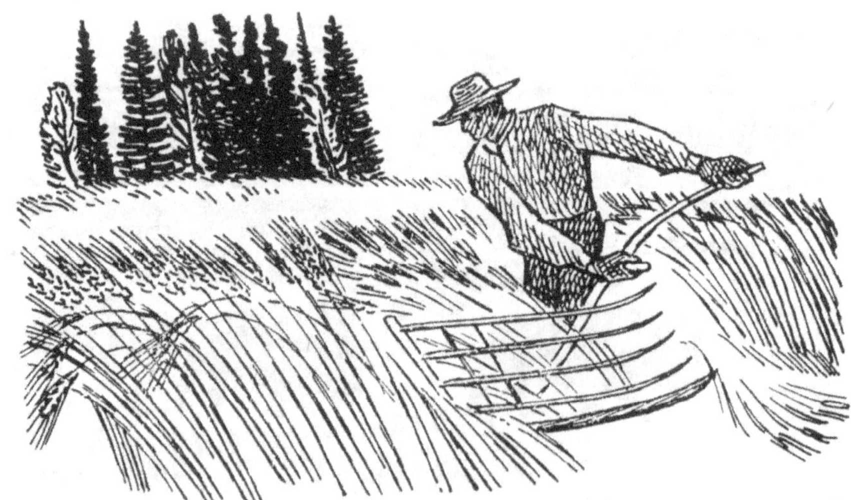

1959

B60
Locke, Clark. *Country Hours.* Toronto, Ryerson Press [1959] 105 p
63 drawings (22 vignettes), jacket design

1961

B61
Fred S. Haines, 1879-1960; Memorial Exhibition. [Toronto, Art Gallery of Toronto, 1961] [7] p
Travelling exhibition
Design

B60

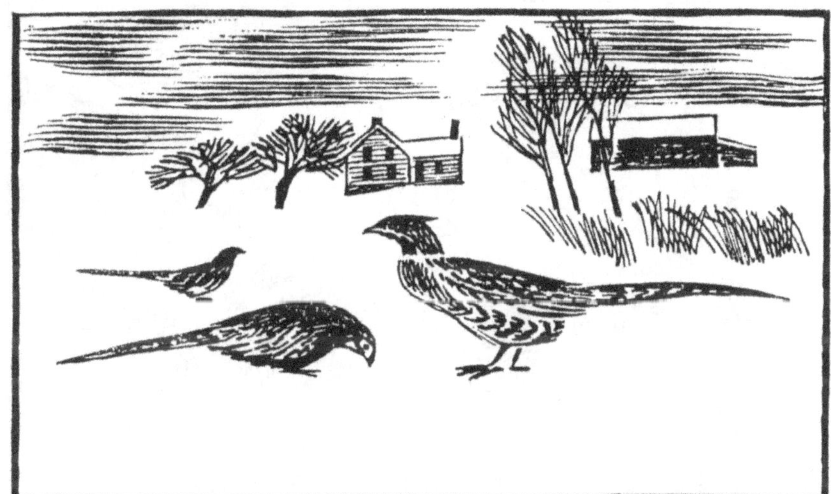

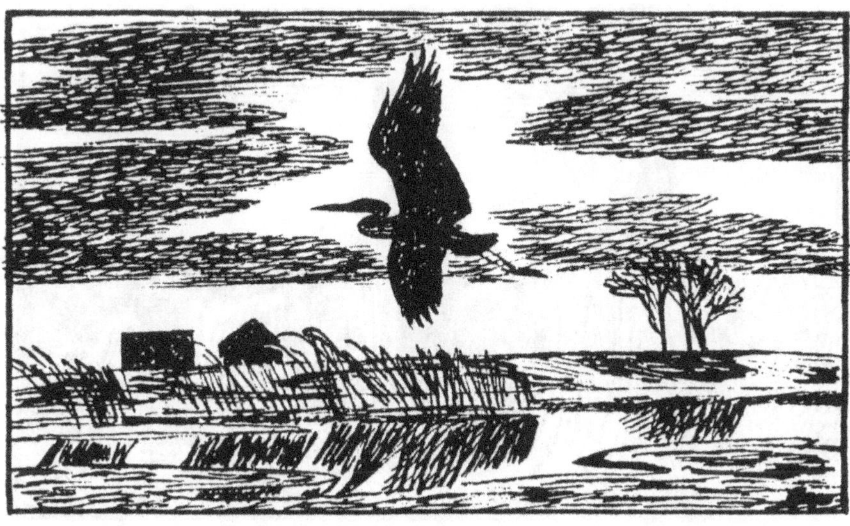

B60

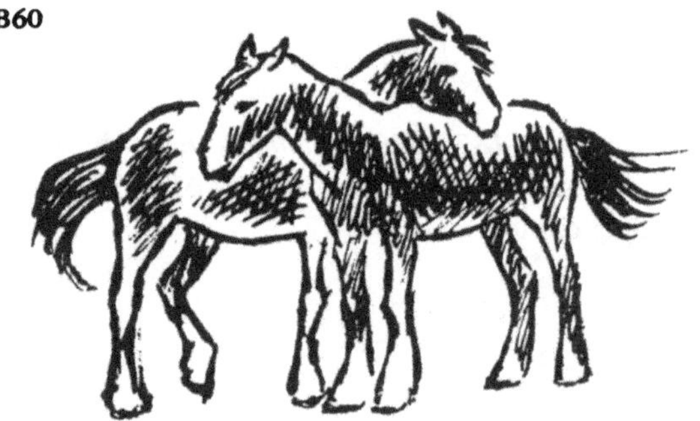

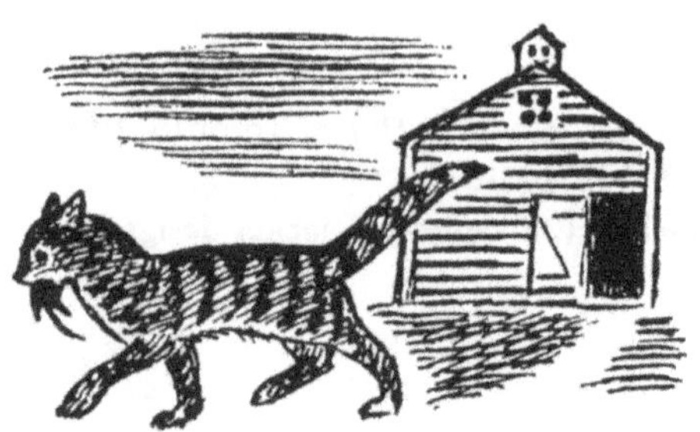

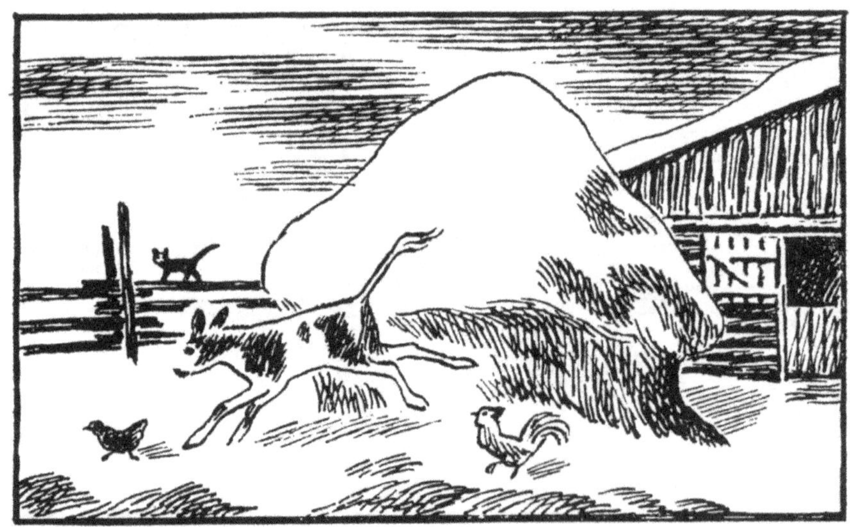

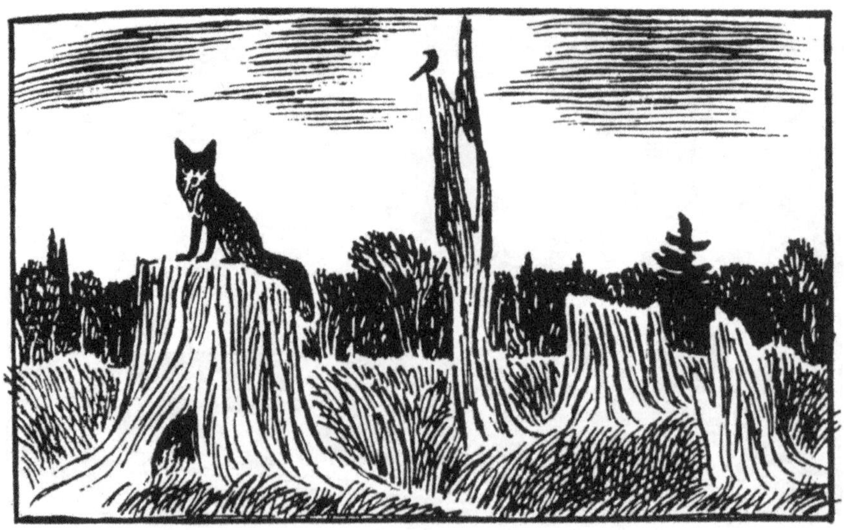

B62
Locke, Clark. *Country After-Hours.* [Toronto]
The Birches End Press [1961] [27] p
8 drawings (2 vignettes), title page, and cover

1964

B63
Rady, George Russell. *Thoreau and the Telegraph.*
[Thornhill, privately printed, 1964] [8] p
Design and 3 drawings (2 vignettes)
Reprinted in 1969
Article, without drawings, first published in *The Blue Bell* (house organ of Bell Telephone) 1956; reprinted in *Fragments*, 5, 2 (April–June 1967)

B62

COUNTRY
AFTER-HOURS

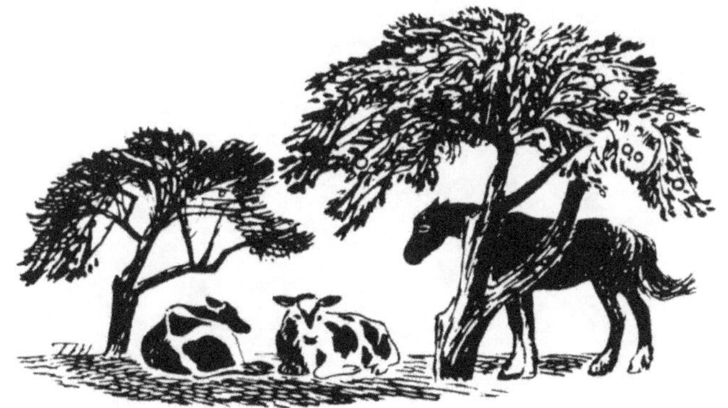

By CLARK LOCKE

1966

B64
MacDonald, Thoreau. *Book plate Designs by J.E.H. MacDonald.* Thornhill [Woodchuck Press] 1966 [18] p
15 book plate designs by J.E.H. MacDonald.
'The cover design is from an unused lino cut.'
Woodchuck Press device
'MacDonald worked as a designer all his life but made only about 20 bookplates. A list follows of those we have been able to trace and some of the better ones are reproduced. The best of these is Dr. MacCallum's and it and A.Y. Jackson's design for F.B. Housser are probably the most characteristic Canadian bookplates ever made.'

1967

B65
MacDonald, James E.H. *The Decorations at St. Anne's Church, Toronto.* [Thornhill, privately printed, 1967] [6] p
Cover title
Edition limited to 150 copies
'Reprinted 1967, from The Journal, Royal Architectural Institute of Canada, 1925.'
Photograph of 'Raising of Lazarus,' TM's painting in chancel
2 vignettes (1 on cover)

B66
Thoreau Society. *Annual Meeting, Concord, Massachusetts, July 15th, 1967.* [4] p
Cover drawing and vignette

1970

B67
FitzGerald, Doris, M. *Old Time Thornhill.* [Thornhill, privately printed] 1970. 56 p
Edition limited to 500 copies
6 drawings and cover design
2d printing 1971, 500 copies

B66

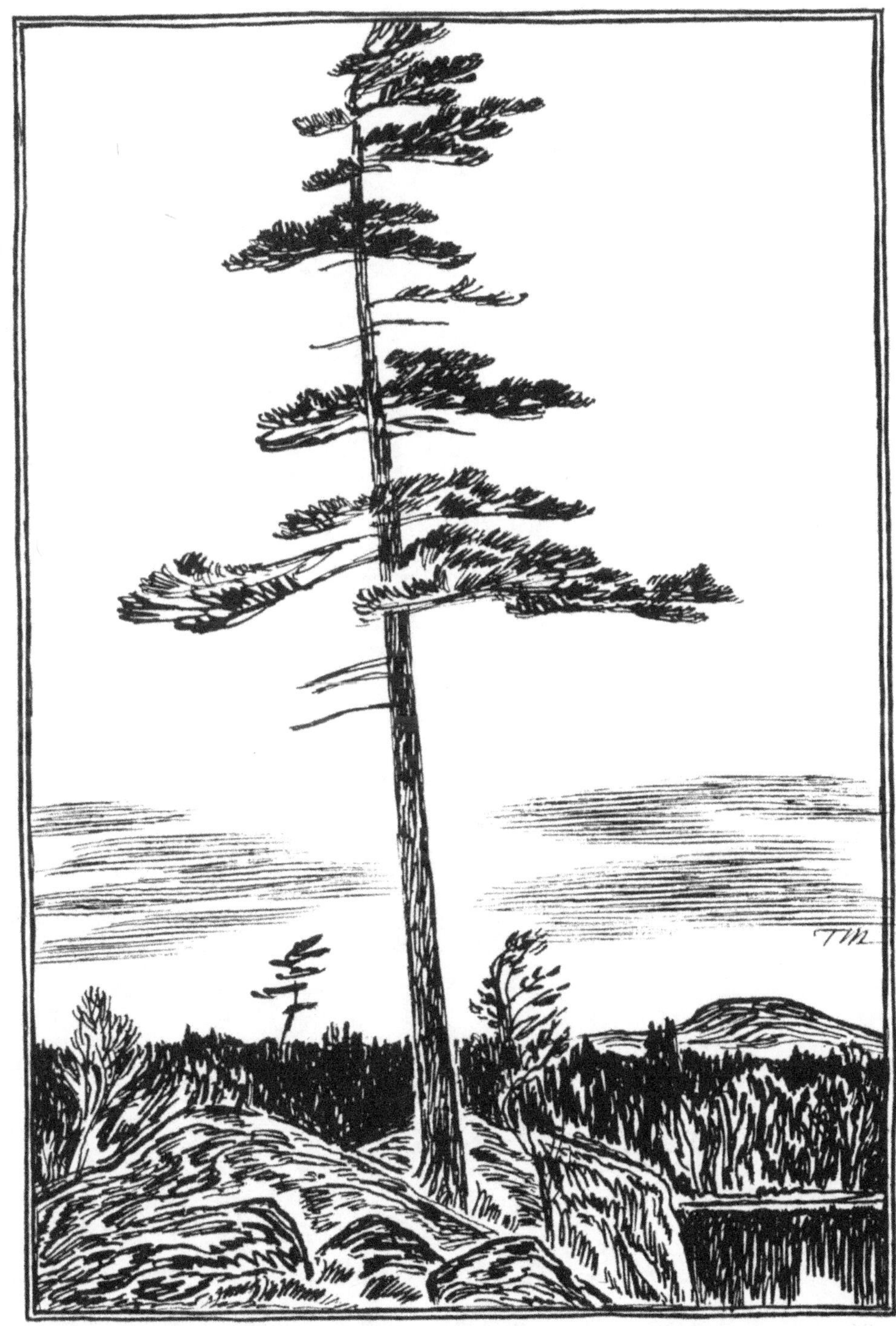
Annual Meeting · Thoreau Society Inc.
Concord Massachusetts · July 15th 1967

C · Books containing Designs or Lettering

1923

C1
King, Ben. *Ben King's Verse.* Toronto, McClelland and Stewart [1923] 238 p
Lettering on title page, cover, spine, and jacket

C2
Nasmith, George G. *Timothy Eaton.* Toronto, McClelland & Stewart [1923] xi, 312 p
Title, jacket lettering, and 4 drawings

C1

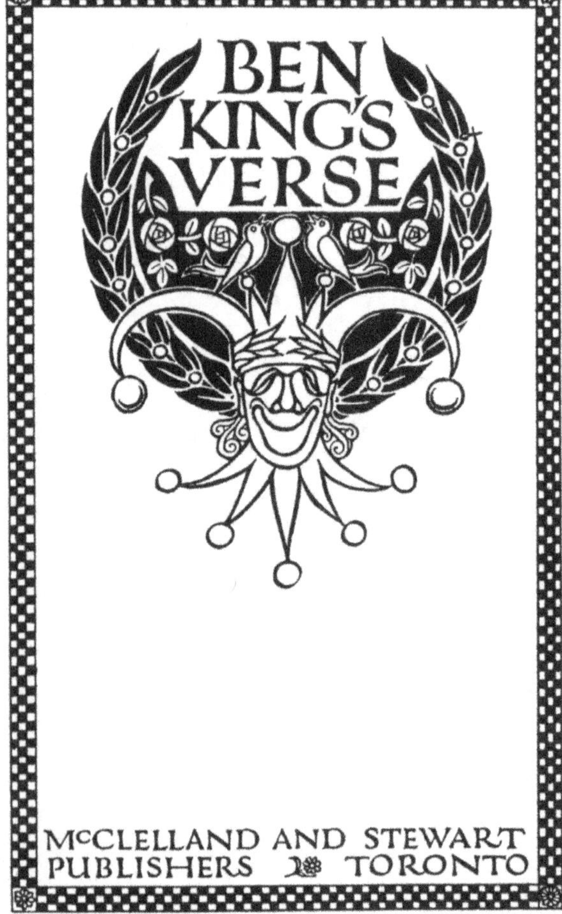

1924

C3
Johnson, E. Pauline. *Flint and Feather.* Toronto, Musson Book Co. [1924]
Ninth edition; first published 1912
Introduction by Theodore Watts-Dunton
Cover stamp; stamp first used for this edition.

C4
Rivard, Adjutor. *Chez Nous (Our Old Quebec Home).* Toronto, McClelland & Stewart [1924] 201 p
Translated by W.H. Blake
Lettering, jacket, and cover designs
Decorations by A.Y. Jackson.

1925

C5
Canadian Drawings, by Members of the Group of Seven. Toronto, Rous & Mann, 1925. [23] leaves. (loose in portfolio)
Edition limited to 100 copies; each drawing signed by the artist
Title leaf and cover label

C6
Groves, Edith Lelean. *The Kingdom of Childhood.* Toronto, Warwick Bros. and Rutter [1925] 106 p
Author's edition limited to 500 copies
Reprinted nine times. Decorations by Maude MacLaren
Lettering on jacket, cover, and end papers

C7
Lampman, Archibald. *Lyrics of Earth: Sonnets and Ballads.* Toronto, Musson Book Co. [1925] xi, 276 p
With an introduction by Duncan Campbell Scott
Jacket, cover and title page
Once attributed to J.E.H. MacDonald (see C50)

1926

C8
Drummond, William Henry. *Complete Poems.*
Toronto, McClelland & Stewart [1926] xxxiii, 449 p
With an introduction by Louis Frechette and an appreciation by Neil Munro
Jacket, cover stamp, frontispiece, title page, and end papers
Binding variants

C9
Hale, Katherine. *Canadian Houses of Romance.*
Toronto, Macmillan of Canada, 1926. xv, 213 p
Drawings by Dorothy Stevens
Jacket, cover, and title page lettering
Binding variants

C8

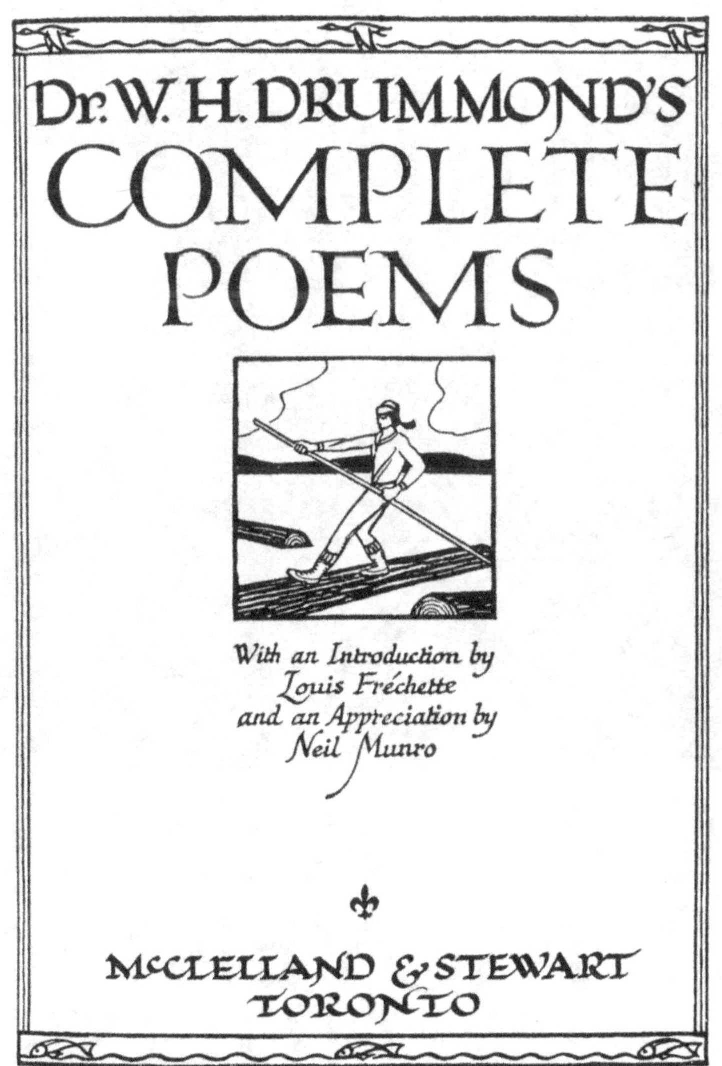

C11

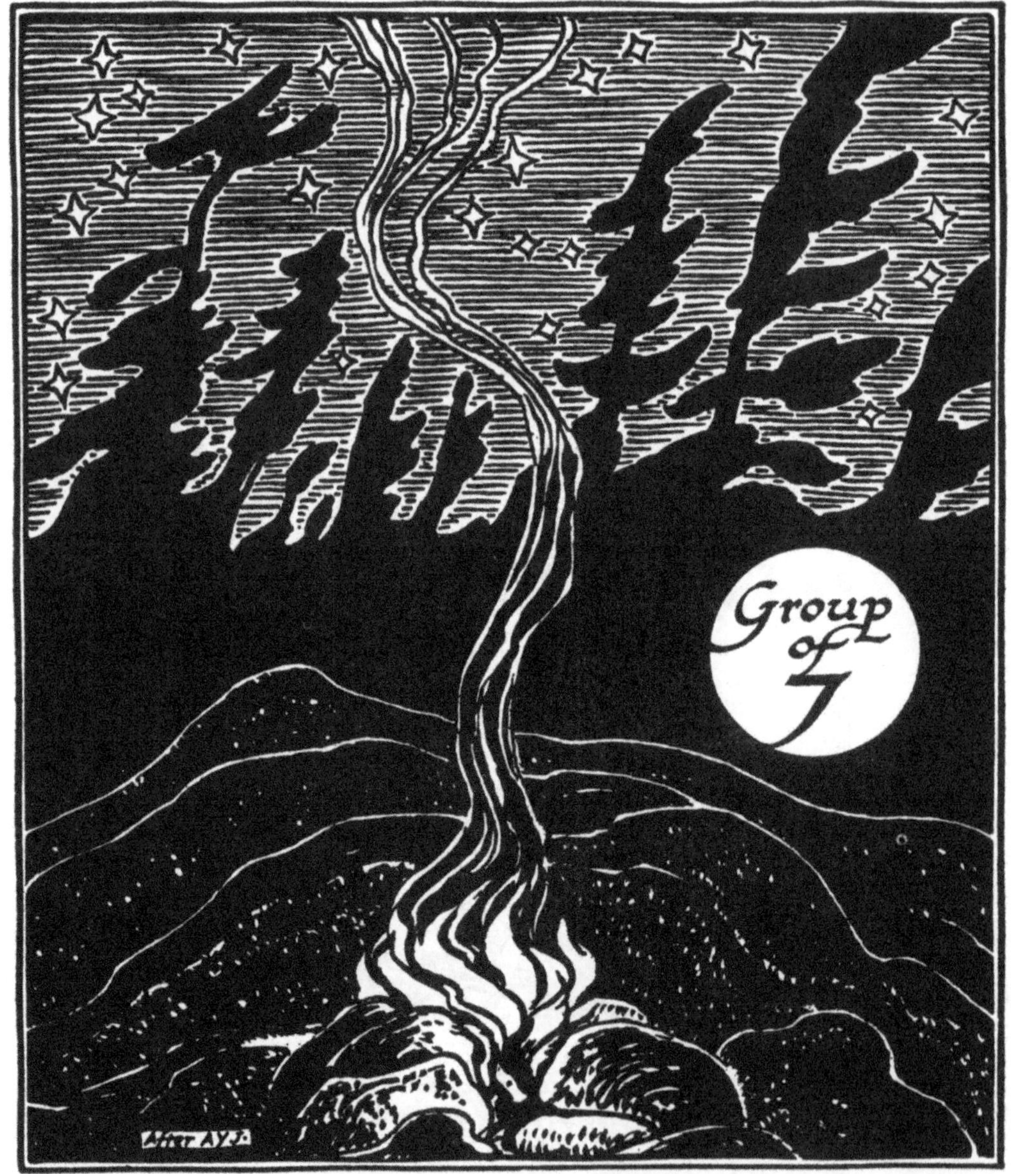

C10
Hammond, Melvin O. *Canadian Footprints: A Study in Foregrounds and Backgrounds.* Toronto, Macmillan of Canada, 1926. xvi, 305 p
Illustrated with photographs
Jacket, cover, and title page design

C11
Housser, Fred B. *A Canadian Art Movement: The Story of the Group of Seven.* Toronto, Macmillan of Canada, 1926. 221 p
Jacket, end papers (maps), cover, and title page
Group of Seven symbol by Franklin Carmichael

C12
Pickthall, Marjorie. *Little Hearts.* Toronto, McClelland and Stewart [1926]
Cover lettering

C13
Scott, Duncan Campbell. *Poems.* Toronto, McClelland & Stewart [1926] 341 p
Jacket, cover, and title page lettering
- Another edition. London, J.M. Dent, 1927
  Lettering on jacket, spine, and title page different from 1926 edition

C14
Sheard, Virna. *Candle Flame.* Toronto, McClelland and Stewart [1926] 79 p
Lettering on title page, cover, and jacket

C15
Stevenson, Lionel. *Appraisals of Canadian Literature.* Toronto, Macmillan of Canada, 1926. xviii, 272 p
Lettering on spine and cover, and on spine of jacket

1927

C16
Guthrie, Norman Gregor. *The Poetry of Archibald Lampman.* Toronto, Musson Book Co. [1927] 58 p
Edition limited to 250 copies; autographed
Lettering on cover
A soft cover edition was issued for the Annual Convention of the American Library Association at Toronto, June 1927.

C17
Harris, W. Eric. *Stand to Your Work: A Summons to Canadians Everywhere.* Toronto, Musson Book Co. [1927] 269 p
Jacket design

C18
Jackson, Alexander Y. *The Far North: A Book of Drawings.* Toronto, Rous and Mann [1927] 11 p
Introduction by Dr F.G. Banting
Edition of 1000 copies, including 50 signed
Lettering on cover label, decorated initials, and map

C13

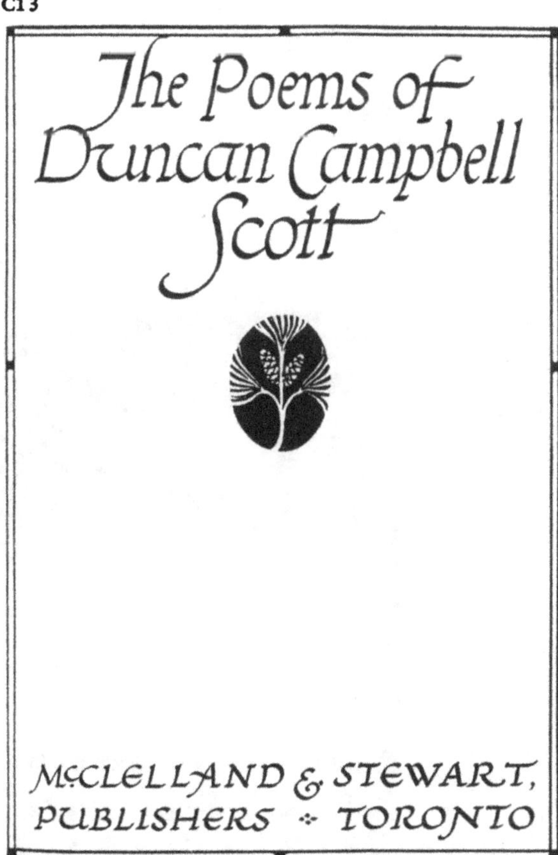

C19 THE BOOK OF ULTIMA THULE

by Archibald MacMechan

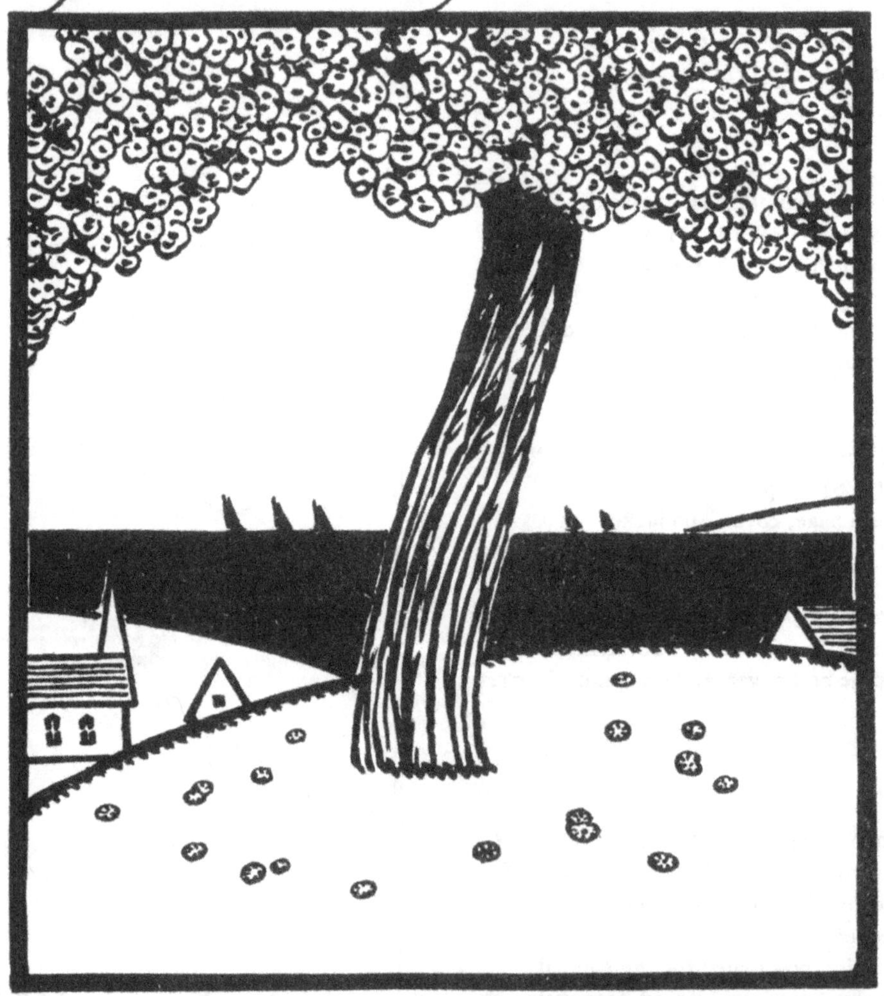

MCCLELLAND & STEWART
PUBLISHERS — TORONTO

C19
MacMechan, Archibald. *The Book of Ultima Thule.*
Toronto, McClelland & Stewart [1927] 368 p
Jacket, cover, endpapers, half-title, and title page

1928

C20
Barbeau, Marius. *The Downfall of Temlaham.*
Toronto, Macmillan of Canada, 1928. xii, 253 p
Jacket design (map), and label; lettering on cover and spine
Decorated initials by A.Y. Jackson; illustrations by Jackson and other artists

C20

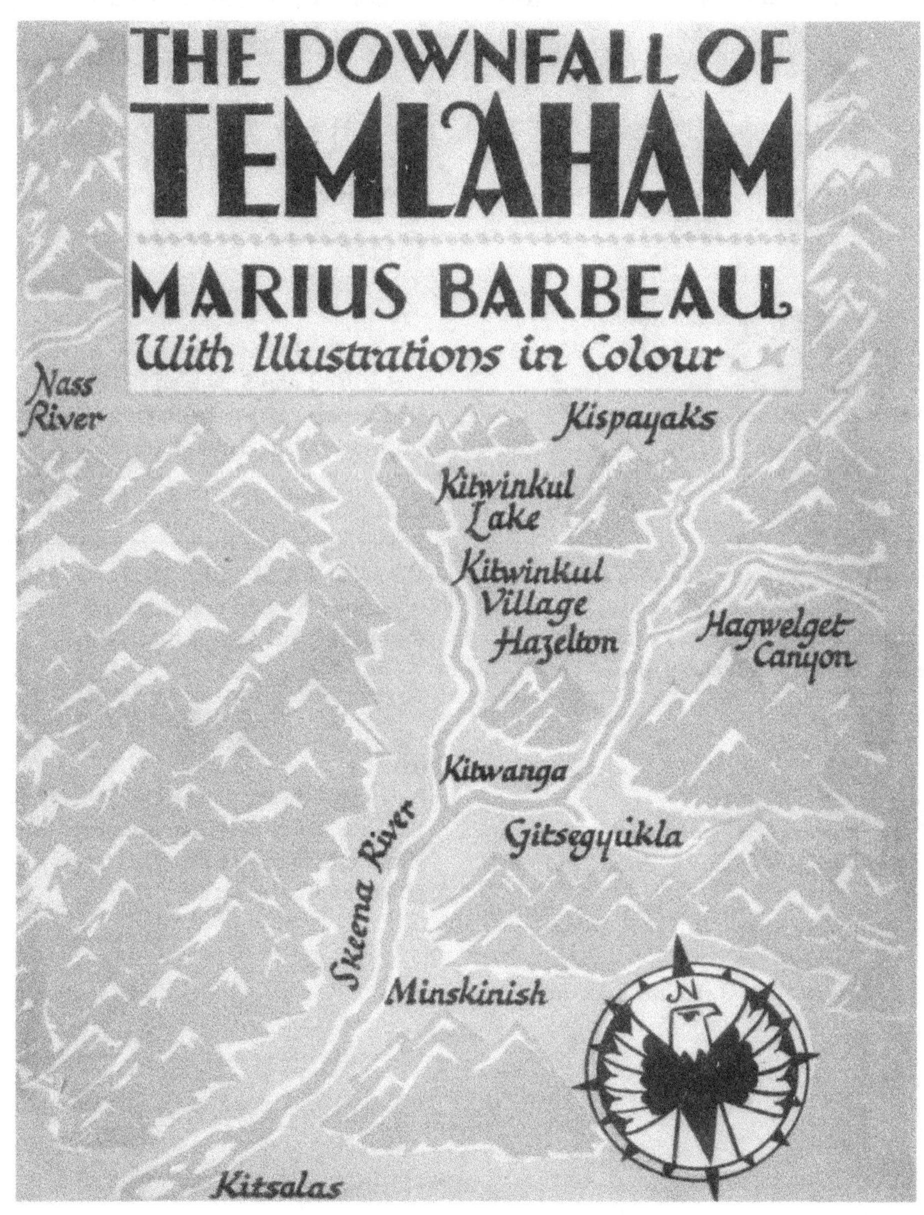

C21
Chauvin, Jean. *Ateliers: Etudes sur vingt-deux peintres et sculpteurs canadiens. Illustrées de reproductions d'oeuvres.* Montreal, New York, Louis Carrier & Cie, Les Editions du Mercure, 1928. 266 p
Edition of 1000 copies
Title page and lettering on cover
One reference in Bibliography of Canadian illustrated works to TM: *The Chopping Bee and other Laurentian Stories.* Traduit de Croquis laurentiens du frère Marie-Victorin. Traduction de James Ferres. Illustrations de TM. Toronto, Musson, 1922

C22
The Oxford Course in Canadian History: [Book 3] Settlement and Social Progress. Toronto, The Makers of Canada Ltd. [1928] 39 p
Title page drawing and cover design

C23
Waugh, W.T. *James Wolfe: Man and Soldier.* Montreal, New York, Louis Carrier & Cie, 1928. 333 p
Lettering on title page, jacket, and cover

1929

C24
Cameron, W.A. *Not by Eastern Windows Only: Messages from Modern Prophets.* Toronto, McClelland & Stewart [1929] xi, 243 p
Jacket, lettering on cover, and end papers

1930

C25
Davies, Blodwen. *Saguenay, 'Saginawa': The River of Deep Waters.* Toronto, McClelland & Stewart [1930] 204 p
Jacket, cover, endpapers (map), half title and title page
Illustrations by Paul Caron & G.A. Cuthbertson

C26
Wallis, Ella Bell. *The Exquisite Gift.* Ottawa, Ariston [1930] 248 p
Cover stamp
Also issued in wrappers, designed by TM

1931

C27
MacMechan Archibald. *Red Snow on Grand Pré.* Toronto, McClelland & Stewart [1931] 224 p
Jacket and title page

C28
Ranns, Horace D. *Careers for Canadians.* Toronto, Ryerson Press [1931] 72 p
Cover design

1932

C29
Davies, Blodwen. *The Charm of Ottawa.* Toronto, McClelland and Stewart [1932] 250 p
End papers (map) signed G.P. and T.M.
Illustrations by Barbara Stephens

C30
Davies, Blodwen. *Romantic Quebec.* Toronto, McClelland & Stewart [1932] vii, 213 p
Illustrated by Barbara Stephens
End papers and jacket (both a map)

1933

C31
Burt, Alfred Leroy. *The Old Province of Quebec.* Toronto, Ryerson Press; Minneapolis, University of Minnesota Press, 1933. xiii, 551 p
Jacket and cover stamp

C25

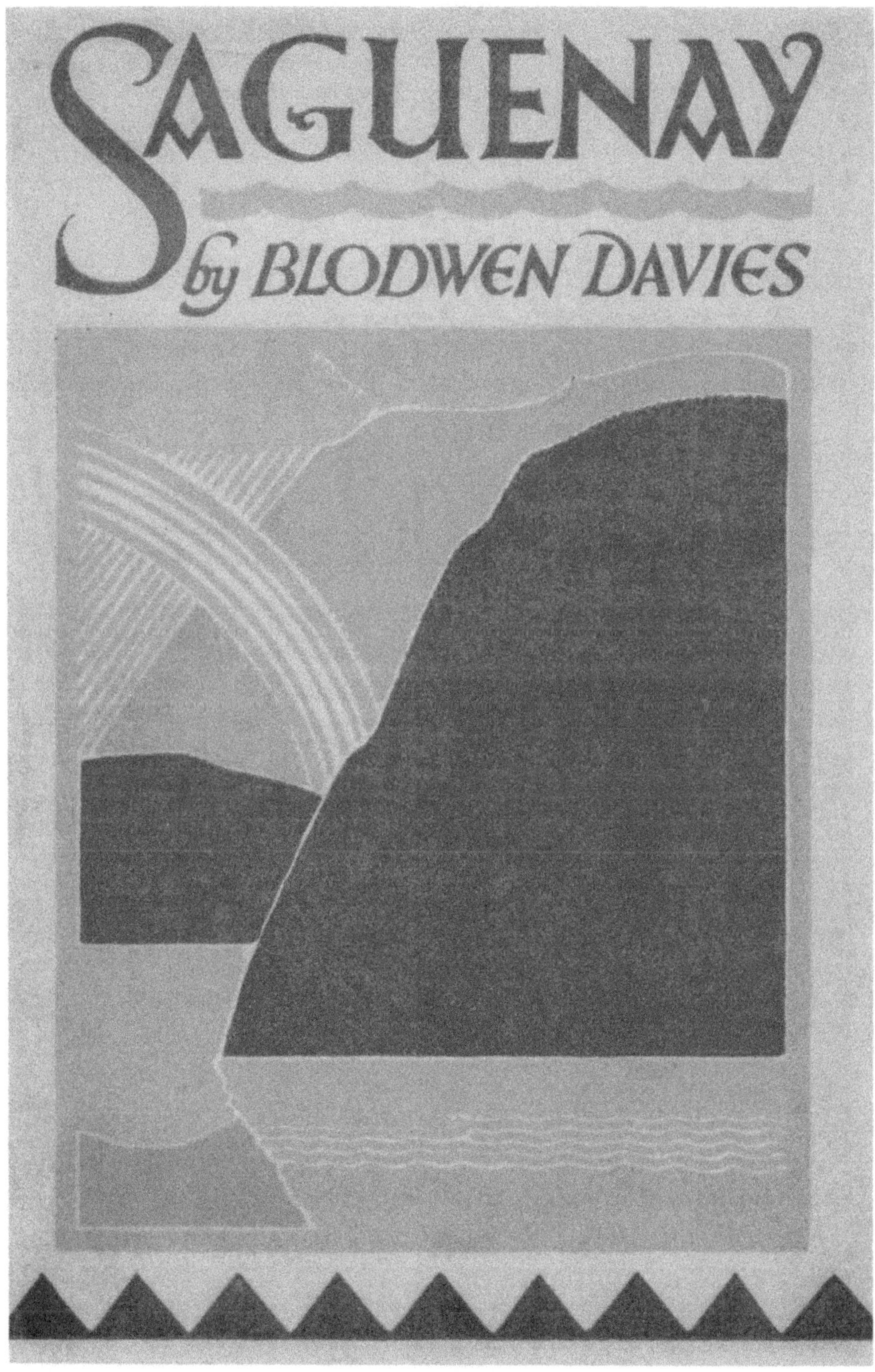

1934

C32
Dennis, Clara. *Down in Nova Scotia: My Own, My Native Land.* Toronto, Ryerson Press [1934] xii, 410 p
Lettering on jacket and cover
Illustrated with photographs taken by the author

C33
Roberts, Theodore Goodridge. *The Leather Bottle.* Toronto, Ryerson Press, 1934. viii, 87 p
Title page and cover stamp

C35

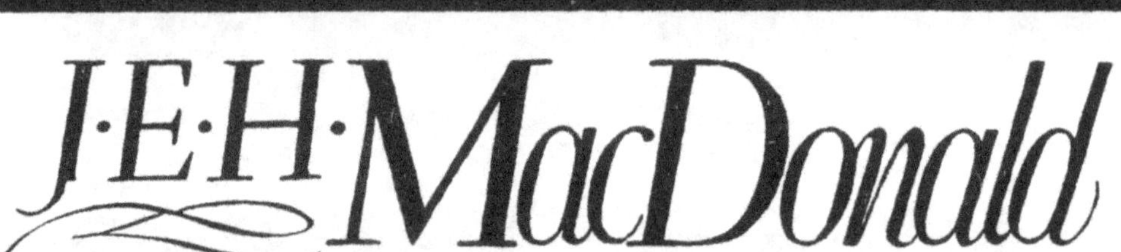

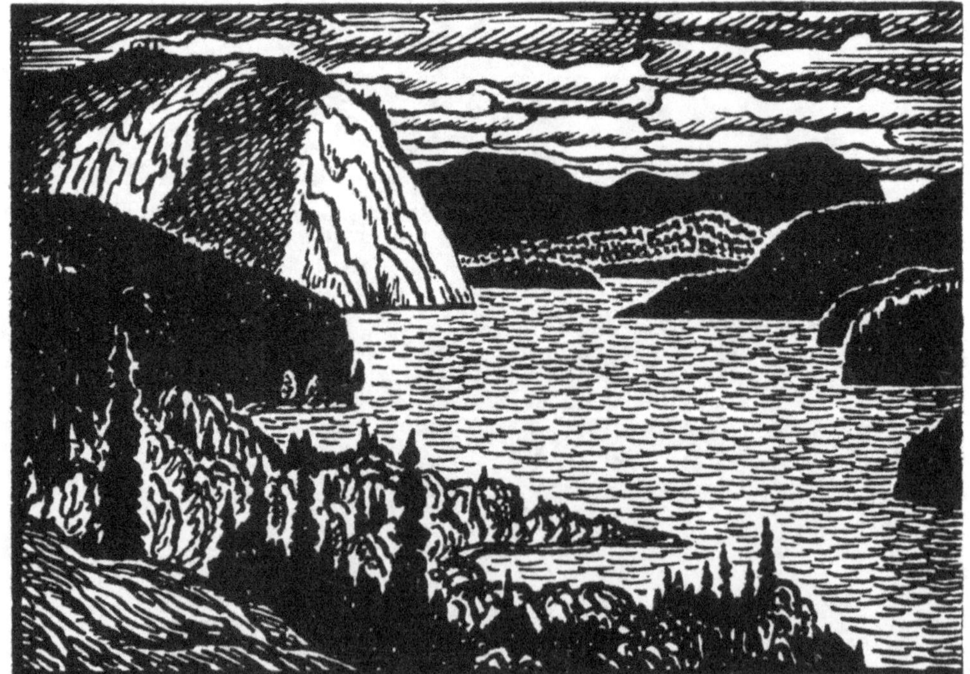

CANADIAN ARTISTS SERIES

1937

C34
Dennis, Clara. *More About Nova Scotia: My Own, My Native Land.* Toronto, Ryerson Press [1937] xii, 412 p
Jacket and cover design
Illustrated with photographs taken by the author

C35
Robson, Albert H. *J.E.H. MacDonald R.C.A.* Toronto, Ryerson Press [1937] 32 p (Canadian Artists Series)
Wrapper design for soft cover issue

1938

C36
Lewis, Nellie M. *Games and Parties the Year Round.* Toronto, Ryerson Press [1938] xiv, 130 p
Jacket and cover design

C37
MacDonald, James E.H. *The Elements.* Toronto, Ryerson Press, 1938. [4] p folder
Reproduction of J.E.H. MacDonald painting 'With the season's greetings; the Ryerson Press'
Cover lettering

C38
Robson, Albert H. *A.Y. Jackson.* Toronto, Ryerson Press [1938] 32 p (Canadian Artists Series)
Wrapper design for soft cover issue

C39
Robson, Albert H. *Paul Kane.* Toronto, Ryerson Press [1938] 32 p (Canadian Artists Series)
Wrapper design for soft cover issue

1939

C40
Merriman, Robert Owen and Mackintosh, W.A. *Trade and Industry.* Toronto, Ryerson Press [1939] x, 257 p
Cover design

C41
Robson, Albert H. *Canadian Landscape Painters.* Toronto, Ryerson Press, 1932. 227 p
Specially bound in full apricot leather with birch bark end papers by William L. Cope for the Golden Gate International Exposition, 1939
Binding design, one copy only
'Catalogue of Fine Book Bindings' (San Francisco, Grabhorn Press, 1939) issued.

1940

C42
Hunter, E. Robert. *J.E.H. MacDonald: A Biography and Catalogue of his Work.* Toronto, Ryerson Press [1940] xiv, 60 p
Edition limited to 500 copies
Design and introduction (p xi-xiii)

C42

J·E·H·MacDonald
A Biography & Catalogue of his Work

BY E·R·HUNTER

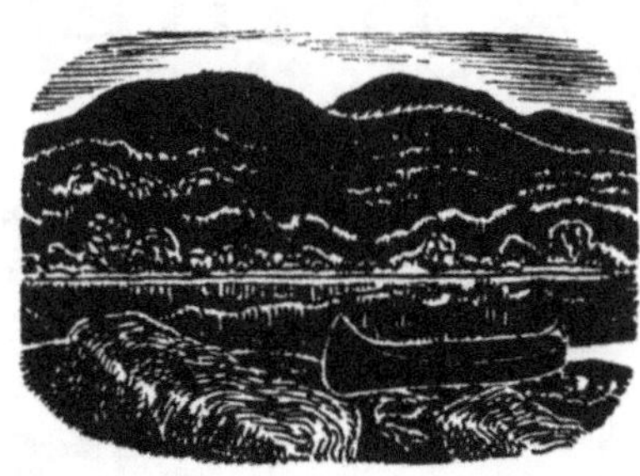

THE RYERSON PRESS TORONTO

C43
Pierce, Lorne. *A Postscript on J.E.H. MacDonald, 1873-1932.* Toronto, Ryerson Press, 1940. 12 p
Edition limited to 100 copies
Title page and some cover lettering

1941

C44
Barbeau, Marius. *Henri Julien.* Toronto, Ryerson Press [1941] 44 p (Canadian Art Series)
Wrapper design for soft cover issue

1942

C45
Beston, Henry. *The St. Lawrence.* New York, Toronto, Farrar & Rinehart [1942] xi, 274 p
Map facing p 3
Jacket and other illustrations by A.Y. Jackson

C46
Birney, Earle. *David and Other Poems.* Toronto, Ryerson Press [1942] 40 p
Edition limited to 500 copies
Lettering on jacket, cover, and title page
Reprinted December 1942 with slightly different jacket and in different colours

C47
Colman, Mary Elizabeth. *For this Freedom, Too.* [Toronto, Ryerson Press, 1942] 16 p (Ryerson Poetry Chapbooks, no 99)
Edition limited to 250 copies
Cover design and series statement on first page
The original cover design for the series was by J.E.H. MacDonald. It was redrawn by TM in 1942, for Chap Book no. 99., and signed 'JM & TM.'

C46

DAVID

and other Poems by

EARLE BIRNEY

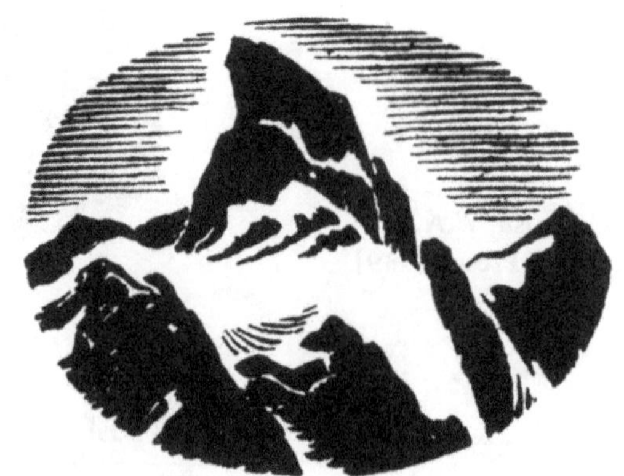

C48
Dennis, Clara. *Cape Breton Over.* Toronto, Ryerson Press [1942] xiii, 342 p
Introduction by Angus L. MacDonald
Jacket and cover design
Illustrated with photographs taken by the author

C49
Maheux, Arthur. *French Canada and Britain: A New Interpretation.* Toronto, Ryerson Press [1942] 121 p
Translated by R.M. Saunders
Also issued in wrappers
Cover design

C48

Cape Breton
Over
BY CLARA DENNIS

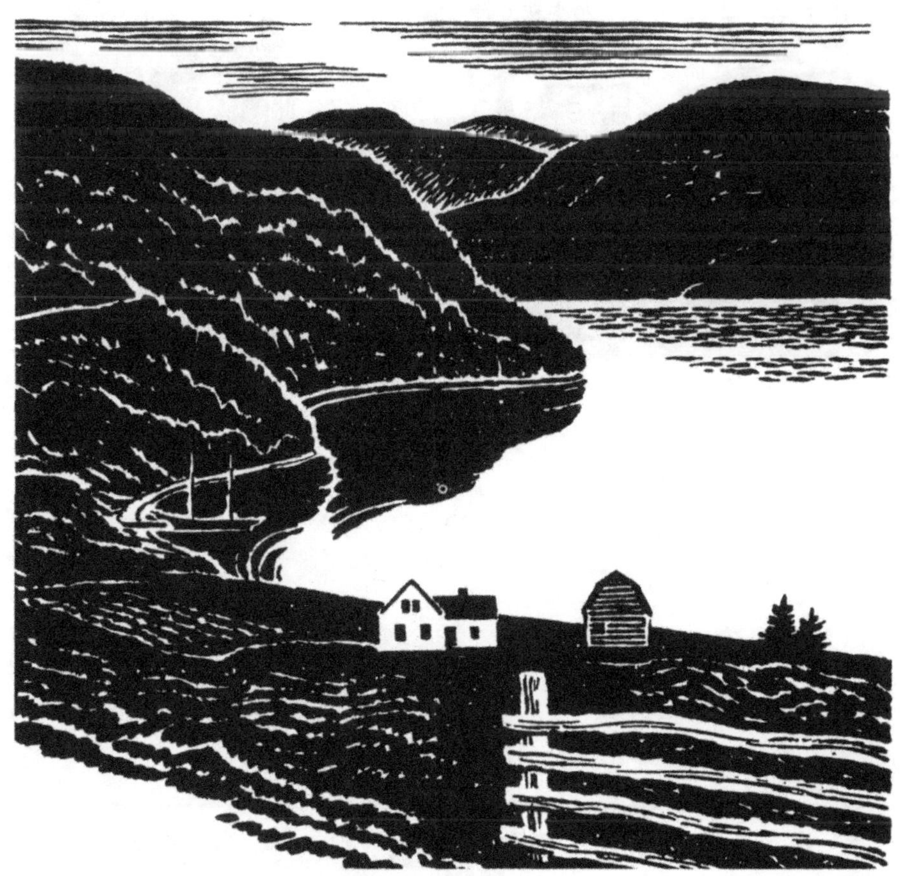

C50
Hunter, Robert E. *Thoreau MacDonald.* Toronto, Ryerson Press [1942] 43 p
(Canadian Art Series)
Wrapper design for soft cover issue

C50 *E. R. HUNTER*

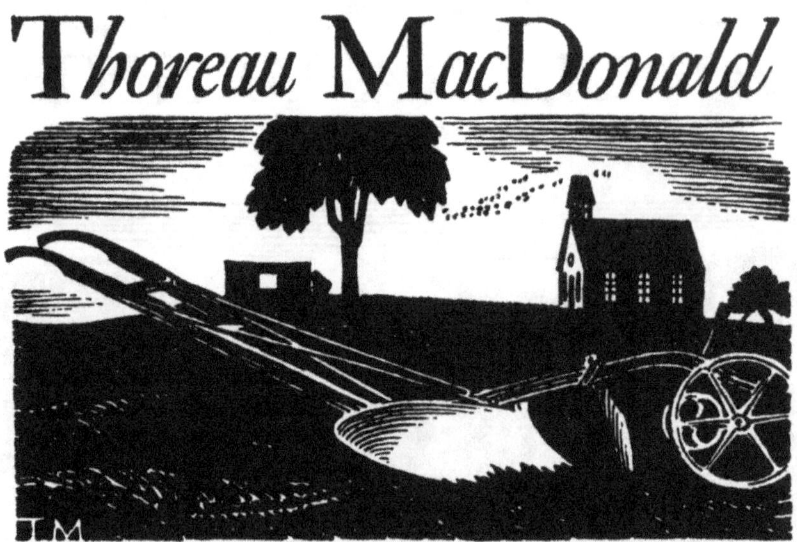

CANADIAN ART SERIES

C51
Montgomery, Lucy M. *Anne of Green Gables.* Toronto, Ryerson Press [1942] viii, 396 p
Cover and title page vignette
TM also designed covers and title page vignettes for other L.M. Montgomery books.

C52
Queen's University: A Centenary Volume 1841-1941. Toronto, Ryerson Press [1942] xi, 189 p
Edition limited to 500 copies; 150 for sale
Spine and title page

C53
Sharman, Lyon. *Town and Forest.* Toronto, Macmillan of Canada, 1942. 73 p
Cover and frontispiece (see also D16)

C52

QUEEN'S
UNIVERSITY
A Centenary Volume
1841 1941

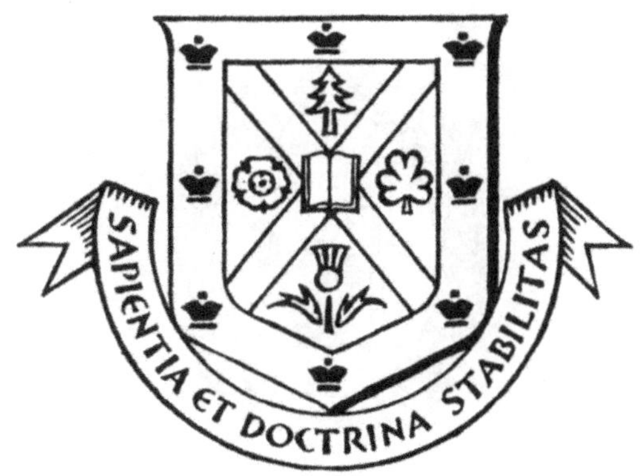

The Ryerson Press Toronto

1943

C54
Anderson, Violet (ed). *The United Nations, Today and Tomorrow.* Toronto, Ryerson Press [1943] vi, 166 p
Lettering, and device for the Canadian Institute of Public Affairs on cover

C55
Baker, John H. (ed). *The Audubon Guide to Attracting Birds.* Garden City, N.Y., Halcyon House [1943] xviii, 268 p
First edition; New York, Doubleday, Doran, 1941
Three diagrams

C58

CANADIAN ART *its origin & development*

BY WILLIAM COLGATE

with a foreword by C.W. Jefferys, R.C.A., LL.D.

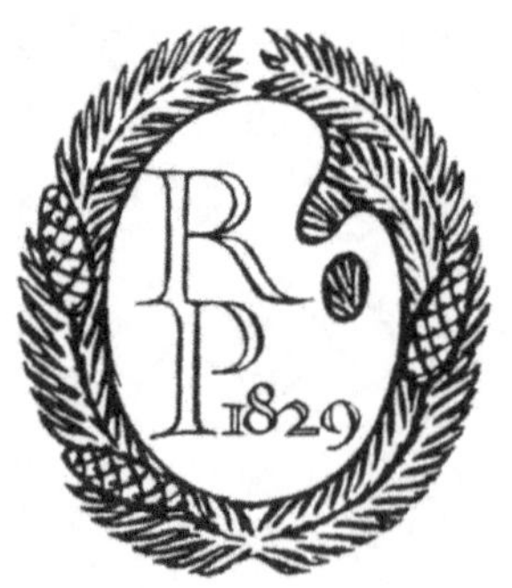

TORONTO · THE RYERSON PRESS

C56
Barbeau, Marius. *Côté, the Wood Carver.* Toronto, Ryerson Press [1943] 43 p (Canadian Art Series)
Wrapper design for soft cover issue

C57
Brown, Edward K. *On Canadian Poetry.* Toronto, Ryerson Press [1943] ix, 157 p
Jacket and title page

C58
Colgate, William. *Canadian Art: Its Origin and Development.* Toronto, Ryerson Press [1943] xvii, 278 p
Foreword by C.W. Jefferys
Jacket and title page
An edition in wrappers, reduced in size and using the same title page, was published by Ryerson in 1967

C59
Douglas, Mary. *Road's End.* Toronto, Ryerson Press, 1943. xi, 150 p
Jacket, cover, and title page

C60
Jackson, Alexander Y. *Banting as an Artist.* Toronto, Ryerson Press, 1943. 37 p
With a memoir by Frederick W.W. Hipwell
Cover design

C61
Lampman, Archibald. *At the Long Sault, and Other New Poems.* Toronto, Ryerson Press, 1943. xxix, 45 p
Foreword by Duncan Campbell Scott, introduction by E.K. Brown
Jacket and cover design

C62
MacDonald, Malcolm. *Down North.* London, Toronto, Oxford University Press, 1943. xiii, 274 p
Lettering, end papers, and title page drawing
Painting on jacket by A.Y. Jackson
Reprinted, 1945, with title *Canadian North*

C63
Pickthall, Marjorie. *The Worker in Sandalwood.* [Toronto, Ryerson Press, 1943] 12 p
Edition limited to 500 copies
Cover and one vignette

C60

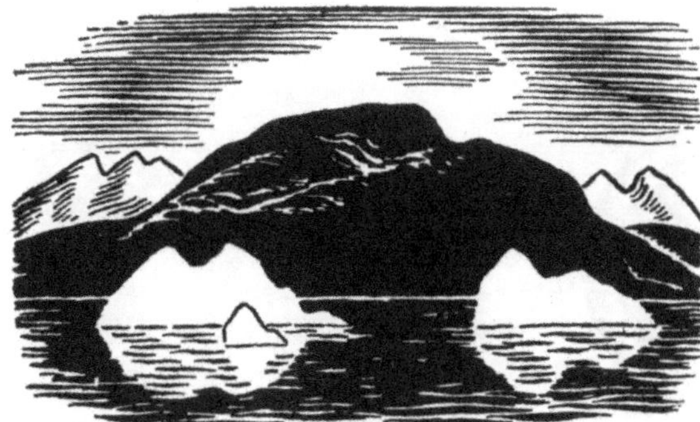

C61

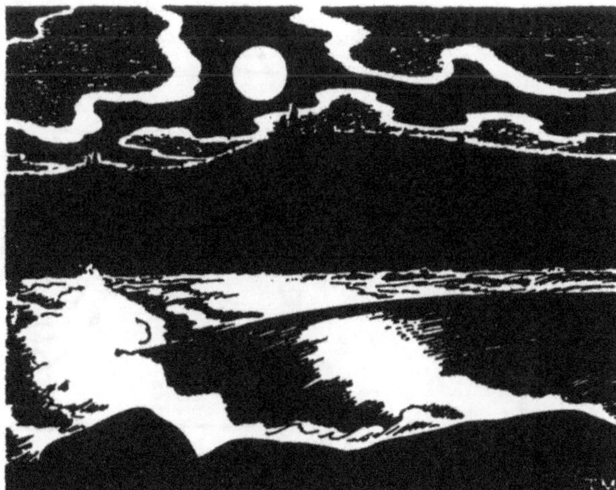

C64
Smith, Arthur J.M. *News of the Phoenix, and Other Poems.* Toronto, Ryerson Press; New York, Coward-McCann, 1943. 42 p
Jacket, cover, title page, and half title

1944

C65
Buchanan, Donald (ed). *This is Canada.* Toronto, Ryerson Press [1944] [84] p
Title page

C66
Creighton, Donald Grant. *Dominion of the North: A History of Canada.* Toronto, Thomas Allen [1944] vii, 535 p
Jacket design

C67
Hambleton, Ronald (ed). *Unit of Five: Louis Dudek, Ronald Hambleton, P.K. Page, Raymond Souster, James Wreford.* Toronto, Ryerson Press [1944] ix, 87 p
Jacket design

C64

News of the Phoenix

AND OTHER POEMS

BY A · J · M · SMITH

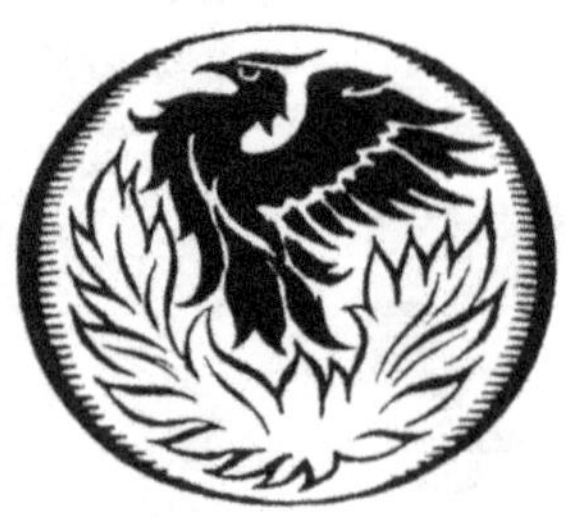

1943

Toronto · The Ryerson Press
New York · Coward-McCann, Inc.

C68
Livesay, Dorothy. *Day and Night.* Toronto, Ryerson Press [1944] 48 p
Jacket, cover, and title page

C69
Livesay, John F.B. *Peggy's Cove.* Toronto, Ryerson Press [1944] viii, 100 p
Jacket, cover, and title page

C70
Pierce, Lorne. *Prime Ministers to the Book.* Toronto, Ryerson Press [1944] [12] p (The Beverley Papers, VII)
Edition limited to 100 copies; reprinted from *Quill & Quire*
Colophon device (on cover) adapted by TM from the device of Christopher Plantin.

C71
Sullivan, Alan. *And from that Day.* Toronto, Ryerson Press [1944] xiv, 195 p
Jacket, spine, and title page

1945

C72
As the Camera Catches C.L.B., Pictures of the President in Many Moods. Toronto, 1945. xiv, 71 leaves. 67 plates
'Presented to Charles Luther Burton, C.B.E., President of the Robert Simpson Company Limited by the Officers of the Company at Toronto.'
'Format by Thoreau MacDonald'
Title page and cover monogram
One copy known

C73
Birney, Earle. *Now is Time.* Toronto, Ryerson Press [1945] 56 p
Jacket, cover, and title page

C74
Bruce, Charles. *Grey Ship Moving.* Toronto, Ryerson Press, London, British Authors' Press [1945] vii, 34 p
Jacket, cover, and title page

C75
Calvin, Delano D. *A Saga of the St. Lawrence: Timber and Shipping through three Generations.* Toronto, Ryerson Press [1945] x, 176 p
Jacket, title page, and frontispiece

C76
Colgate, William. *C.W. Jefferys.* Toronto, Ryerson Press [1945] 42 p (Canadian Art Series)
Lettering on wrapper of soft cover issue, wrapper drawing by C.W. Jefferys

C77
Creighton, William Black. *Life is Like That.* Toronto, Ryerson Press [1945] x, 254 p
Jacket, spine, and colophon device

C78
Klinck, George A. (ed). *Allons Gai! A Topical Anthology of French Canadian Prose and Verse.* Toronto, Ryerson Press [1945] x, 154 p
Foreword by Lorne Pierce
Cover, title page vignette, and frontispiece

C79
Leechman, Douglas. *Eskimo Summer.* Toronto, Ryerson Press [1945] ix, 247 p
Jacket and spine

C72

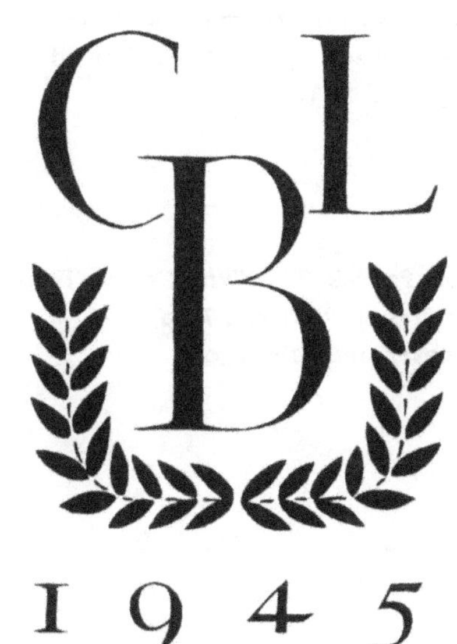

C80
Marriott, Anne. *Sandstone, and Other Poems.* Toronto, Ryerson Press [1945] 42 p
Jacket, cover, and title page

C81
Pacey, Desmond. *Frederick Philip Grove.* Toronto, Ryerson Press [1945] ix, 150 p (Canadian Men of Letters)
Title page

C82
Pierce, Lorne. *A Canadian People.* Toronto, Ryerson Press [1945] viii, 84 p
Issued also in wrappers
Jacket and cover design

C83
Scott, Frank R. *Overture: Poems.* Toronto, Ryerson Press [1945] 79 p
Jacket, cover, and title page

C84
Shaw, John Mackintosh. *Life after Death: The Christian View of the Future Life.* Toronto, Ryerson Press [1945] ix, 110 p
Jacket design

C85
A Word to Us All. [Toronto, Ryerson Press, 1945] [8] p
Ryerson Press Christmas greeting, 1945
Decorated borders by J.E.H. MacDonald
Prefatory note by TM

1946

C86
Anderson, Patrick. *The White Centre.* Toronto, Ryerson Press [1946] viii, 72 p
Jacket, cover, and title page

C87
Barbeau, Marius. *Painters of Quebec.* Toronto, Ryerson Press [1946] 48 p (Canadian Art Series)
Wrapper design for soft cover issue

C88
Colgate, William. *Two Letters of Tom Thomson, 1915 and 1916.* Weston, Ont. The Old Rectory Press, 1946. 15 p
'First published in Saturday Night, Toronto, November 9, 1946, now reprinted ... in a limited edition ... as a ... Christmas message for Dr. and Mrs. Arnold D.A. Mason.'
2 vignettes

C89
Coulter, John. *The Blossoming Thorn.* Toronto, Ryerson Press [1946] 54 p
Jacket, cover, and title page

C90
Dudek, Louis. *East of the City.* Toronto, Ryerson Press [1946] 51 p
Jacket, cover, and title page

C91
Heeney, William Bertal. *The Great Certainty.* Toronto, Ryerson Press [1946] ix, 160 p
Jacket and cover lettering

C92
Macnaughton, John. *Essays and Addresses.* [Kingston] Queen's University, 1946. x, 319 p
Selected by D.D. Calvin
Title page design

C93
Page, Patricia K. *As Ten As Twenty.* Toronto, Ryerson Press [1946] 43 p
Jacket, cover, and title page

C94
Sissons, Constance Kerr. *John Kerr.* Toronto, Oxford University Press, 1946. ix, 282 p
Jacket and spine design

C94

JOHN
KERR

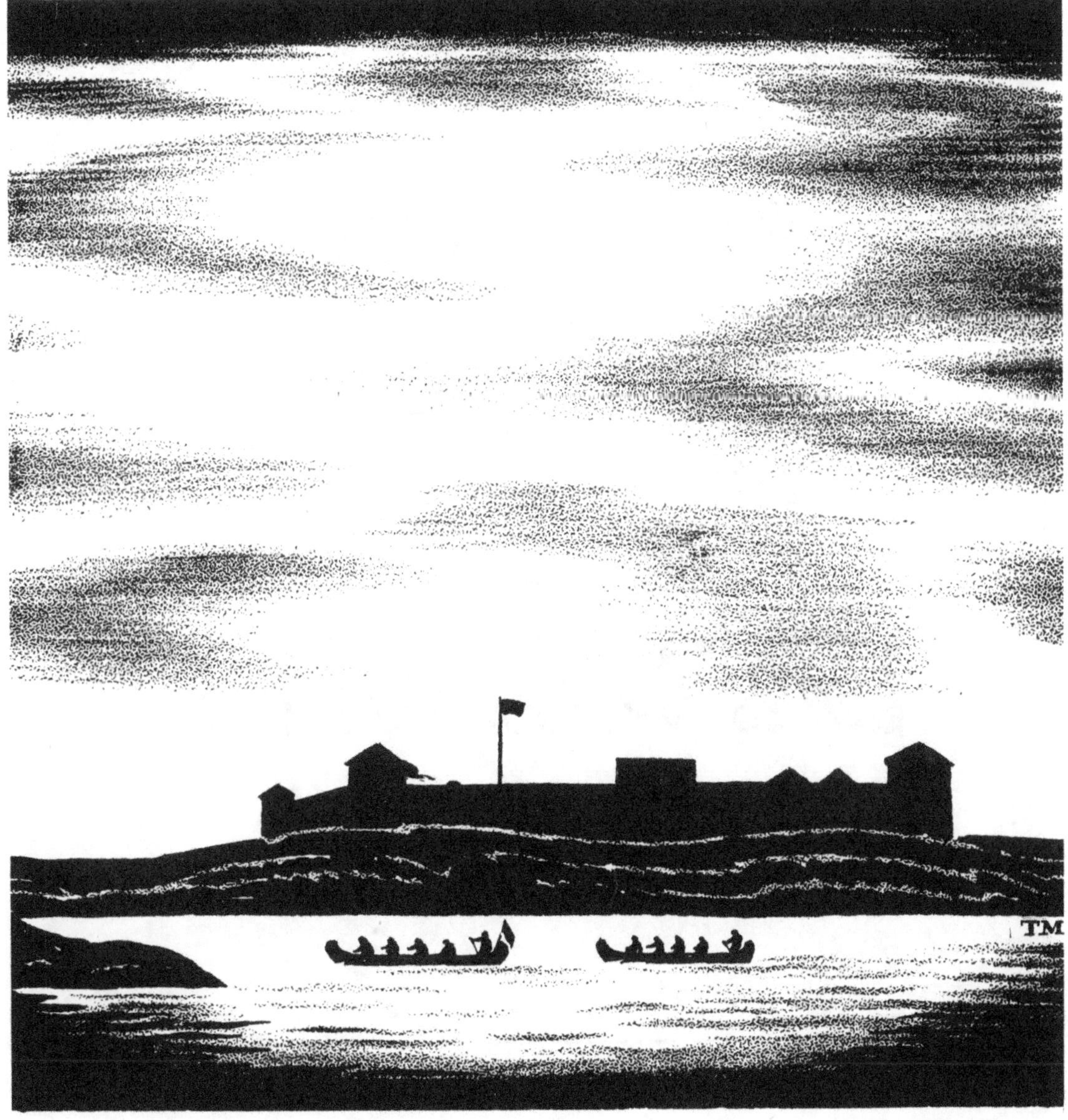

1947

C95
Buchanan, Donald W. *James Wilson Morrice.* Toronto, Ryerson Press [1947] 38 p (Canadian Art Series)
Wrapper design for soft cover issue

C96
Klinck, George A. (ed). *En Avant!: A Junior Anthology of French Canadian Prose and Verse.* Toronto, Ryerson Press [1947] x, 195 p
Foreword by Lorne Pierce
Cover and 2 vignettes

C95

DONALD W. BUCHANAN

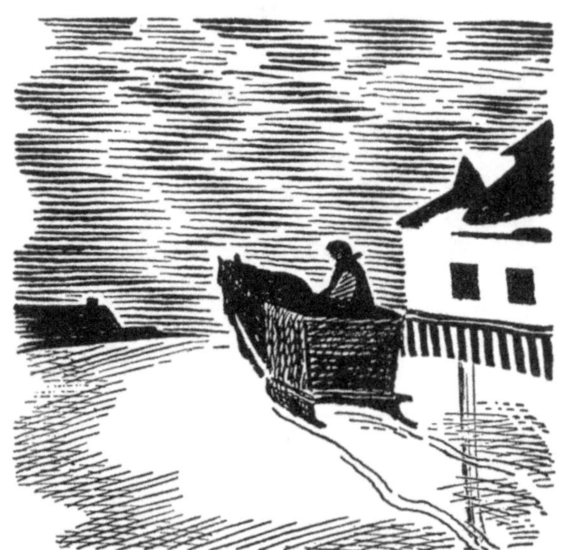

James Wilson Morrice

CANADIAN ART SERIES

C97
Livesay, Dorothy. *Poems for People.* Toronto, Ryerson Press [1947] 40 p
Jacket, cover and title page

C98
MacDonald, Malcolm. *The Birds of Brewery Creek.* London, Geoffrey Cumberlege, Oxford University Press, 1947. x, 334 p
Title page vignette, and lettering on jacket and cover
Illustrated with photographs by Dr Arthur A. Allen and W.V. Crich

C99
MacInnes, Tom. *In the Old of My Age: A New Book of Rhymes.* Toronto, Ryerson Press [1947] viii, 55 p
Title page and jacket by T.H. Varley and TM

C100
McRaye, Walter. *Pauline Johnson and her Friends.* Toronto, Ryerson Press [1947] xv, 182 p
Jacket lettering

C101
Souster, Raymond. *Go to Sleep, World.* Toronto, Ryerson Press [1947] vii, 59 p
Jacket, cover, and title page

C102
Wilson, Clifford (ed). *The New North in Pictures.* Toronto, Ryerson Press [1947] 223 p
Chiefly photographs
Cover, title page, and lettering on jacket

1948

C103
Barbeau, Marius. *Cornelius Krieghoff.* Toronto, Ryerson Press [1948] 36 p (Canadian Art Series)
Wrapper design for soft cover issue

C104
Beattie, A.M. and Swayze, J.G. (ed). *Reading for Today: Prose, Book Two.* Toronto, Ryerson Press [1948] x, 183 p
Title lettering on cover and title page

C105
Birney, Earle. *The Strait of Anian: Selected Poems.* Toronto, Ryerson Press [1948] viii, 84 p
Jacket, cover, and title page

C106
Brown, Audrey Alexandra. *All Fools' Day.* Toronto, Ryerson Press [1948] 56 p
Jacket, cover, and title page

C107
Canadian Pulp and Paper Association. *10 Pulp and Paper Paintings.* [Montreal, 1948] 24 p
Cover title
Reproduction of oil painting 'The Forest' on p 4

C108
Chalmers, Randolph Carleton. *The Pure Celestial Fire: An Evangelical Interpretation of Christianity.* Toronto, Ryerson Press [1948] xi, 238 p
Jacket design

C109
Grayson, Ethel Kirk. *Beggar's Velvet.* Toronto, Ryerson Press [1948] 42 p
Jacket, cover, and title page

C110
The National Society of the Deaf and the Hard of Hearing. *Annual Report. Fiscal year 1947-48.* [Toronto, 1948] 26 p
Lettering on cover

C111
Percival, Walter P. (ed). *Leading Canadian Poets.* Toronto, Ryerson Press [1948] x, 271 p
Spine, jacket, and title page

1949

C112
Coates, Carol. *Invitation to Mood.* Toronto, Ryerson Press [1949] 54 p
Jacket, cover, and title page

C113
Cranston, J. Herbert. *Etienne Brûlé: Immortal Scoundrel.* Toronto, Ryerson Press [1949] xiii, 144 p
Jacket and spine lettering
Jacket drawing by C.W. Jefferys

C114
Leechman, Douglas. *Indian Summer.* Toronto, Ryerson Press [1949] x, 182 p
Jacket and spine
Illustrated by W. Langdon Kihn

C115
Speakman, Horace B. *Faith of a Scientist: Science, Humanism and Christian Education.* Toronto, Clarke, Irwin & Co. Ltd., 1949. v, 79 p
Jacket design, cover, and some lettering on title page

1950

C116
McNaught, Carlton. *The Canadian Forum ... Volume Thirty: A Retrospect.* [Toronto, Canadian Forum] 1950
Reprinted from *The Canadian Forum,* April, May, and June, 1950
Cover drawing, design, and one lino cut

C117
Needler, George H. *Moore and his Canadian Boat Song.* Toronto, Ryerson Press, 1950. 14 p
'Only five hundred copies have been printed, of which two hundred and fifty are for sale.'
Cover, title page, and map
Part of the issue in wrappers

C118
Pacey, Desmond (ed). *A Book of Canadian Stories.* Toronto, Ryerson Press [1950] xxxviii, 310 p
Revised edition; first published 1947
Jacket and spine design

1951

C119
Six Trees. [Montreal, Canadian Pulp and Paper Assoc., 1951] [32] p
Reproductions of 1 oil painting and 13 drawings

C117

MOORE *and his*

Canadian Boat Song

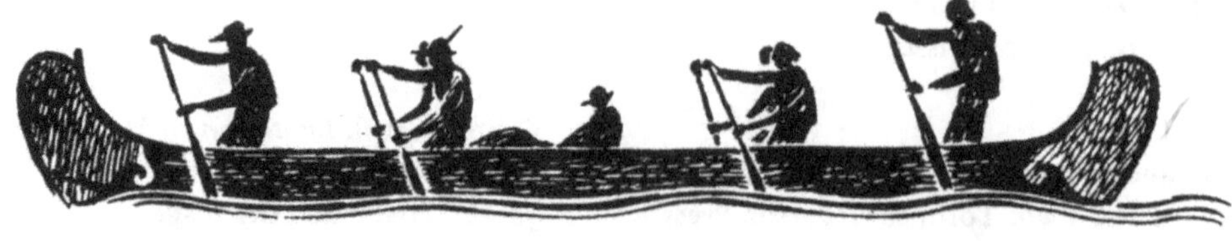

by G·H·Needler

C118

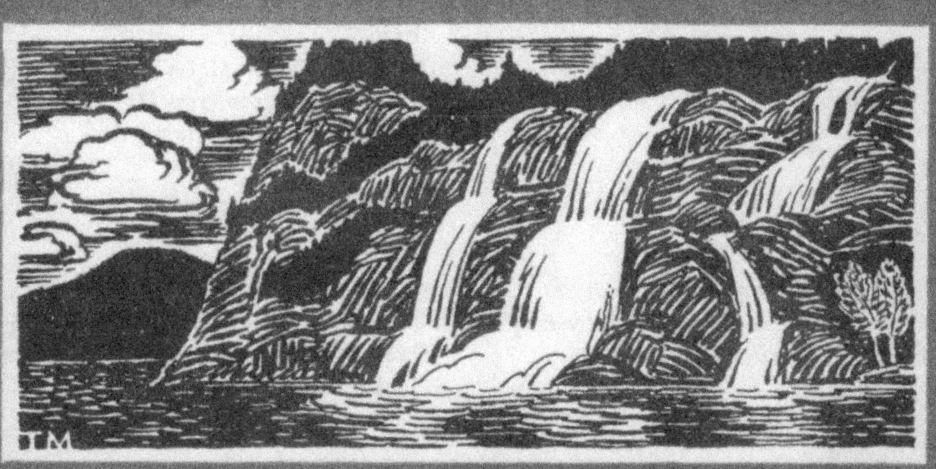

A BOOK OF
CANADIAN
STORIES

Edited with an Introduction and Notes
by DESMOND PACEY
Professor of English in the University of New Brunswick

1952

C120
Fine Paper, Product of a Great Canadian Asset. [Montreal, Canadian Pulp and Paper Association, 1952] 16 p
Cover title
9 drawings (2 vignettes)

C121
Reed, T.A. (ed). *A History of the University of Trinity College, 1852-1952.* [Toronto] University of Toronto Press, 1952. xii, 313 p
Jacket and title page

1953

C122
Lower, Arthur R.M. *Unconventional Voyages.* Toronto, Ryerson Press [1953] xii, 156 p
Jacket, cover, and title page

1954

C123
Canadian Poetry in English: Chosen by Bliss Carman, Lorne Pierce and V.B. Rhodenizer. Toronto, Ryerson Press [1954] xxxvi, 456 p
Jacket and title page

C121

A History of the University of
Trinity College

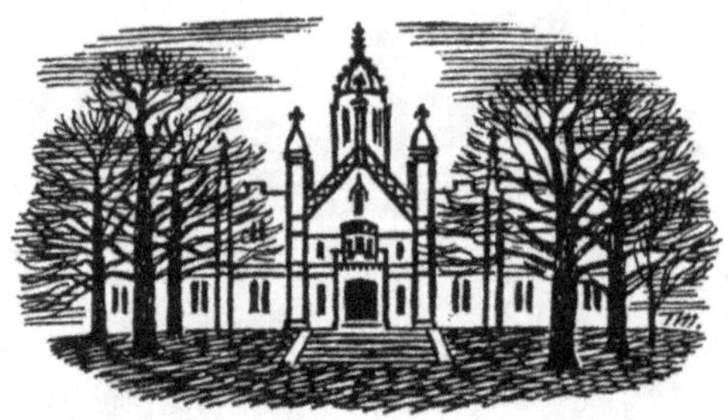

1852 ☆ 1952

C124
Colgate, William. *The Toronto Art Students League, 1886-1904.* Toronto, Ryerson Press, 1954. iv, 34 p
Cover design; drawing by C.W. Jeffreys

C125
Massey, Vincent. *On Books and Reading.* [Toronto, Ryerson Press, 1954] [12] p
Edition limited to 1600 copies
Some lettering

C126
Pierce, Lorne. *The House of Ryerson, 1829-1954.* Toronto, Ryerson Press [1954] ix, 52 p
Foreword by C.H. Dickinson
Cover and title page

1957

C127
Colgate, William. *Archibald Lampman, a Dedication and a Note.* Toronto, privately printed, 1957. 15 p
Edition limited to 70 copies
2 drawings (1 vignette)

1959

C128
Humble, A.H. *The Crisis in Canadian Education.* Toronto, Ryerson Press [1959] 21 p (Saddlebag Books)
Series vignette on title page and cover design

C129
This One Thing: A Tribute to Henry Burton Sharman, 1865-1953. [Toronto, Student Christian Movement of Canada, 1959] 96 p
'Prepared by a group of friends'
3 drawings (2 vignettes)

1960

C130
Pierce, Lorne. *A Canadian Nation.* Toronto, Ryerson Press [1960] viii, 42 p
Jacket and cover design

C131
Wallace, William Stewart. *The Knight of Dundurn.* Toronto, Rous & Mann Press, 1960. 22 p
10 vignettes

1961

C132
Bourinot, Arthur S. *Paul Bunyan, Three Lincoln Poems, and other Verse.* Ottawa, privately printed, 1961. [36] p
Frontispiece

1962

C133
Aegis. Hanover, N.H.
Dartmouth College yearbook
Lettering on cover of issue for 1962

1964

C134
Harris, Lawren. *The Story of the Group of Seven.* Toronto, Rous & Mann, 1964. 29 p
Edition limited to 775 copies; for private distribution
Cover stamp

C135
Orvil E. Dryfoos Conference on Public Affairs, Dartmouth College. Hanover, N.H., Public Affairs Center, Dartmouth College, 1964–
Publication of papers from an annual conference
College arms design

1965

C136
Dickinson, Clarence H. *Lorne Pierce: A Profile.* Toronto, Ryerson Press [1965] xii, 79 p
1 vignette

C137
Ontario Society for Education through Art. *An Evening with Members of the Group of Seven.* Toronto, 20 April 1965. [7] p
Cover design (1 vignette) and lettering
With colour reproductions of 6 paintings by Group of Seven artists

C138
Sterling, John C. *Daniel Webster and a Small College.* Hanover, N.H., Dartmouth Publications, 1965. 62 p
Edition limited to 1000 copies
College arms drawn by TM used as diaper design on printed paper covers in binding.
Designed by Ray Nash

1966

C139
Graham, M. Audrey. *150 Years at St. John's, York Mills.* Toronto, General Publishing Co. [1966] xi, 275 p
Frontispiece

C140
Official Opening, the McMichael Conservation Collection of Art. Kleinburg, Ontario, Friday, 8 July 1966, 2 PM [8] p folder
Cover drawing

1969

C141
Addison, Ottelyn. *Tom Thomson: the Algonquin Years [by] Ottelyn Addison in collaboration with Elizabeth Harwood; with drawings and an appendix by Thoreau MacDonald.* Vancouver, Ryerson Press [1969] 98 p
4 drawings (3 vignettes), and appendix (pp 84-7)

C142
Brown, Francis (ed). *A Dartmouth Reader.* Hanover, N.H., Dartmouth Publications, 1969. 339 p
College arms on title page, and blind-stamped on front cover

1971

C143
Reaman, G. Elmore. *A History of Vaughn Township.* [Vaughn Township Historical Society, Printed by University of Toronto Press 1971] xii, 346 p
Wash drawing on jacket
20 drawings

D · Designs for and in Periodicals

D1
Acta Victoriana. Toronto
Cover design used from vol 49, no 1 (October 1924) to vol 51, no 7 (Midsummer 1927)
A second cover design used from vol 52, no 1 (October 1927) to vol 53, no 7 (Midsummer 1929)
A third cover design used from vol 54, no 1 (October 1929) to vol 59, no 7 (June 1935)

D2
Canadian Art. Ottawa
Cover lettering used from vol 1, no 1 (October/November 1943) to vol 5, no 1 (October/November 1947)
Reproduction of silkscreen print in vol 1, no 5 (June/July 1944) p 206
Reproduction of silkscreen print on cover of vol 8, no 1 (October 1949); p 61, one drawing

D3
The Canadian Author & Bookman. Toronto
Cover lettering design used from vol 19, no 4 (December 1943) to vol 21, no 1 (March 1945)

D4
The Canadian Bookman. Toronto
Cover design used from vol 5, no 6 to vol 7, no 12 (June 1923 to December 1925)
A second cover design used from vol 8, no 1 to vol 10, no 12 (January 1926 to December 1928)
A third cover design used from vol 11, no 1 to vol 13, no 12 (January 1929 to December 1931)
A fourth cover design used from vol 14, no 1 to vol 16, no 9 (January 1932 to October 1934)
Lettering on cover and pictorial headpiece used from vol 16, no 10 to vol 17, no 11 (November 1934 to December 1935)
A second lettering design used from vol 18, no 1 to vol 19, no 6 (January 1936 to December 1937)
1 drawing in August/September 1938 issue (p 7)
1 drawing in February/March 1939 issue (p 24)
A third lettering design used from vol 20, no 1 to vol 20, no 4 (April/May 1939 to October/November 1939)

D1

ACTA
VICTORIANA

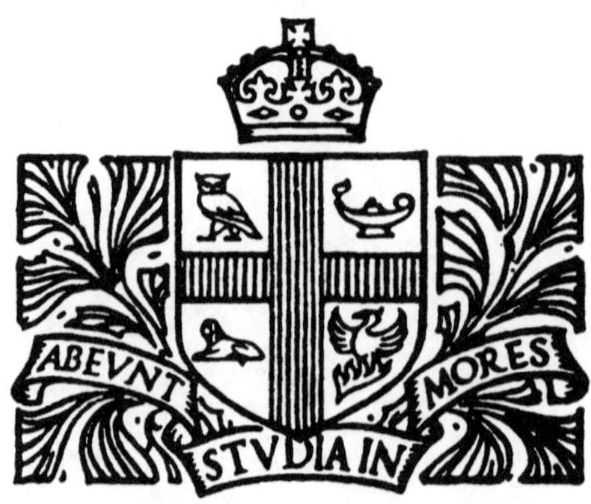

D5

The Canadian Forum. Toronto

Cover designs, including drawings for the following issues: no 47 (August 1924); no 48 (September 1924); no 49 (October 1924); no 50 (November 1924); no 52 (January 1925); no 53 (February 1925); no 54 (March 1925); no 55 (April 1925); no 56 (May 1925); no 57 (June 1925); no 59 (August 1925) (repeat of no 47); no 60 (September 1925); no 61 (October 1925) (repeat of no 49); no 62 (November 1925) (repeat of no 50); no 63 (December 1925); no 64 (January 1926) (repeat of no 52); no 66 (March 1926) (repeat of no 54); no 67 (April 1926) (repeat of no 55); no 68 (May 1926) (repeat of no 56); no 69 (June 1926) (repeat of no 57); no 71 (August 1926) (repeat of no 47); no 72 (September 1926) (repeat of no 60); no 73 (October 1926) (repeat of no 49); no 74 (November 1926) (repeat of no 50); no 75 (December 1926); no 76 (January 1927) (repeat of no 52); no 77 (February 1927) (repeat of no 53); no 78 (March 1927) (repeat of no 54); no 79 (April 1927); no 80 (May 1927); no 81 (June 1927); no 82 (July 1927); no 83 (August 1927); no 84 (September 1927); no 85 (October 1927); no 86 (November 1927); no 87 (December 1927); no 88 (January 1928); no 89 (February 1928); no 90 (March 1928); no 91 (April 1928); no 92 (May 1928); no 93 (June 1928); no 94 (July 1928); no 95 (August 1928); no 96 (September 1928); no 97 (October 1928); no 98 (November 1928); no 99 (December 1928); no 100 (January 1929); no 101 (February 1929); no 102 (March 1929); no 103 (April 1929); no 104 (May 1929); no 105 (June 1929); no 106 (July 1929); no 107 (August 1929); no 108 (September 1929); no 109 (October 1929); no 110 (November 1929); no 111 (December 1929); no 112 (January 1930); no 113 (February 1930); no 114 (March 1930); no 115 (April 1930); no 116 (May 1930); no 117 (June 1930); no 118 (July 1930); no 119 (August 1930); no 120 (September 1930); no 121 (October 1930); no 122 (November 1930); no 123 (December 1930); no 124 (January 1931); no 125 (February 1931); no 126 (March 1931); no 127 (April 1931); no 128 (May 1931); no 129 (June 1931); no 130 (July 1931); no 131 (August 1931); no 132 (September 1931); no 133 (October 1931); no 134 (November 1931); no 135 (December 1931); no 136 (January 1932); no 137 (February 1932); no 138 (March 1932); no 139 (April 1932); no 140 (May 1932); no 141 (June 1932)

Drawings and lino cuts included in the following issues: no 17 (February 1922) '3 linoleum cuts' (these constitute TM's first printed work); no 26 (November 1922) 'A Rocky Pasture' (lino cut); no 31 (April 1923) 'Lake Land' (lino cut); no 47 (August 1924) 'Shingled House'; no 54 (March 1925) 'Fire and Hail ...'; no 56 (May 1925) 'Hepaticas'; no 59 (August 1925) 'Rocks and Hills' (lino cut); no 62 (November 1925) 'Followed the Monarch to his Grave'; no 67 (April 1926) 'Wild Ducks on the Lake'; no 70 (July 1926) 'Northern Summer'; no 77 (February 1927) [no title]; no 81 (June 1927) 'Cathedral Mountain, Lake O'Hara' (from a sketch by J.E.H. MacDonald); no 86 (November 1927) 'Cabin Window'; no 89 (February 1928) 'Thomas Hardy'; no 95 (August 1928) 'Leon Tolstoy'; no 107 (August 1929) 'Fanny and Johnny' (lino cut); no 109 (October 1929) 'W.H. Hudson'; no 119 (August 1930) 'In Ontario'; no 132 (September 1931) 'Pioneer Graves: Autumn'; no 138 (March 1932) 'A House at Thornhill'; no 387 (April 1953) 'Rocks and Mink'; no 395 (October 1953) 'Foxes in an Old Orchard'; no 397 (February 1954) 'Horned Owl'; no 403 (August 1954) 'Haliburton Shoreline'; no 416 (September 1955) 'Farm Sawmill'; no 417 (October 1955) 'Grasshopper Hunt'; no 420 (January 1956) 'The Fisher'; no 427 (August 1956) 'Pair of Loons'; no 453 (October 1958) 'Mink by a Stream'; no 462 (July 1959) 'House Near Lake Cecebe,' 'In the Woods,' [untitled]

Vignettes and head pieces used in the issues of the same period: no 41 (February 1924) drawing, by A.Y. Jackson for a poem by Barker Fairley, lettered by TM; reprinted 1971 in *Wavelengths 32* (Toronto, J.M. Dent & Sons 1971), p 160

D5

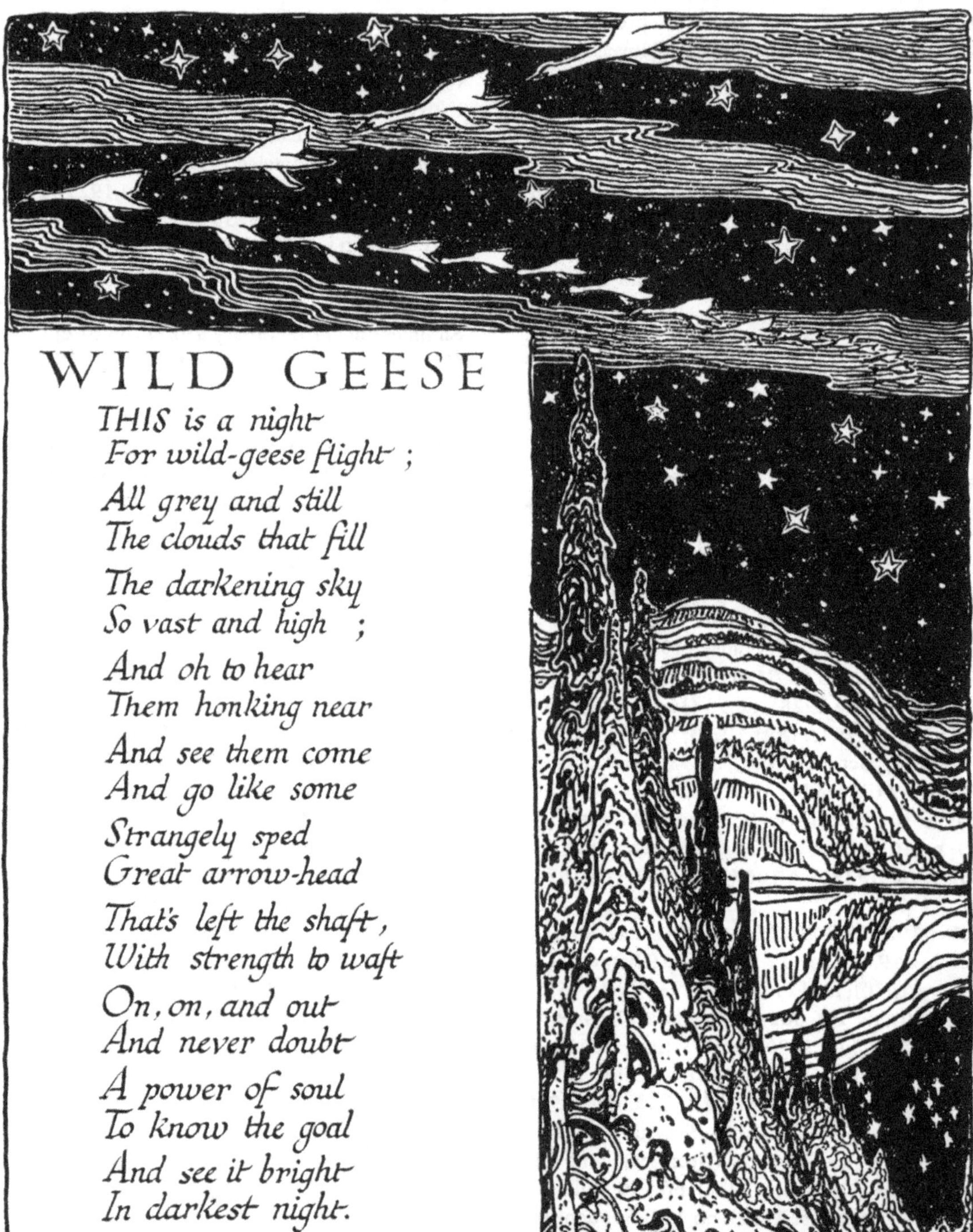
WILD GEESE
THIS is a night
For wild-geese flight ;
All grey and still
The clouds that fill
The darkening sky
So vast and high ;
And oh to hear
Them honking near
And see them come
And go like some
Strangely sped
Great arrow-head
That's left the shaft,
With strength to waft
On, on, and out
And never doubt
A power of soul
To know the goal
And see it bright
In darkest night.
Barker Fairley

D5

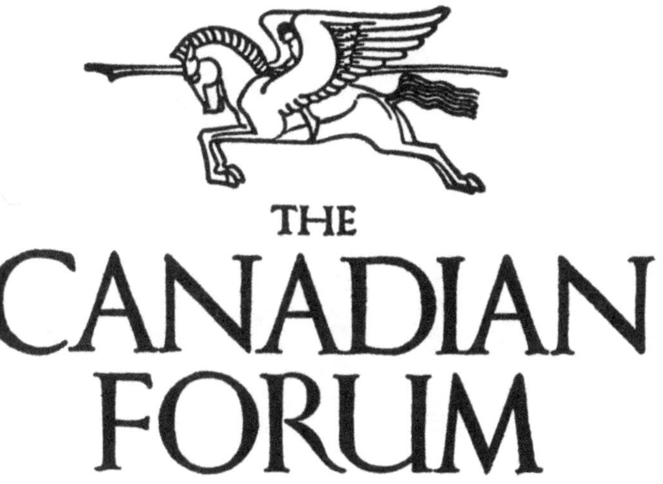

TM

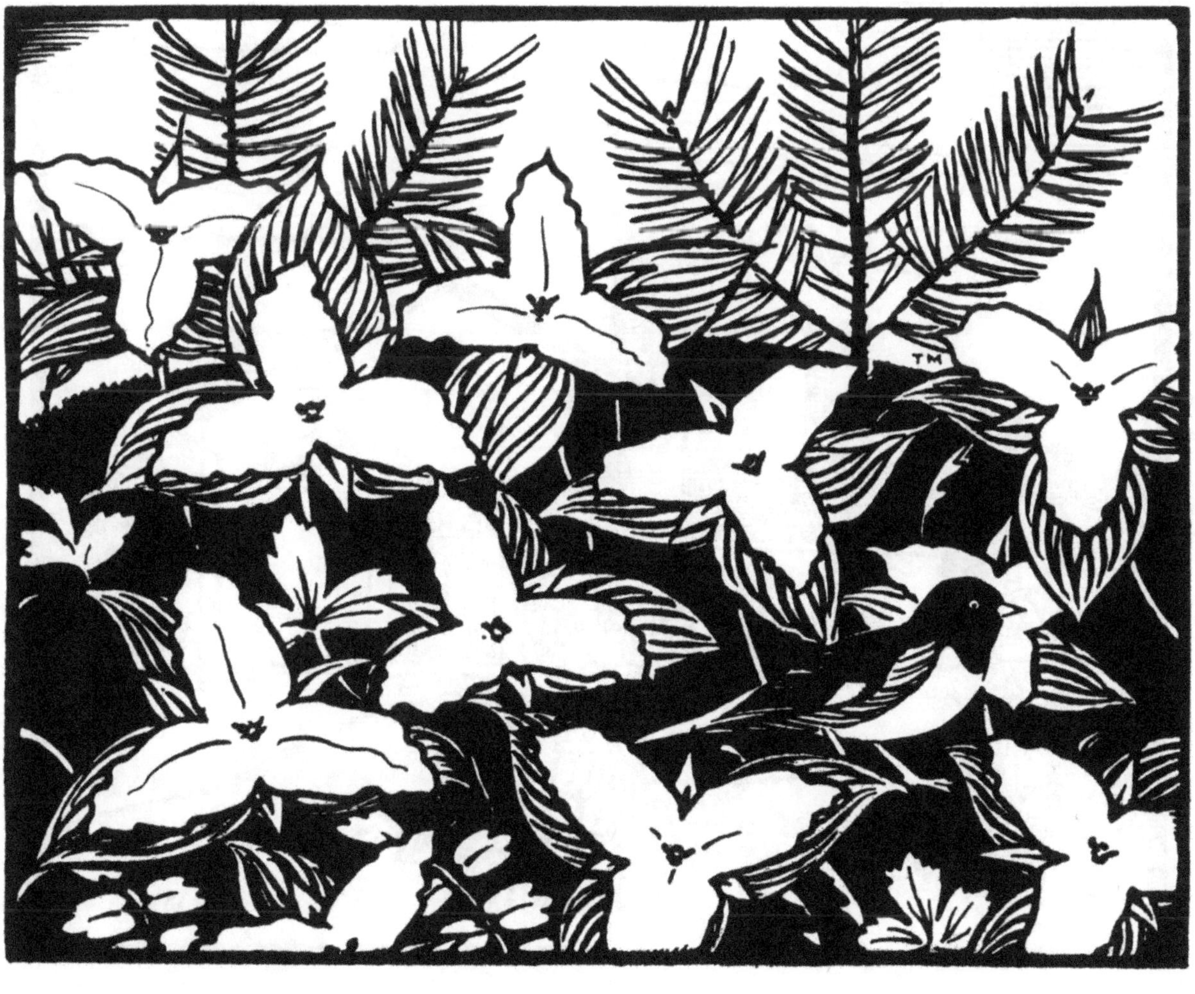

D5

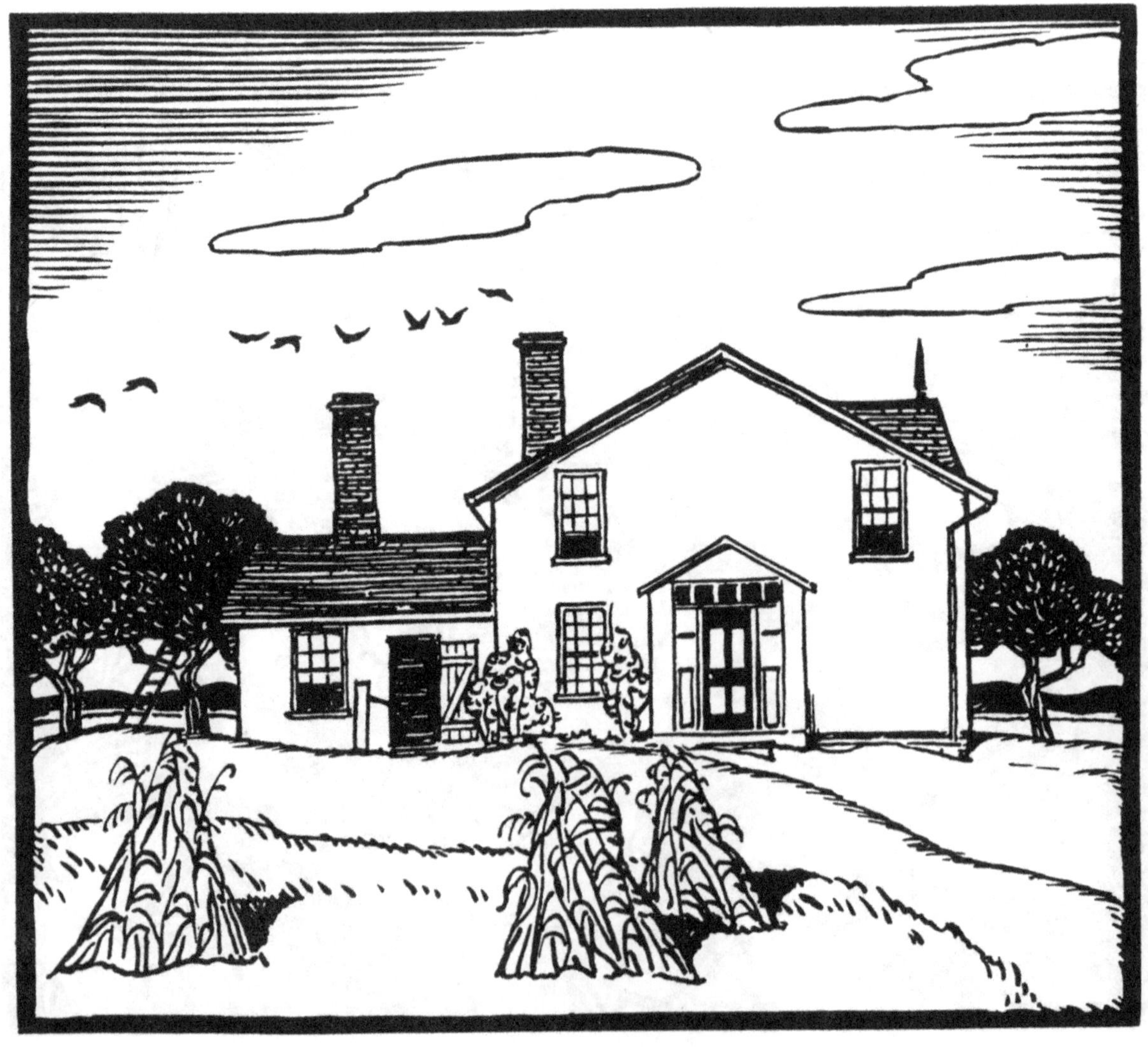

D5

THE CANADIAN FORUM

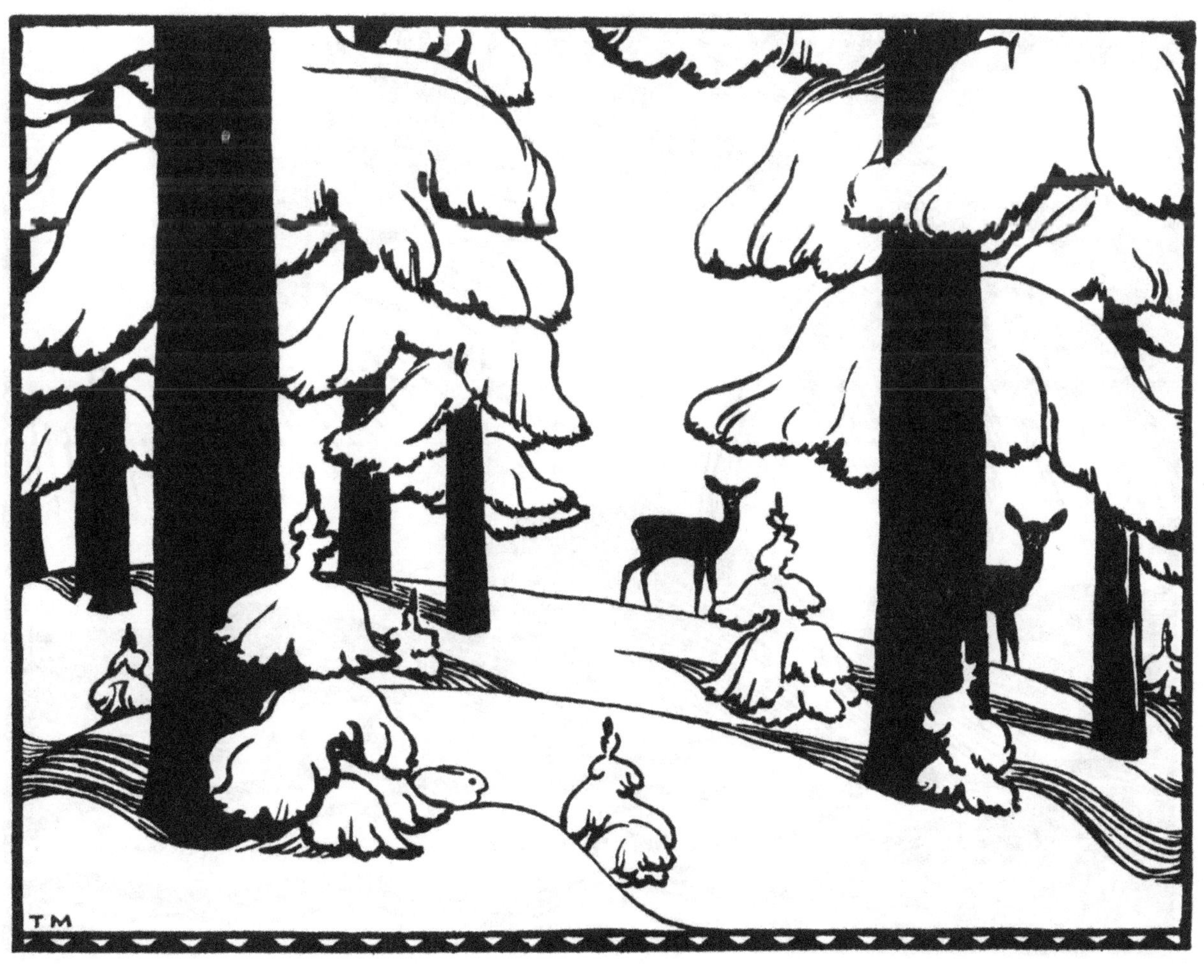

D5

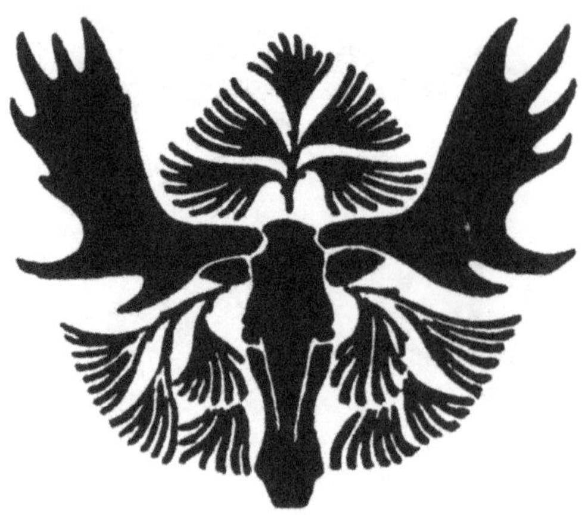

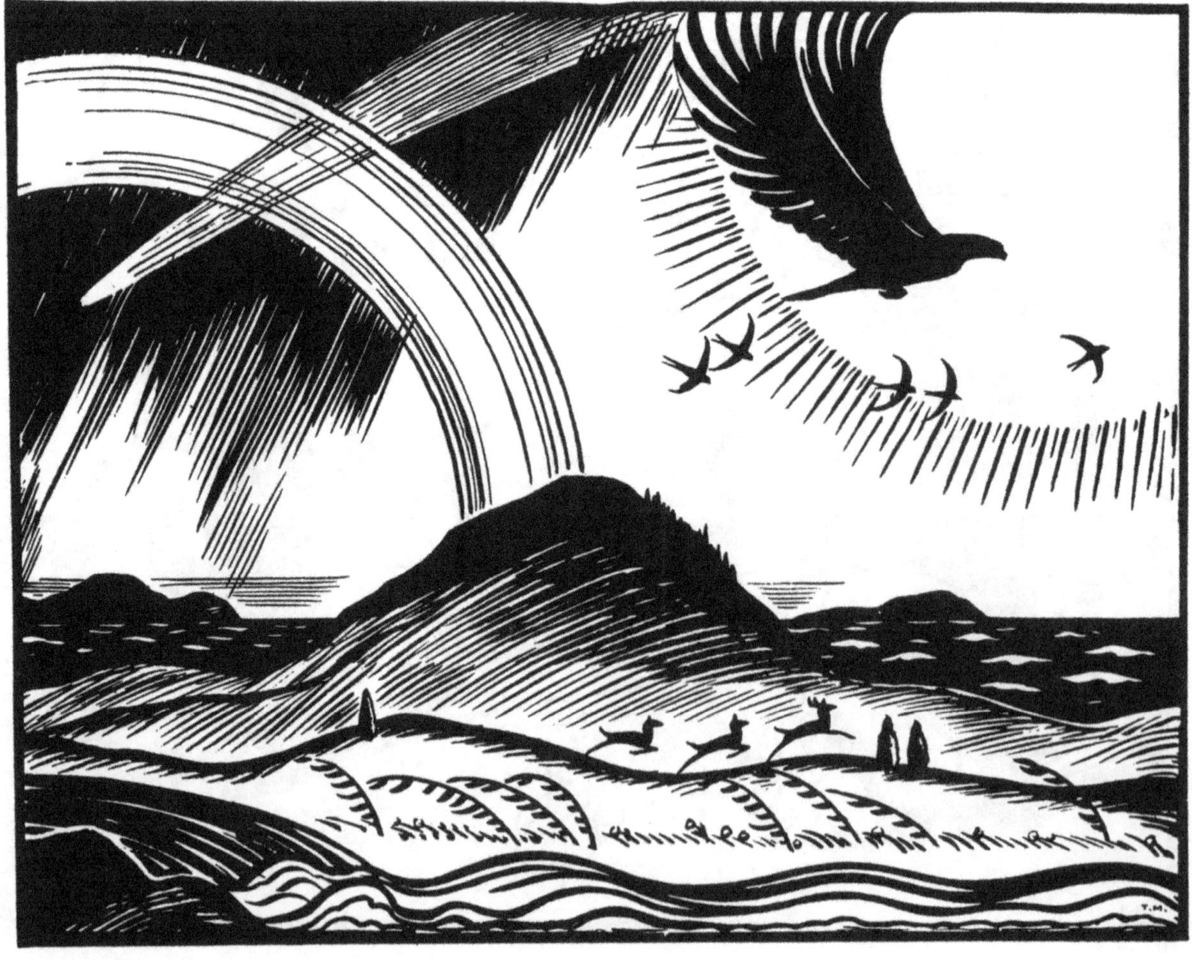

D5

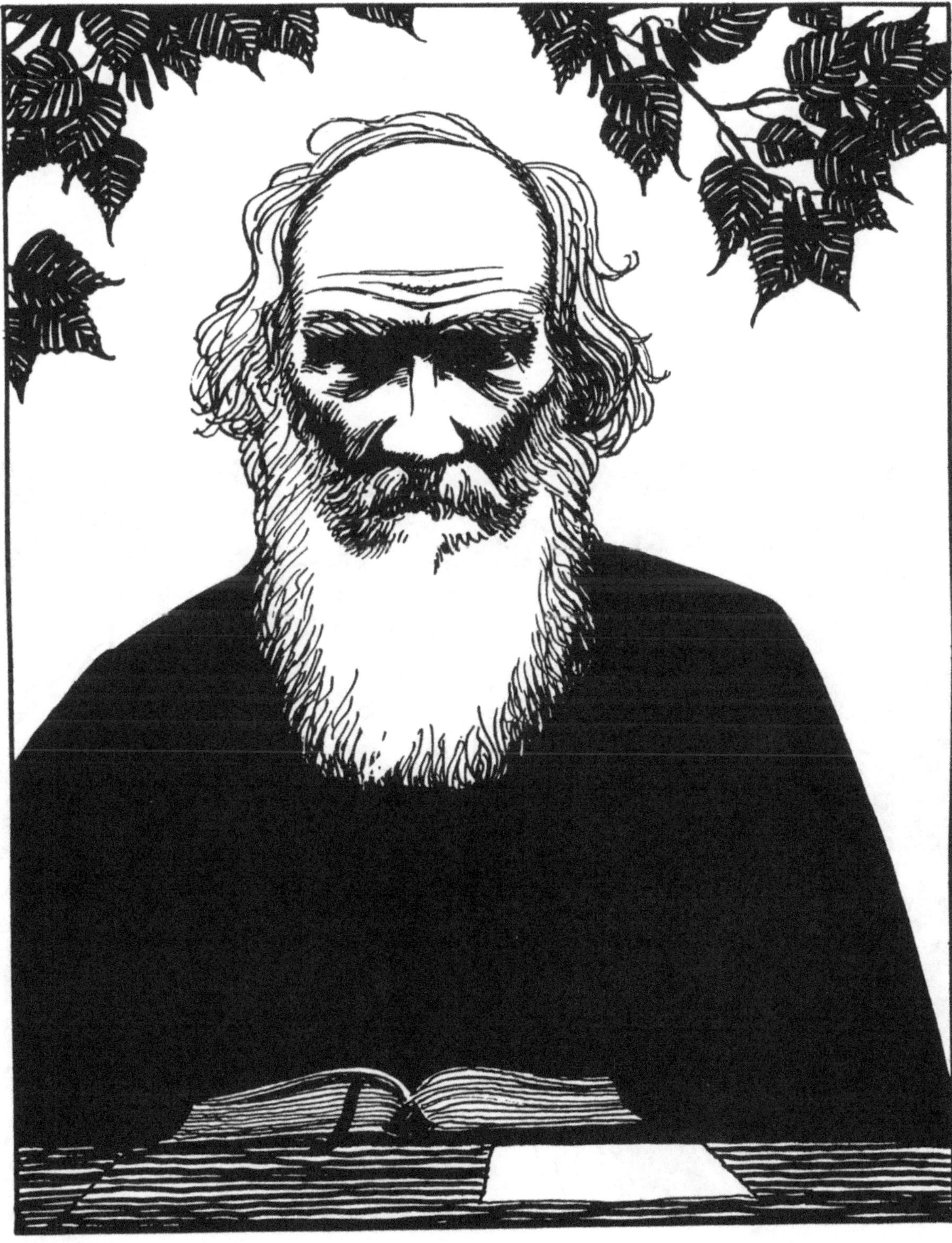

D5

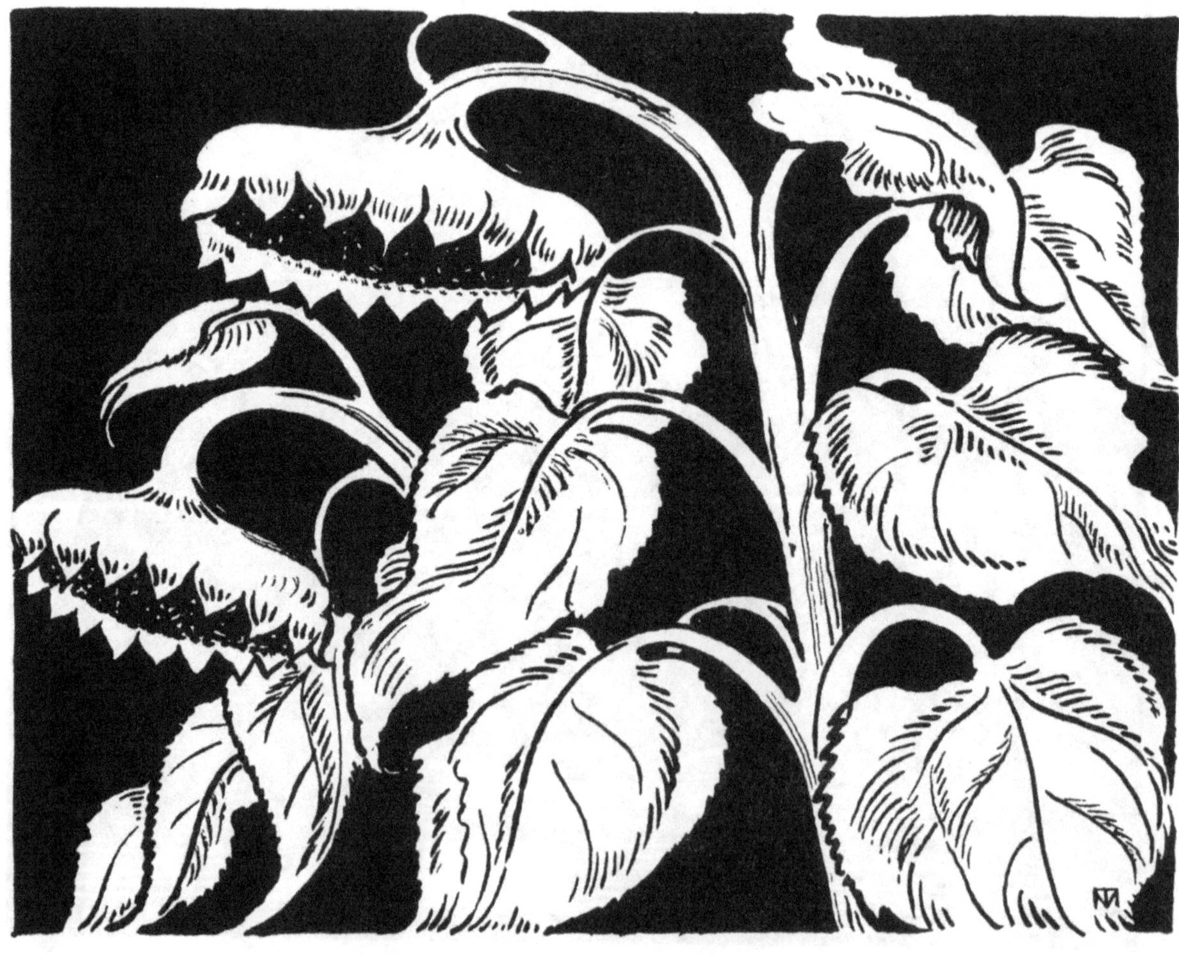

D5

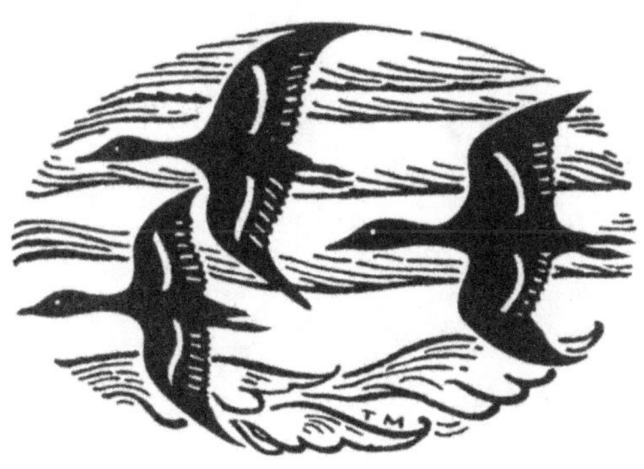

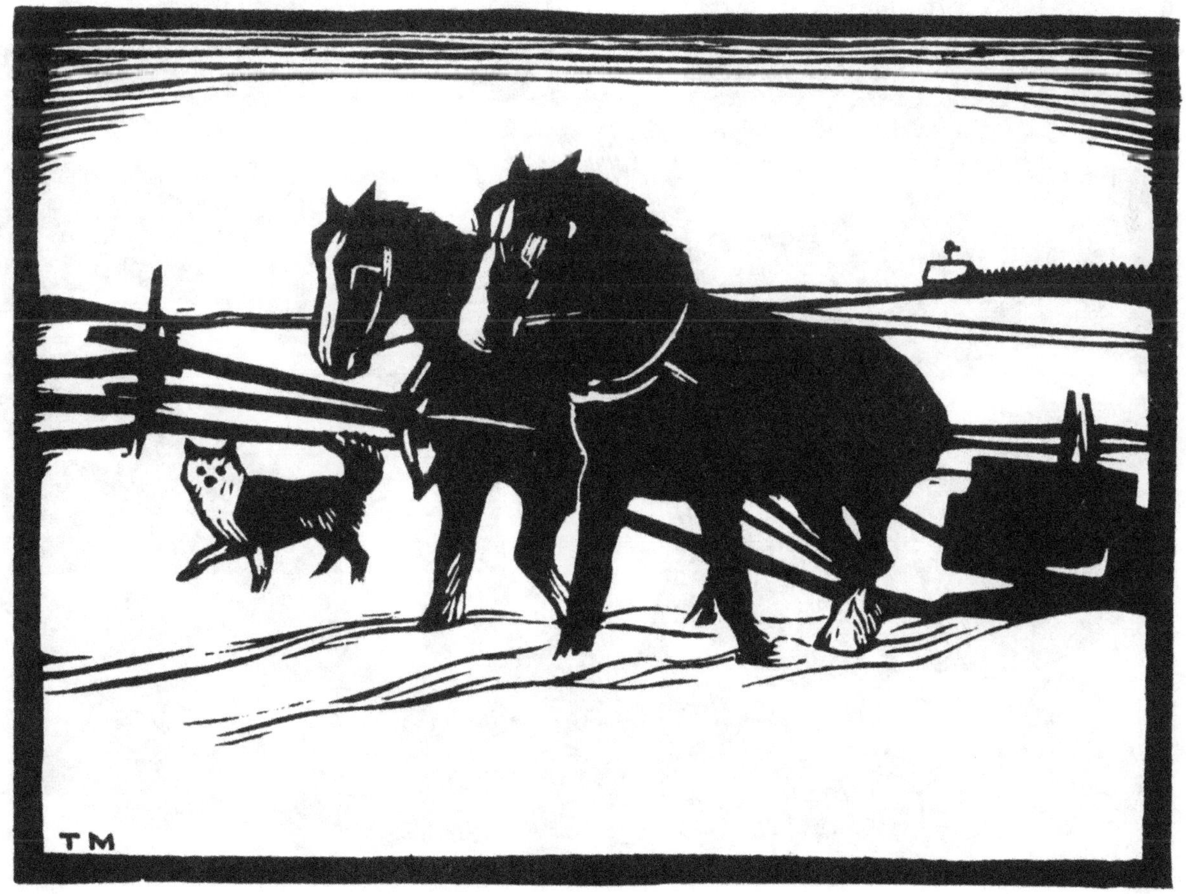

D5

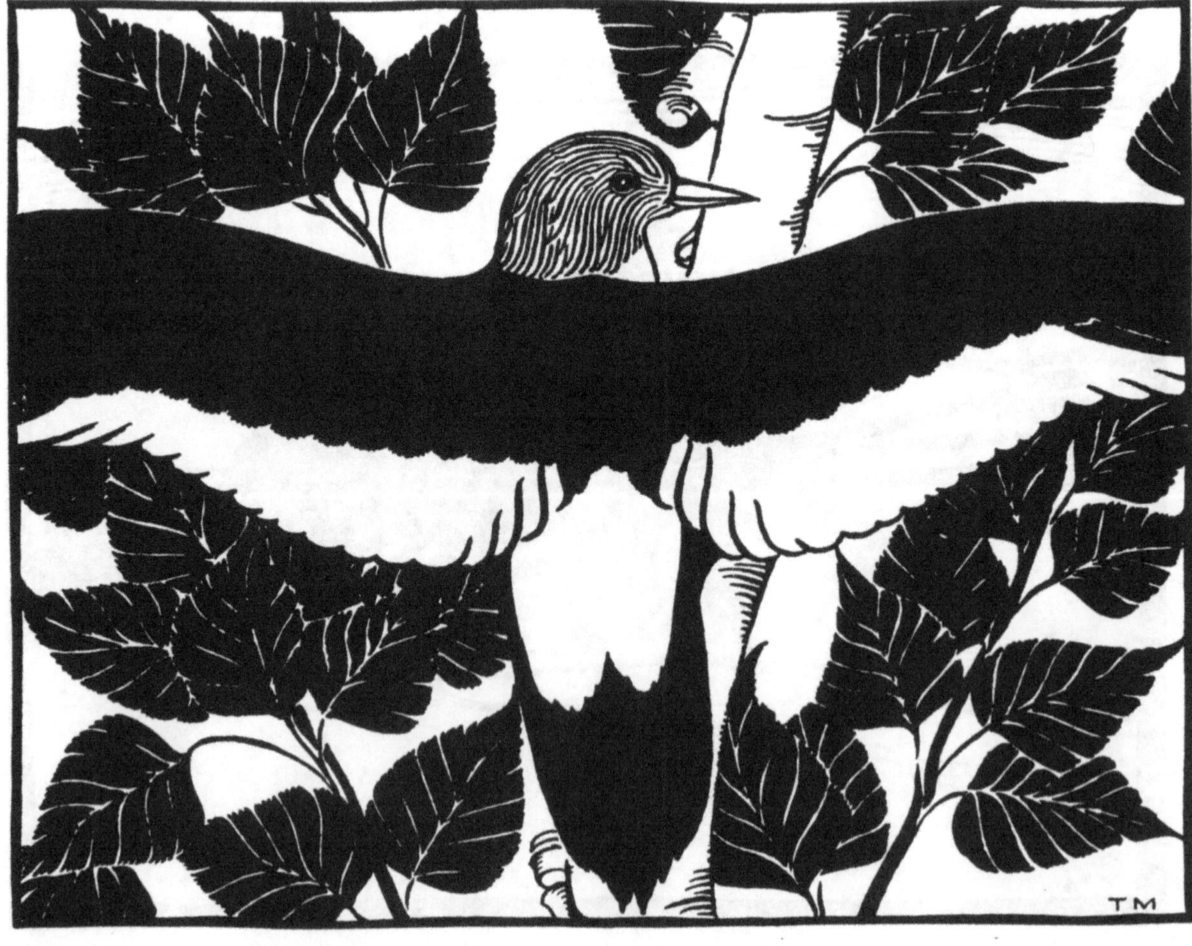

D5

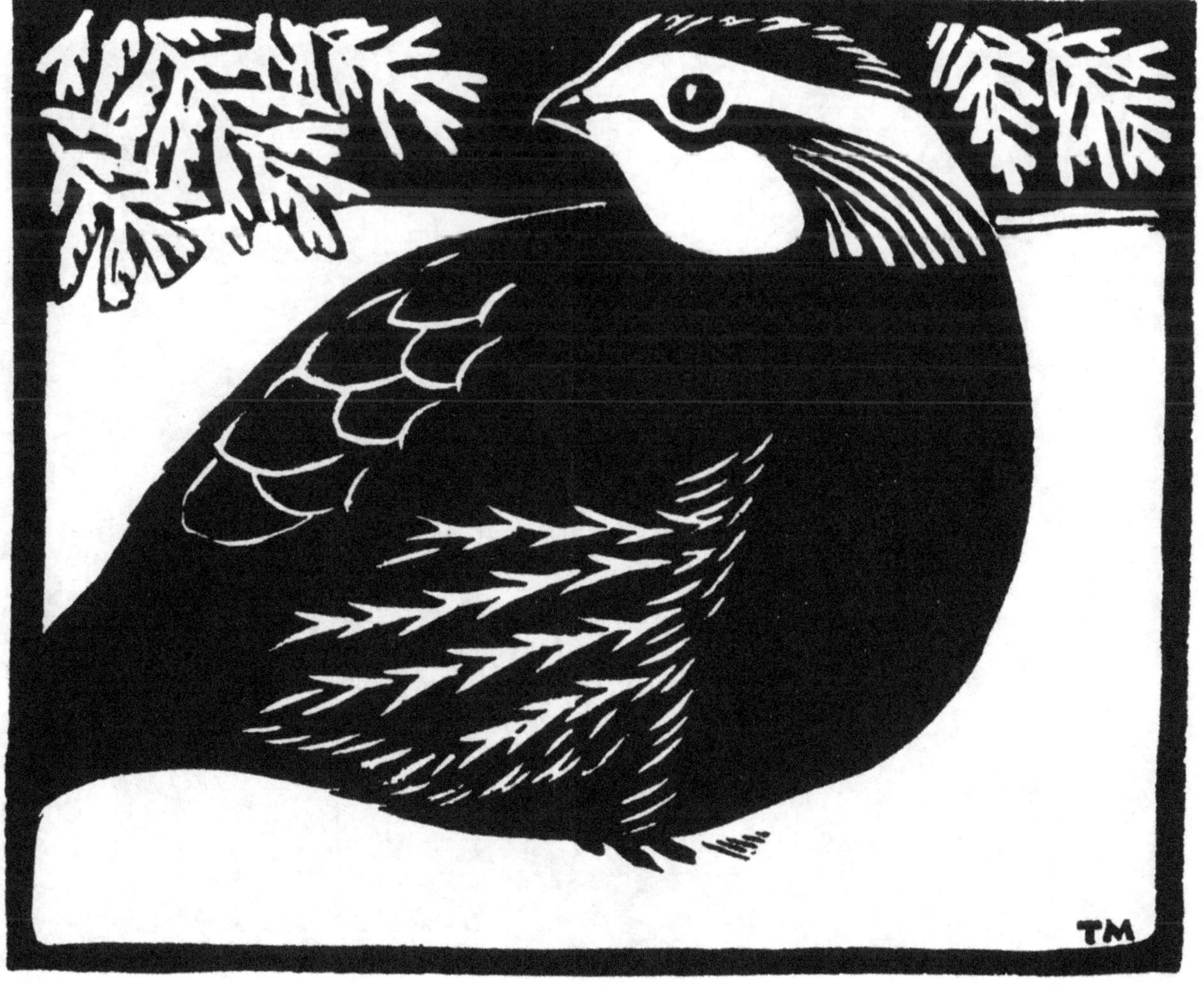

D5

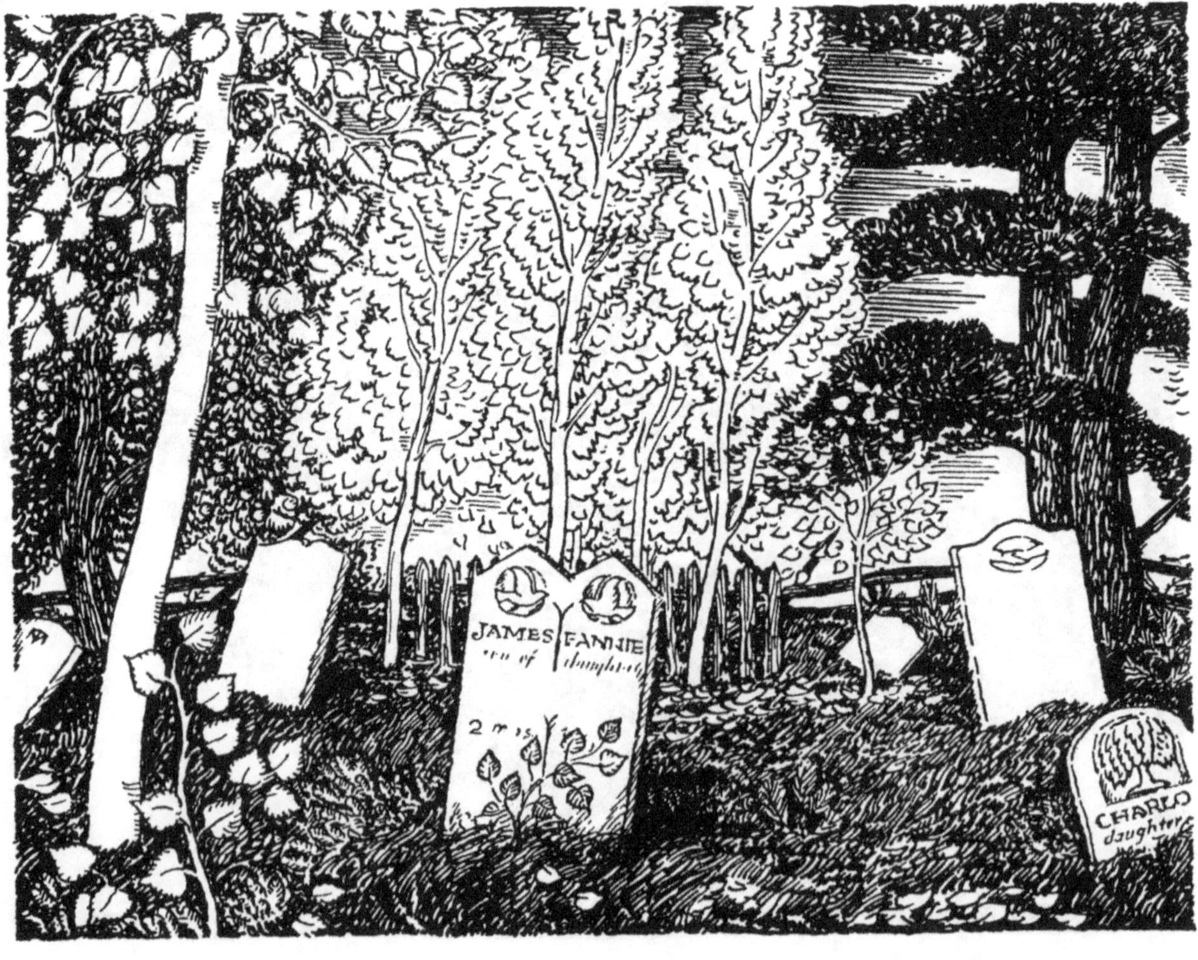

D5

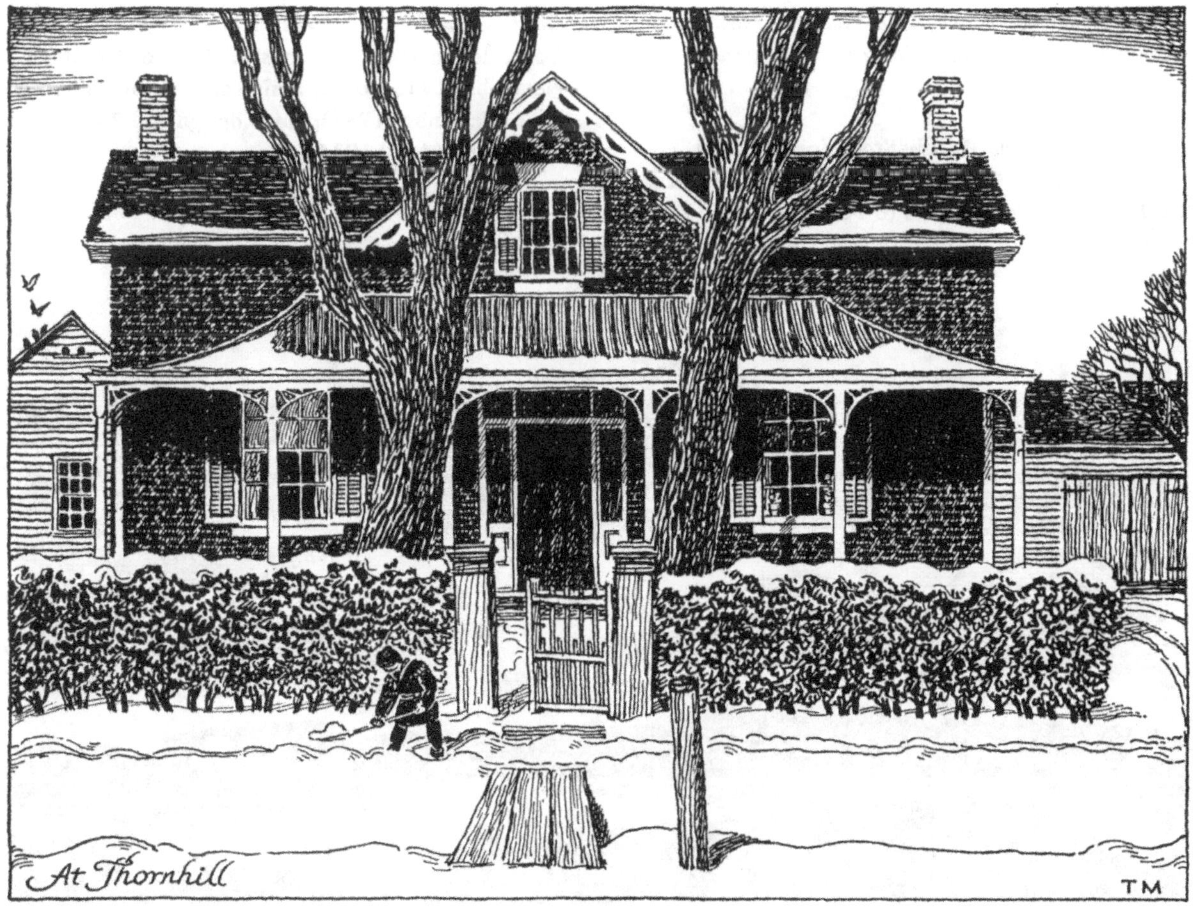

D6
Canadian Library Association Bulletin. Ottawa.
Cover design used for vol 11, no 1 (August 1954)
Design also issued as a poster

D7
The Canadian Student: A Venturer in Opinion. Toronto
Cover design; first known use in vol 6, no 1 (October 1923)
Some vignettes and headpieces

D8
The Dartmouth: The Oldest College Newspaper in America. Hanover, N.H.
Name plate lettering. Used from Wednesday, 21 September 1955 (vol 114, no 1) to Saturday, 25 February 1956 (vol 115, no 106)

D9
Dartmouth Alumni Magazine. Hanover, N.H.
7 vignettes used as fillers from 1960 to present

D10
Family Herald and Weekly Star. Montreal, P.Q.
Illustrations for 'Country Career Woman' by Doris M. Fitzgerald, vol 77, no 6 (6 February 1946)

D11
Federation of Ontario Naturalists. Bulletin. Don Mills, Ont.
Superseded by *The Ontario Naturalist.*
Drawing used with title from no 52 to no 59 (May 1951–January/February 1953). Same drawing featured on first page from no 62 to no 98 (December 1953–December 1962) omitted in no 75 (March 1957).
Crest used on cover from no 63 to no 98 (January 1954–December 1962)

D12
Federation of Ontario Naturalists. Newsletter. Don Mills, Ont.
Crest used with title from October 1958–August/September/October 1969; also used on address panel in some issues.

D13
Gold: Magazine of Canada's North. Toronto
Cover design and 6 drawings vol 1, no 6 (October/November 1933); cover design and 3 drawings vol 2, no 1 (December 1933); cover design and 2 drawings vol 2, no 4 (April 1934)

D11

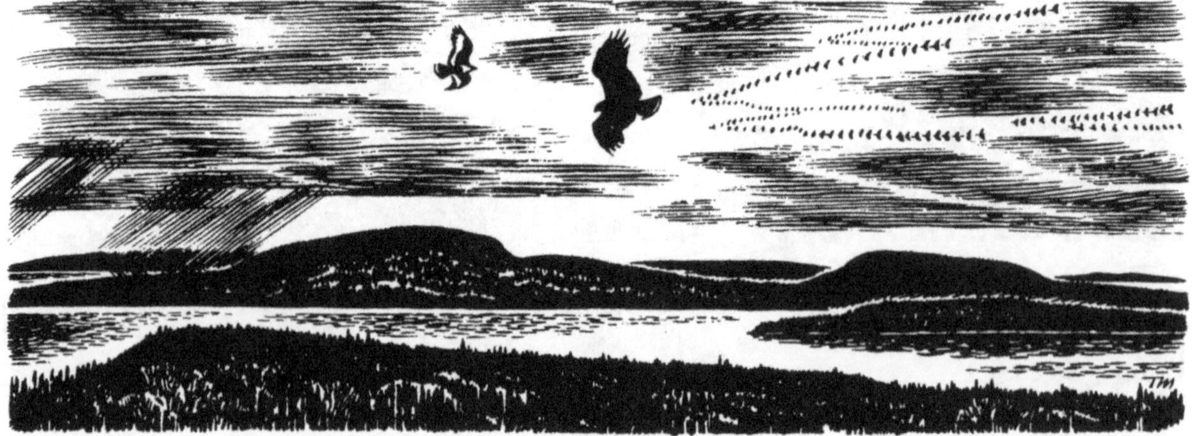

D14
Imperial Oil Review. Toronto
Drawing inside front and back covers, October 1956 issue

D15
International Journal. Toronto
Cover design used from vol 1, no 1 (Winter 1945-6) to vol 25, no 4 (Autumn 1970)

D16
The Narrator: Devoted to Books. Toronto
Reproduction of a cover design on cover of vol 10, no 1 (January 1943) (see also C53)

D17
The Northward Road. Toronto
'Published occasionally'
Cover design for the May 1929 issue

D18
The Ontario Naturalist. Federation of Ontario Naturalists. Don Mills, Ont.
Crest used on contents page from January 1963–November 1970; use of crest discontinued following that issue. Crest also appears on cover for issue of March 1966.

D19
Print: A Quarterly Journal of the Graphic Arts. Woodstock, Vermont
Cover design for vol 3, no 3 (1943) and vol 6, no 1 (1948)
A second cover design for vol 5, no 1 (1947)

D20
Printing and Graphic Arts. Lunenburg, Vermont
2 drawings and 1 decorated capital letter in William Colgate's 'Pointers for Students of Canadian Printing,' vol 2, no 2 (May 1954)

D16

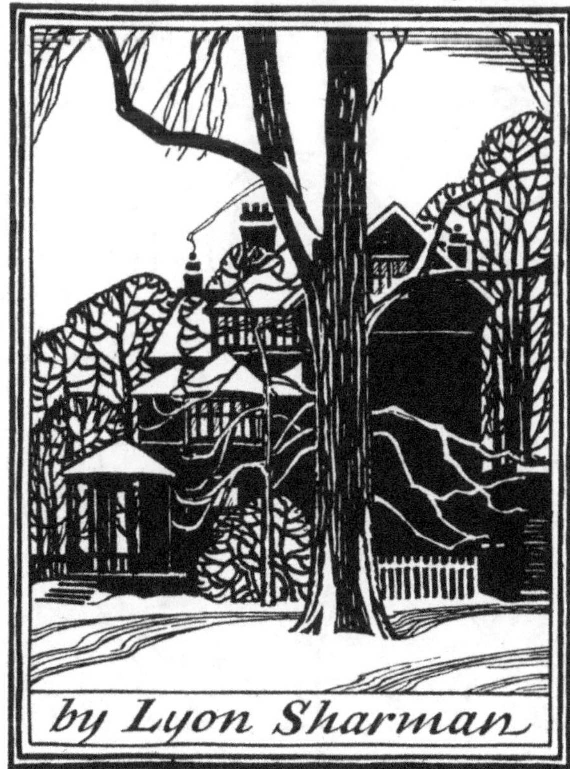

D13

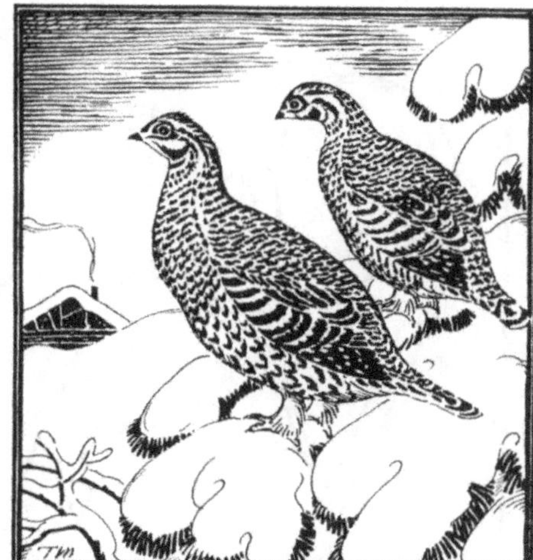

D19

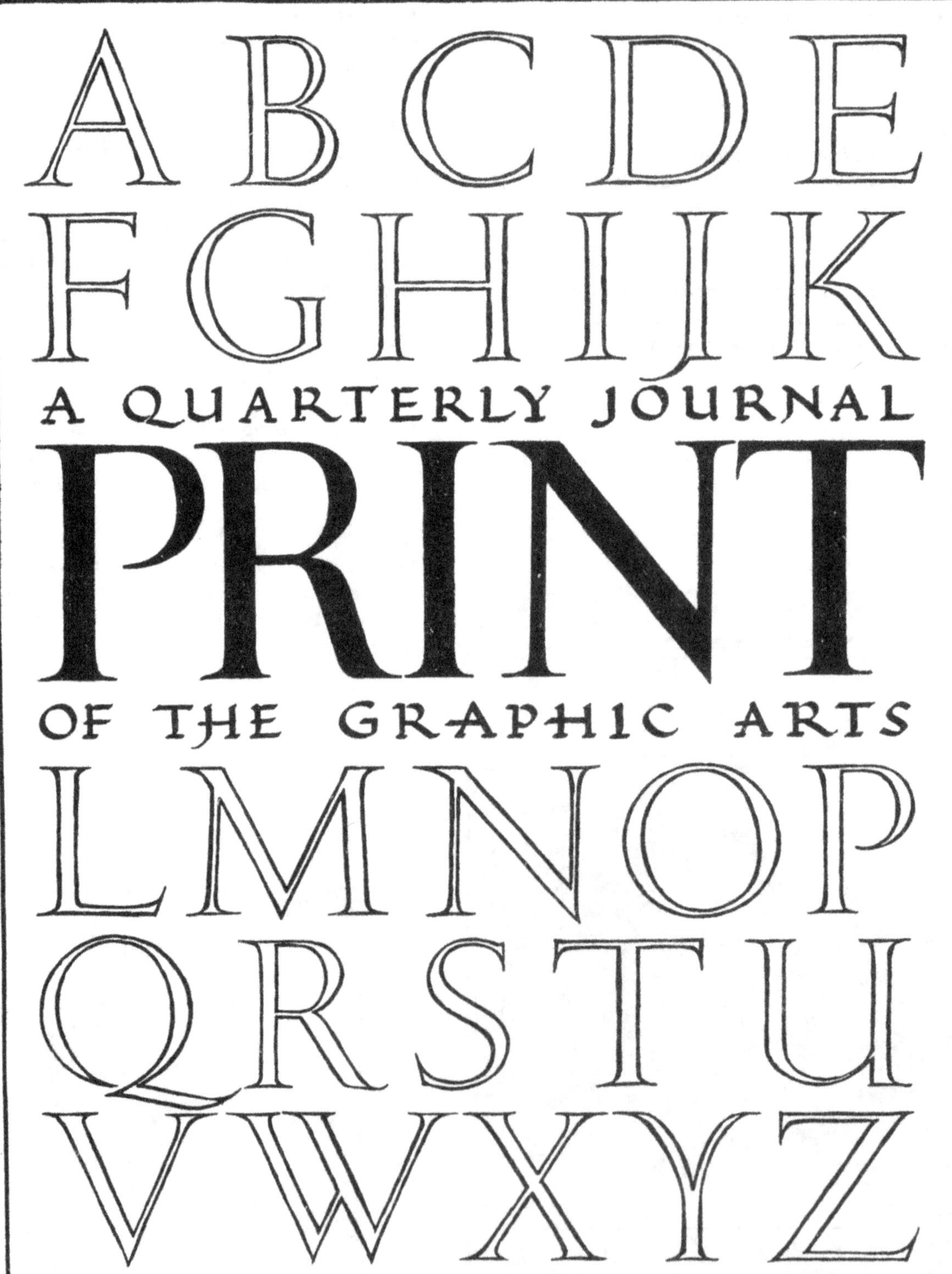

ABCDE
FGHIJK
A QUARTERLY JOURNAL
PRINT
OF THE GRAPHIC ARTS
LMNOP
QRSTU
VWXYZ

D20

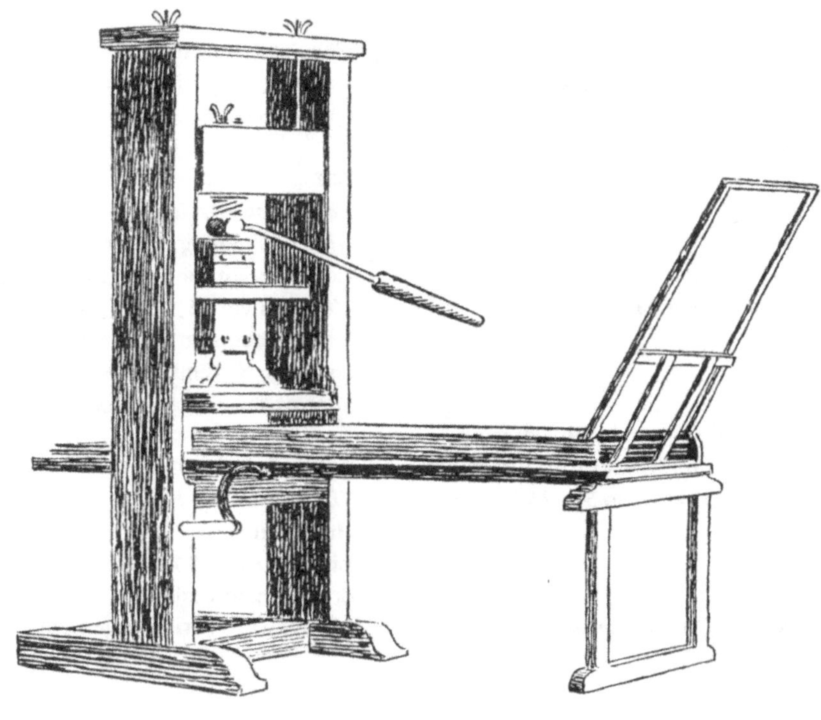

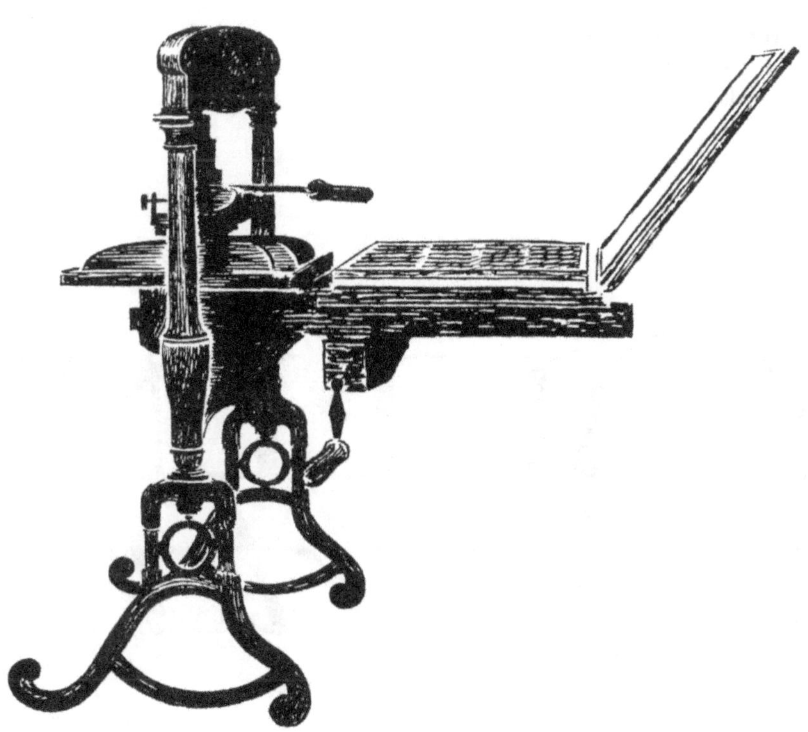

D21
The Progressive. Madison, Wisc.
Country Chronicle, column by Henry Beston, with headpiece and lettering, used from vol 9, no 52 (31 December 1945) to vol 10, no 50 (30 December 1946)

D22
Queen's Quarterly. Kingston
Cover lettering used from vol 51, no 1 (Spring 1944) to the present

D23
Richmond Hill Liberal. Richmond Hill, Ontario
Window on the Past, column by Doris M. Fitzgerald, with headpiece design in vol 90, no 52 (26 June 1968) and in current use

D24
Royal Architectural Institute of Canada. The Journal. Ottawa
Cover design used from vol 10, no 1 (January 1933) to vol 14, no 6 (June 1937)

D25
Ryerson Books. Toronto
Title page and cover designs for Ryerson's semi-annual catalogue of publications were used many times. Examples are the catalogues for 1945, 1946, 1948, and 1954.

D26
The Studio. London
Drawing in special Canadian Issue, vol 129, no 625 (April 1945) p 120

D27
The Torch: A Magazine for Leaders of Canadian Girls in Training. Toronto
Cover design for vol 1, no 1 (September–October 1924) to vol 15, no 3 (January–February 1940)
Design reused in April 1943
Issue for November 1945 contains the final appearance of the Torch symbol on the cover design.

D28
The Tower: By Poets of the Niagara Peninsula. Hamilton
Eighth year (1959) and ninth year (1960): cover drawing and design
1961 to 1964: title page design

D29
The Trinity University Review. Toronto
Printed cover design, drawing of College arms, and title lettering; apparently never used

D22

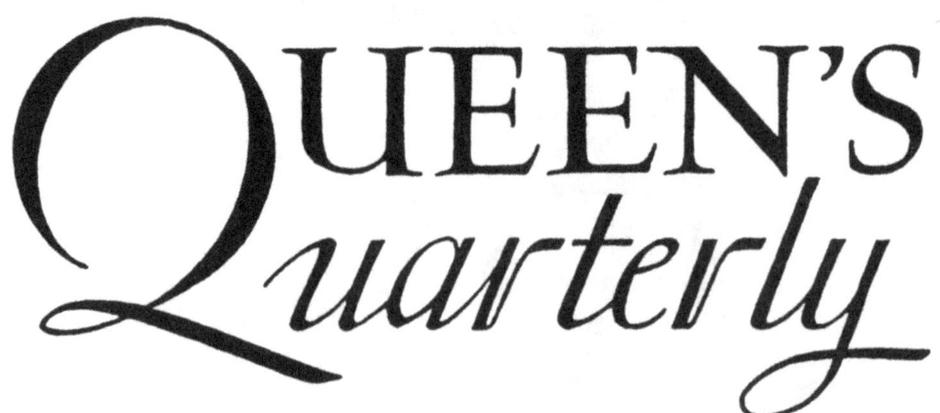

D30
University College Magazine. Toronto
Cover design used from vol 1, no 1 (March 1927) to vol 4, no 4 (December 1930)

D31
University of Toronto Quarterly. Toronto
Cover design used from vol 16, no 2 (January 1945) to vol 24, no 4 (July 1955)

D25

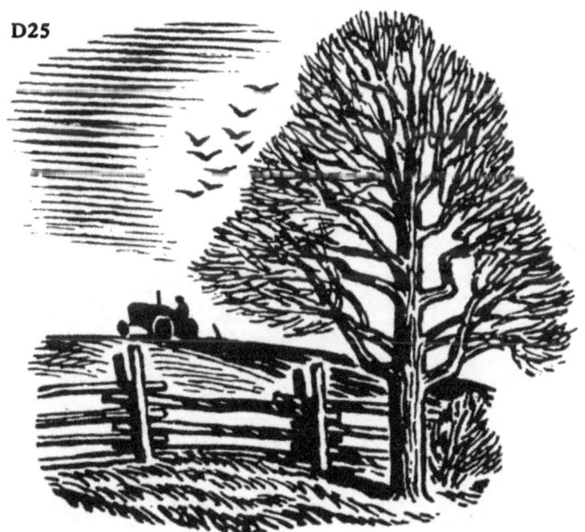

RYERSON
BOOKS SPRING 1945

E · Joint Work of J.E.H. MacDonald and Thoreau MacDonald

1921

E1
Carman, Bliss. *Later Poems.* Toronto, McClelland & Stewart [1921] xxix, 203 p
Reprinted
With an appreciation by R.H. Hathaway
Decorations by J.E.H. MacDonald
Some lettering by TM

E2
University of Toronto Roll of Service 1914-1918. [Toronto] University of Toronto Press, 1921. xlviii, 603 p
Title page by J.E.H. MacDonald
Lettering on coat-of-arms by TM

1922

E3
Johnson, E. Pauline. (Tekahionwake) *Legends of Vancouver.* New edition, illustrated. Toronto, McClelland and Stewart [1922] xvi, 165 p
Reprinted
Illustrated with photographs
Decorations by J.E.H. MacDonald
Lettering by TM
Variant dust jackets

E4
MacKay, Isabel Ecclestone. *Fires of Driftwood.* Toronto, McClelland and Stewart [1922] 139 p
Decorations by J.E.H. MacDonald
Lettering by TM

E5
Pickthall, Marjorie L.C. *The Wood Carver's Wife.* Toronto, McClelland and Stewart [1922] 105 p
Edition limited to 250 copies
Decorations by J.E.H. MacDonald
Lettering by TM
Trade edition issued in smaller format

1923

E6
Carman, Bliss. *Ballads and Lyrics.* Toronto, McClelland & Stewart [1923] x, 298 p
Designed by J.E.H. MacDonald
Some lettering by TM

E7
Denison, Merrill. *The Unheroic North: Four Canadian Plays.* Toronto, McClelland & Stewart [1923] 183 p
Jacket designed by J.E.H. MacDonald
Lettering by TM

E4

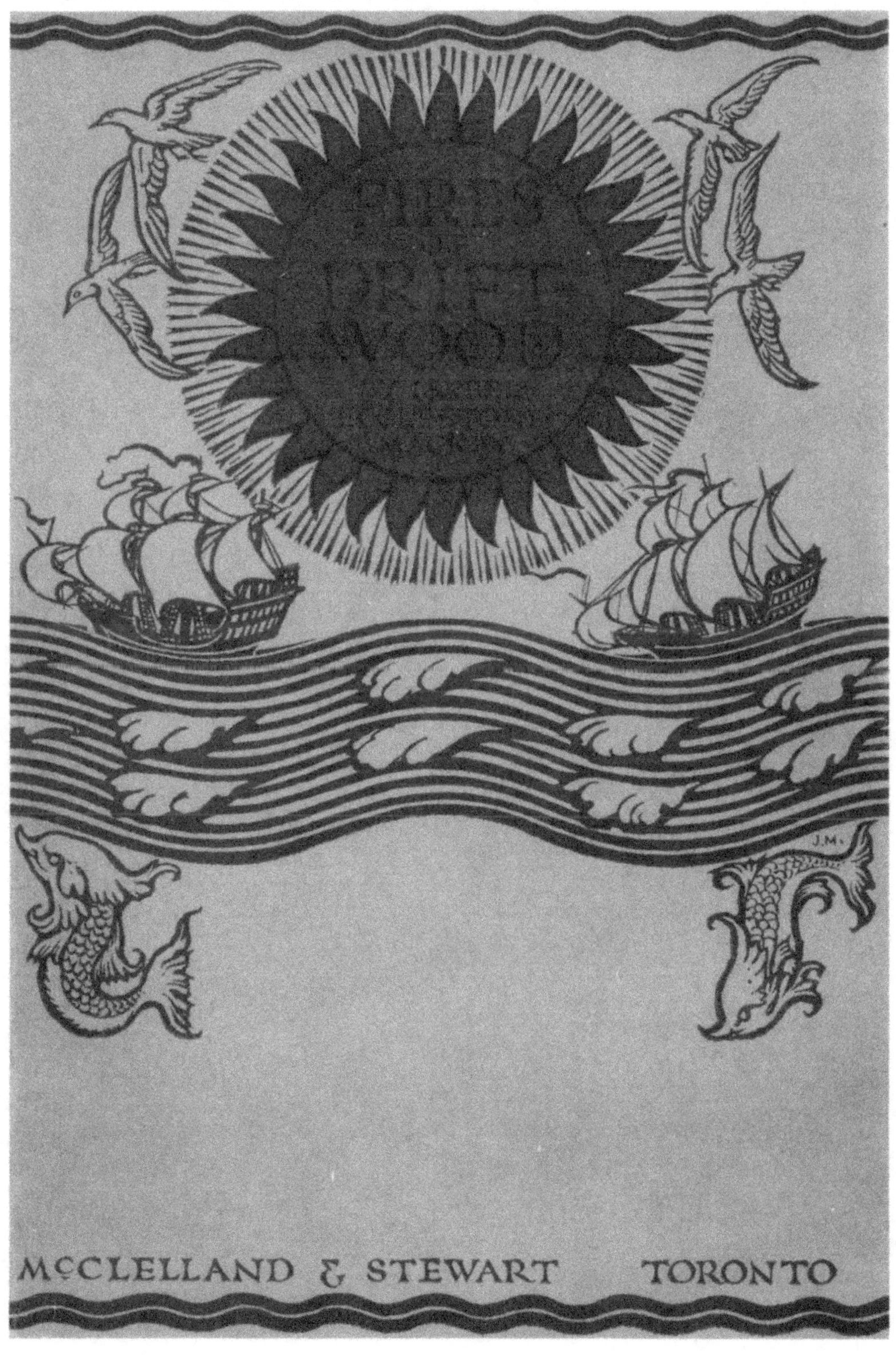

E8

Rogers, Grace McLeod. *Stories of the Land of Evangeline.* Toronto, McClelland & Stewart [1923] 341 p

Design by J.E.H. MacDonald

Lettering, frontispiece figure, and some drawings by TM

- Another edition, 1923; binding variant
- Another edition, 1923; without decorated end papers; binding variant; jacket variant

E9

Shepard, Odell. *Bliss Carman.* Toronto, McClelland & Stewart [1923] xv, 184 p

Decorations by J.E.H. MacDonald

Some lettering by TM

E8

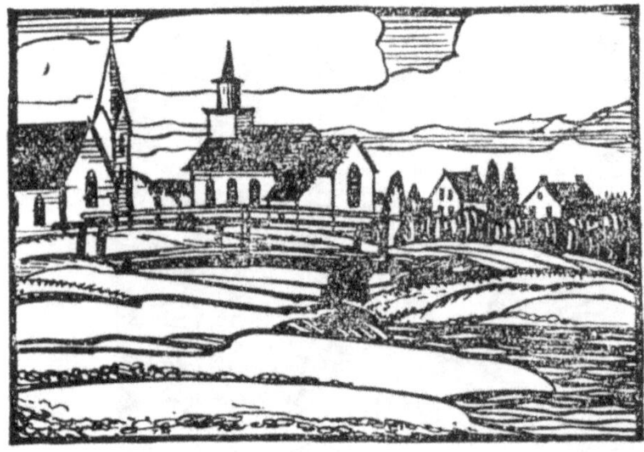

E8

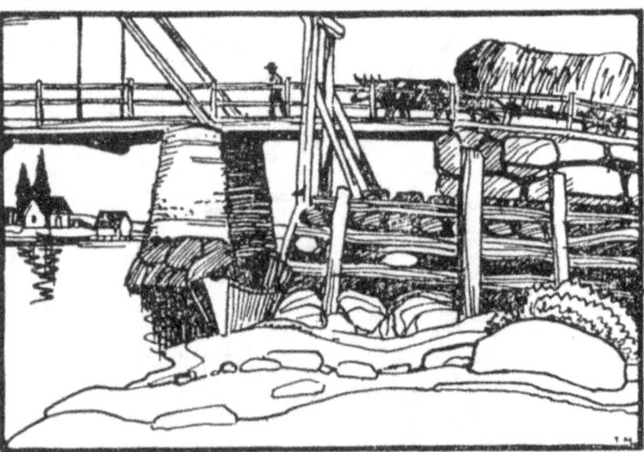

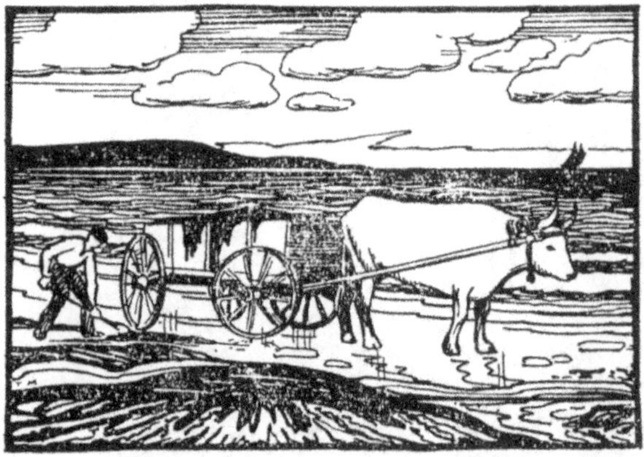

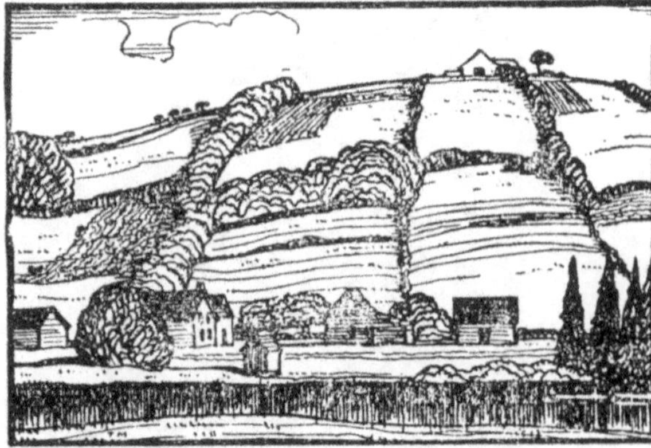

E10

Stephen, Alexander M. *The Rosary of Pan.* Toronto, McClelland & Stewart [1923] 137 p
Decorations by J.E.H. MacDonald
Lettering by TM

E10

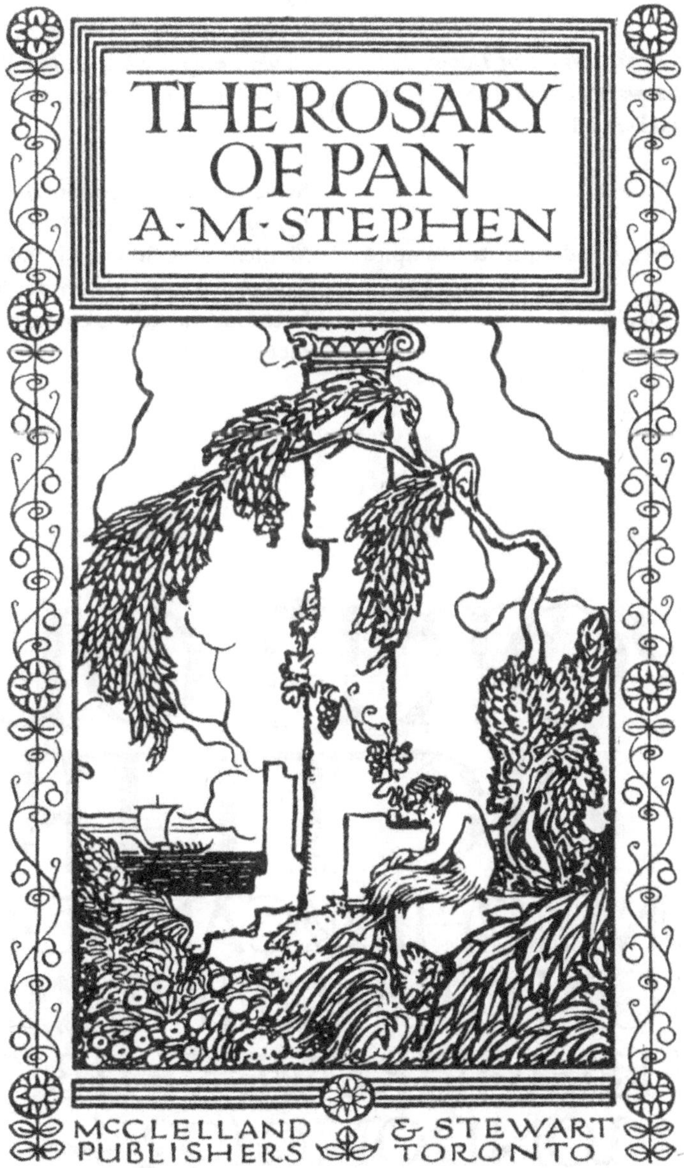

THE ROSARY
OF PAN
A·M·STEPHEN

McCLELLAND & STEWART
PUBLISHERS TORONTO

1924

E11
MacMechan, Archibald. *Old Province Tales.* Toronto, McClelland & Stewart [1924] 345 p
Decorations by J.E.H. MacDonald
Lettering by TM
First edition said to have contained drawings by TM (Cf E.R. Hunter, p 41)
No trace of illustrations in any editions examined; this now thought to describe E8 (M.E.E.)

E12
Taylor, Frances Beatrice. *White Winds of Dawn.* Toronto, McClelland & Stewart [1924] 128 p
Decorations by J.E.H. MacDonald
Some lettering by TM

E13
Canadian Section: Fine Arts. London, British Empire Exhibition, 1924. 35 p
Designed by J.E.H. MacDonald
Some lettering by TM
Cover design reused for 1925 Exhibition

E14
A Portfolio of Pictures from the Canadian Section of Fine Arts. London, British Empire Exhibition, 1924. [32] p
Designed by J.E.H. MacDonald
1 drawing (vignette), and cover lettering by TM

1927

E15
Exposition d'art canadien. Paris, Musée de Jeu de Paume, 1927
Exhibition, 10 April–10 May 1927.
Cover design by J.E.H. MacDonald
Some lettering by TM

E16
Salverson, Laura Goodman. *Lord of the Silver Dragon: A Romance of Lief the Lucky.* Toronto, McClelland & Stewart [1927] 343 p
End papers and title border by J.E.H. MacDonald
Lettering on jacket, cover, title page, and frontispiece by TM

E14

A PORTFOLIO OF PICTURES
FROM THE CANADIAN
SECTION OF FINE ARTS
BRITISH EMPIRE EXHIBITION
LONDON 1924

F · Ephemera

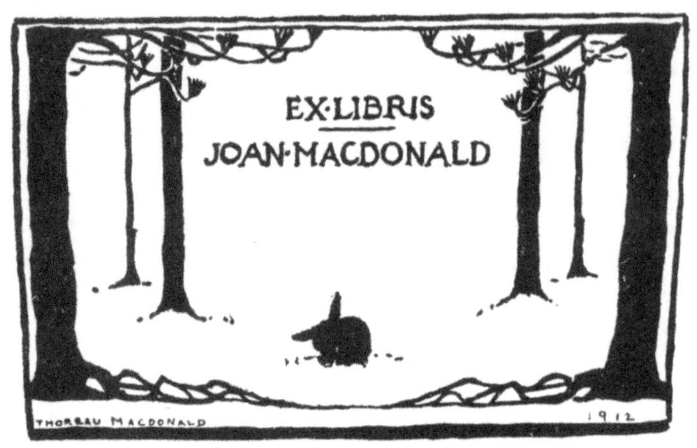
EX·LIBRIS
JOAN·MACDONALD
THOREAU MACDONALD
1912

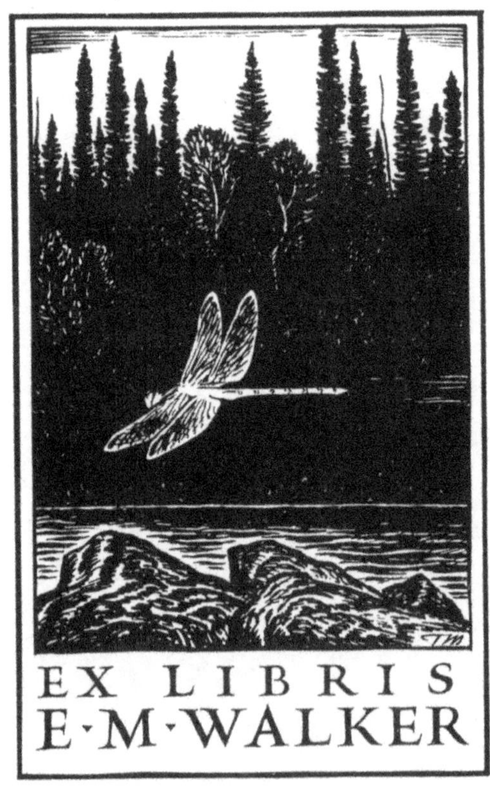
TM
EX LIBRIS
E·M·WALKER

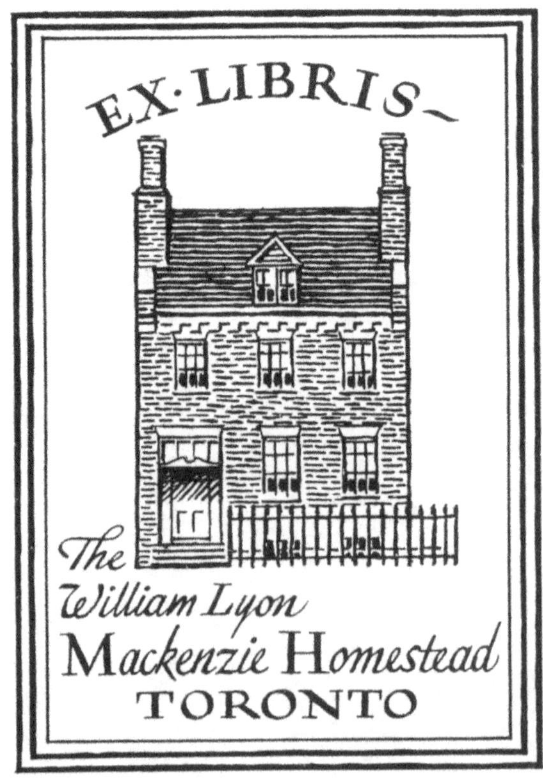
EX·LIBRIS
The
William Lyon
Mackenzie Homestead
TORONTO

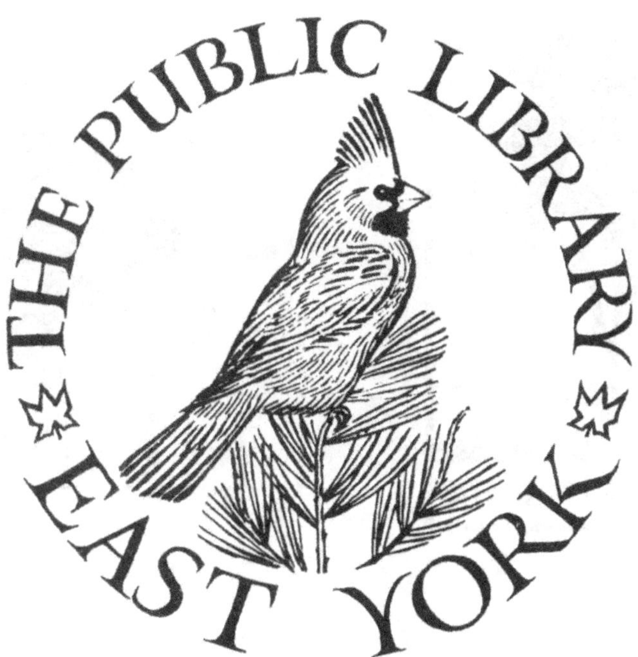
THE PUBLIC LIBRARY
EAST YORK

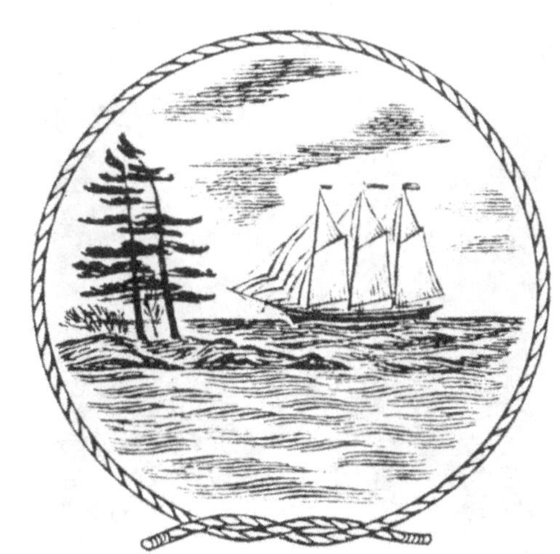
IN MEMORY OF
Thomas Tupper Whittier
DARTMOUTH 1899

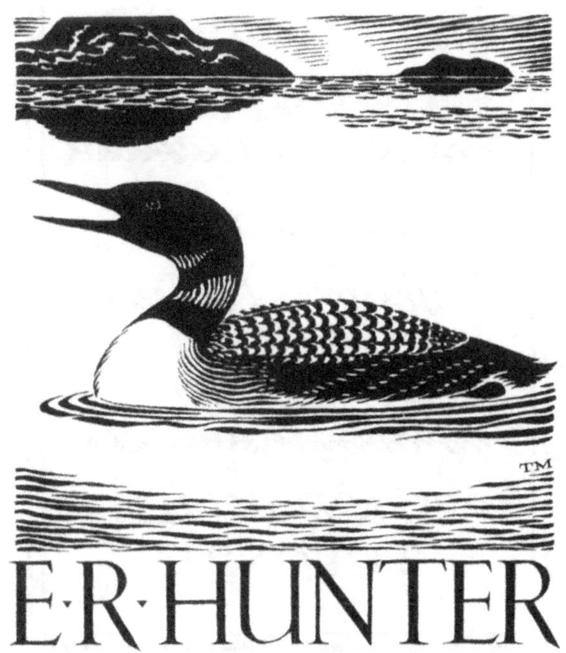
TM
E·R·HUNTER

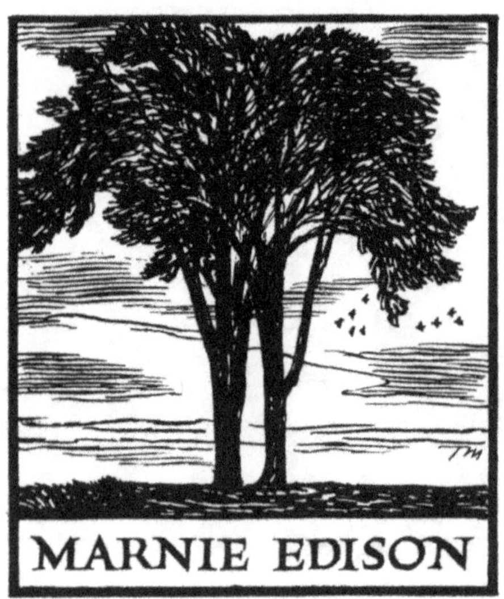
MARNIE EDISON

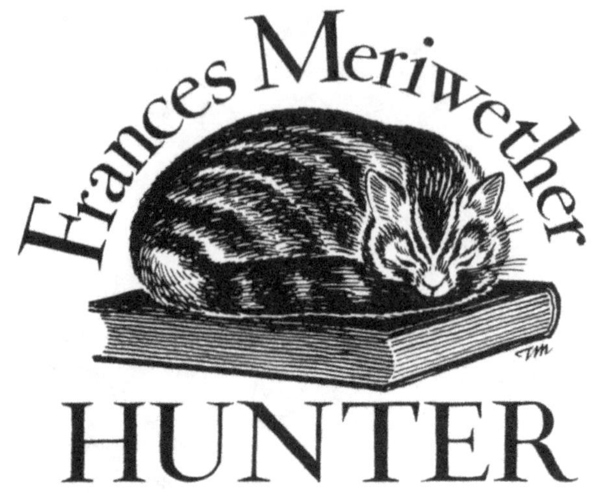
Frances Meriwether
HUNTER

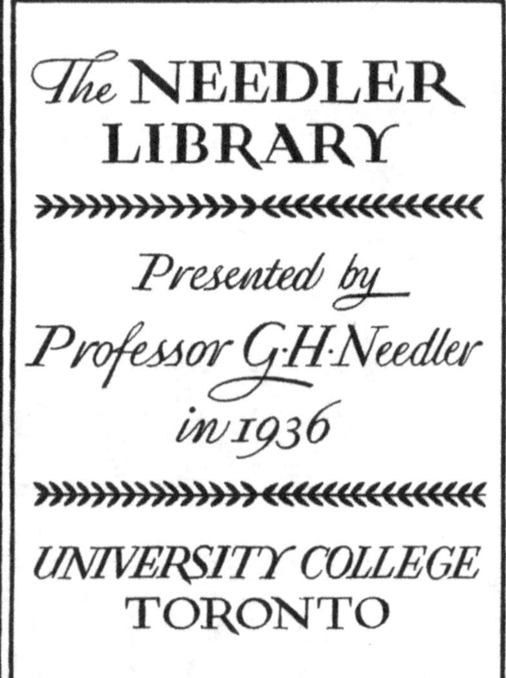
The NEEDLER
LIBRARY
Presented by
Professor G·H·Needler
in 1936
UNIVERSITY COLLEGE
TORONTO

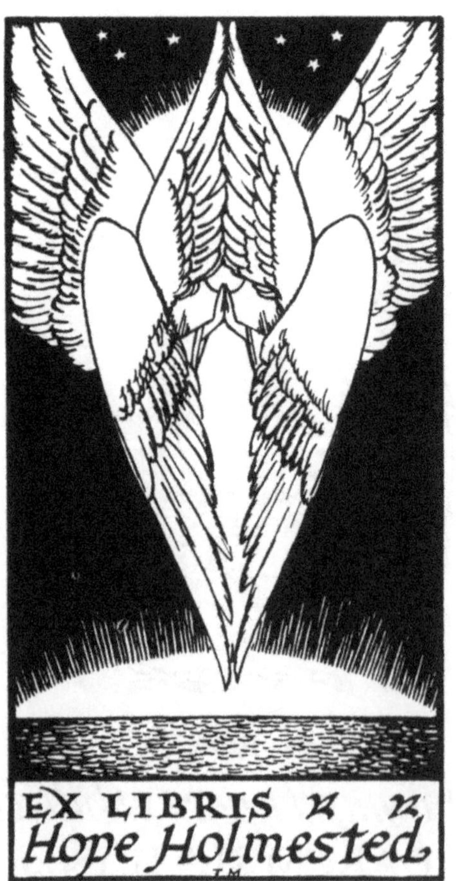
EX LIBRIS
Hope Holmested

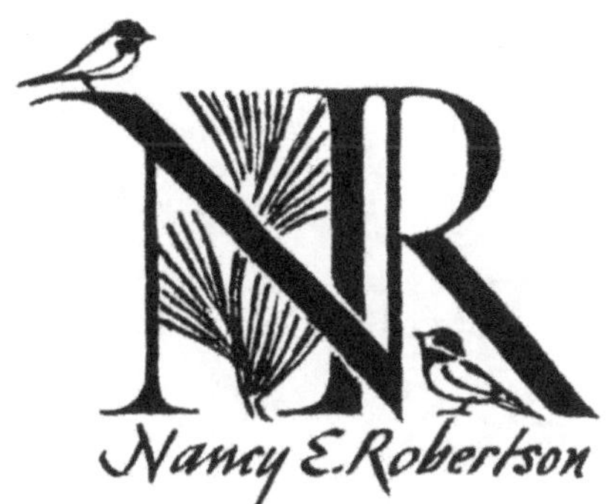

EX LIBRIS
H·NAHABEDIAN

Յ· ՆԱՀԱՊԵՏԵԱՆ

TM

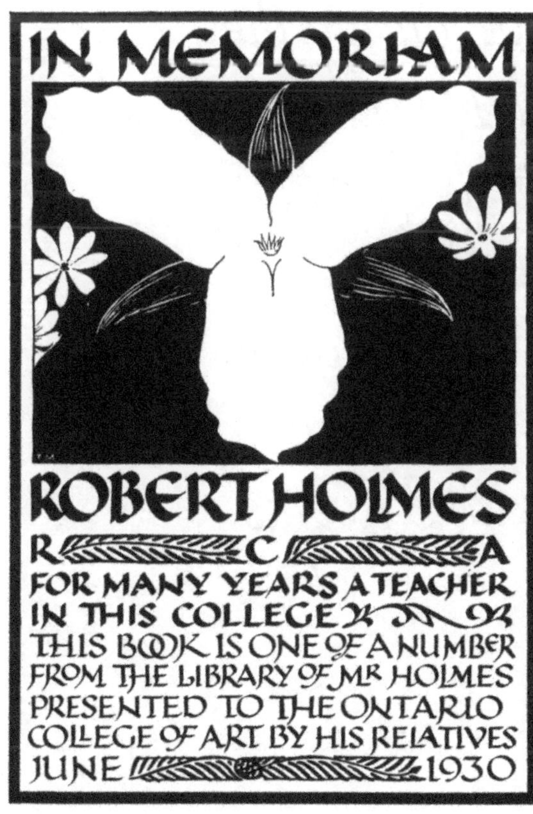

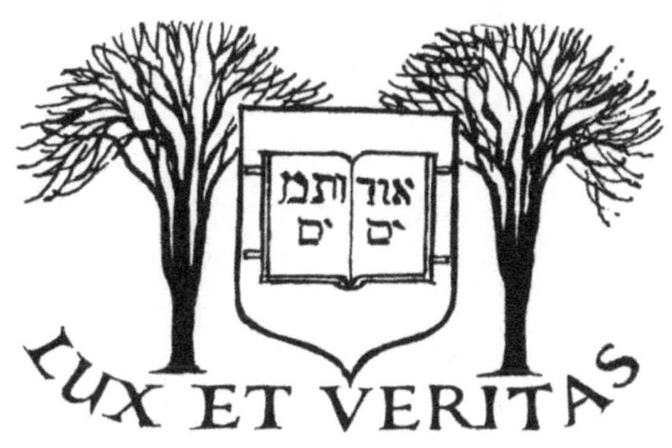

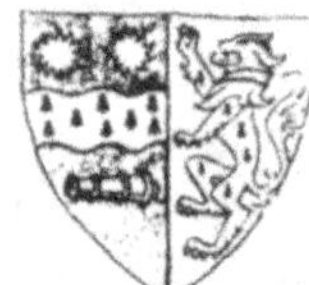

The COLOURS OF THE "QUEEN'S RANGERS, FIRST AMERICANS" (1776–1783) who served with great distinction on the Loyalist side under the command of Colonel John Graves Simcoe, during the War of the American Revolution.

Presented to the Public Library of Toronto through the efforts of the Chief Librarian, George H. Locke, & through the interest, liberality, & public spirit of Frederick B. Robins, Esq.

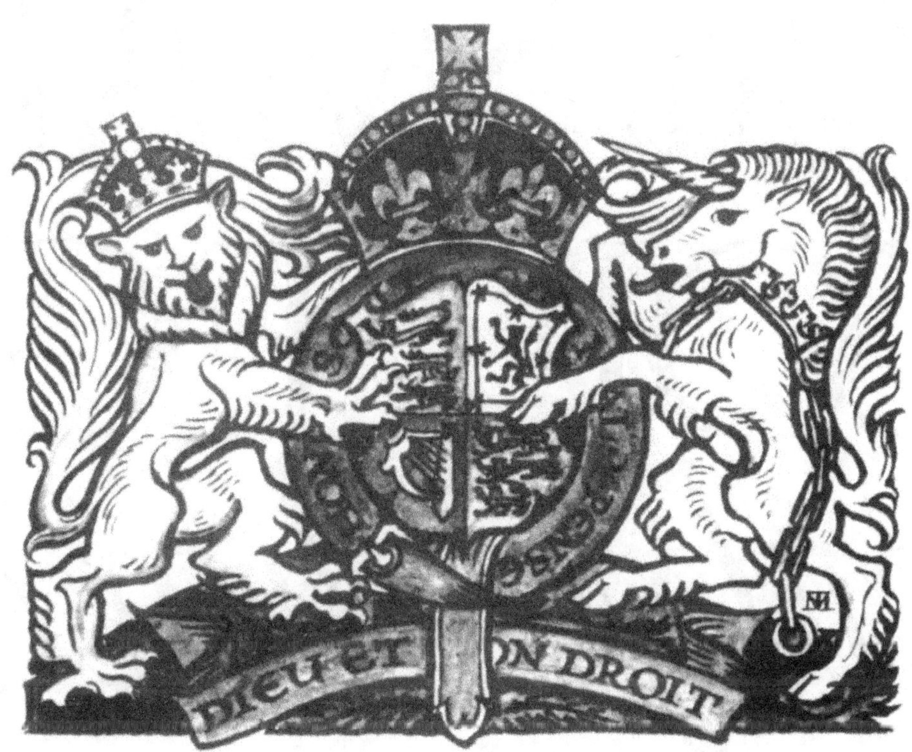

ON THE OCCASION
OF THE PRESENCE
IN TORONTO OF
Their Most Gracious Majesties
KING GEORGE VI
AND
QUEEN ELIZABETH

MAY 22 1939

It is a SMALL COLLEGE *and yet there are* THOSE *who* LOVE IT

WEBSTER

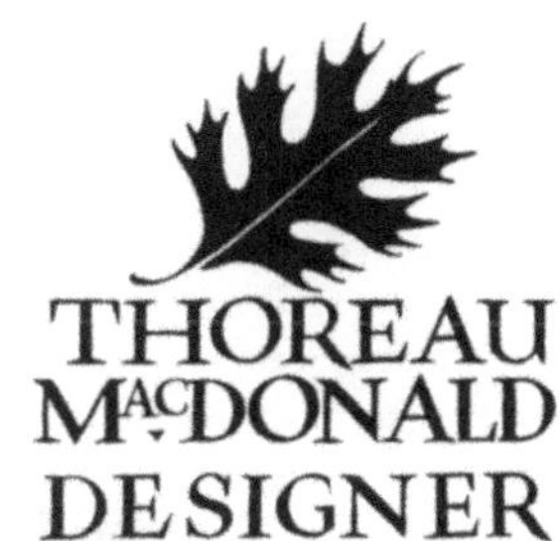

THOREAU MacDONALD

ALL THINGS
NOBLE
ARE AS DIFFICULT
AS THEY ARE RARE

SPINOZA

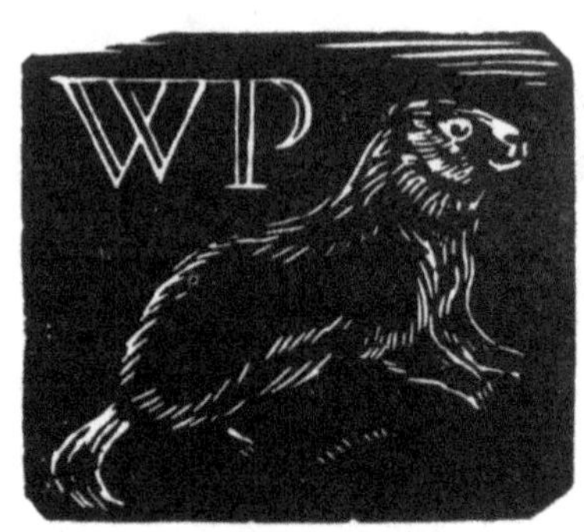
WP

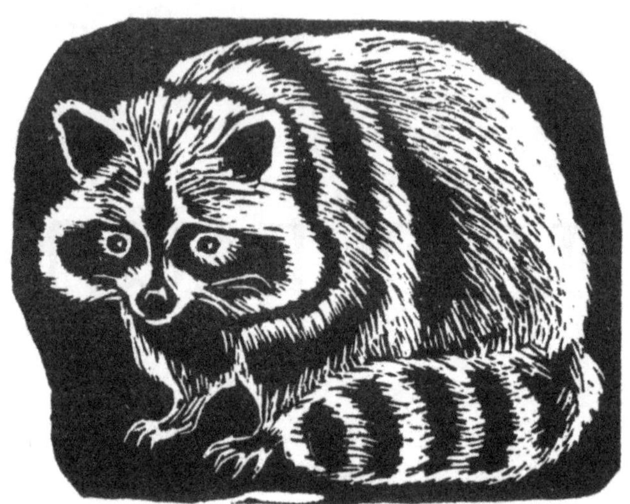

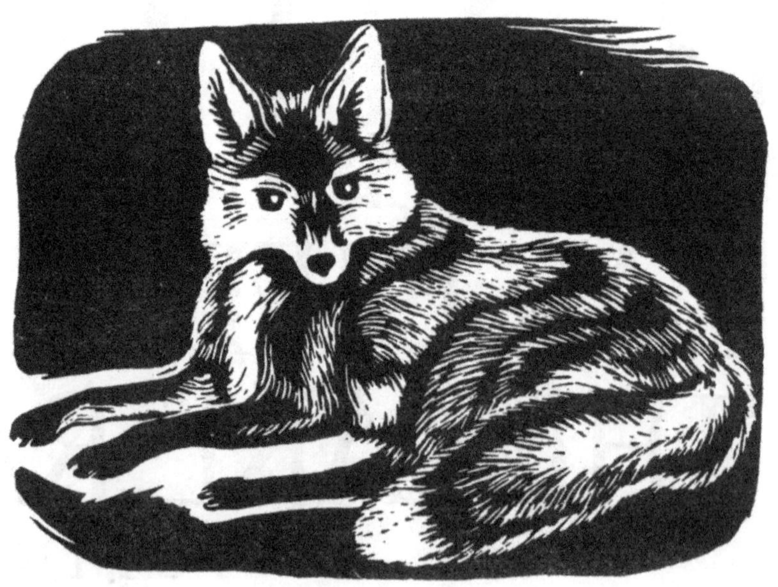

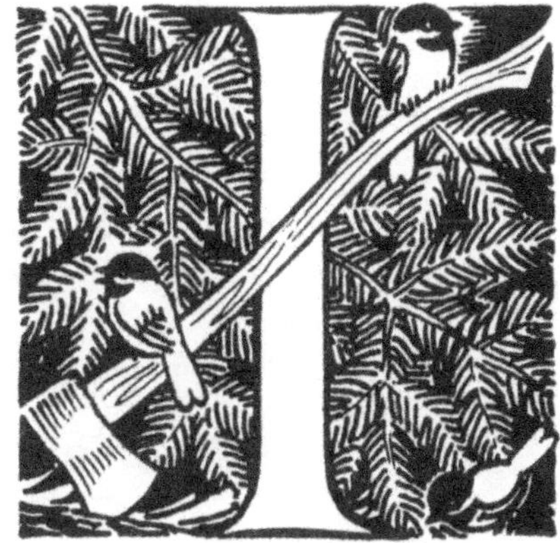

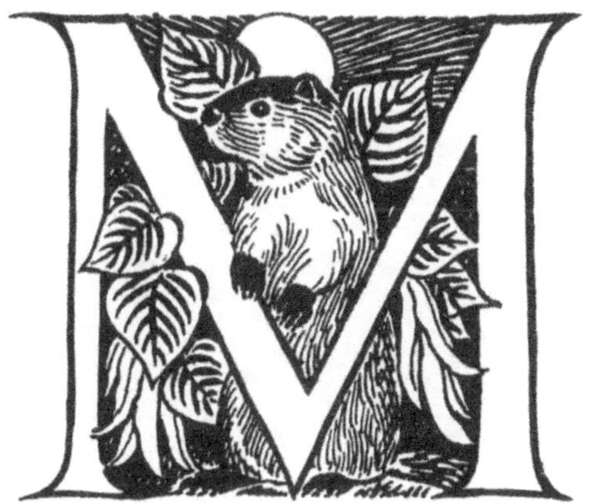

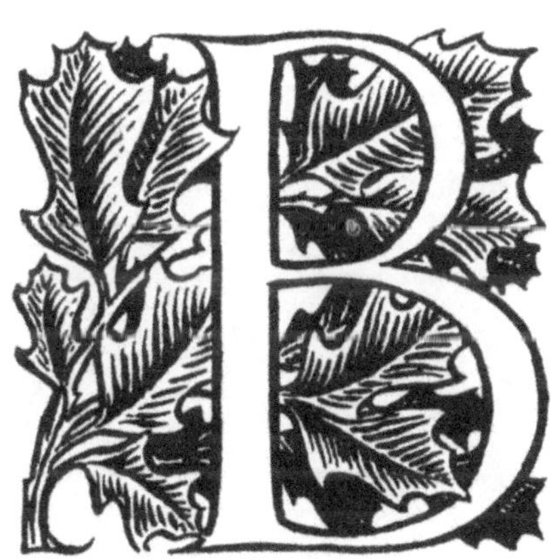

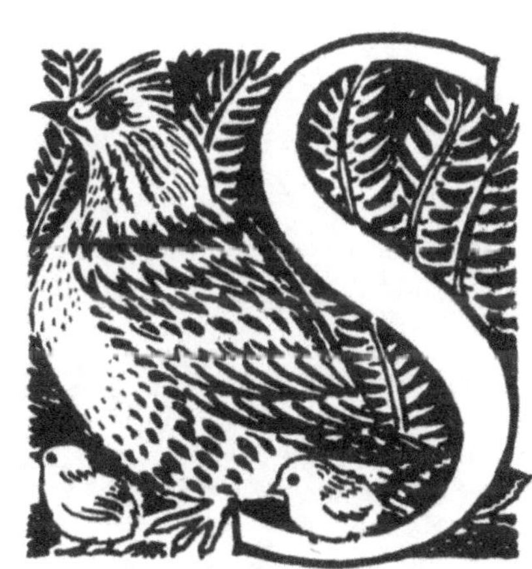

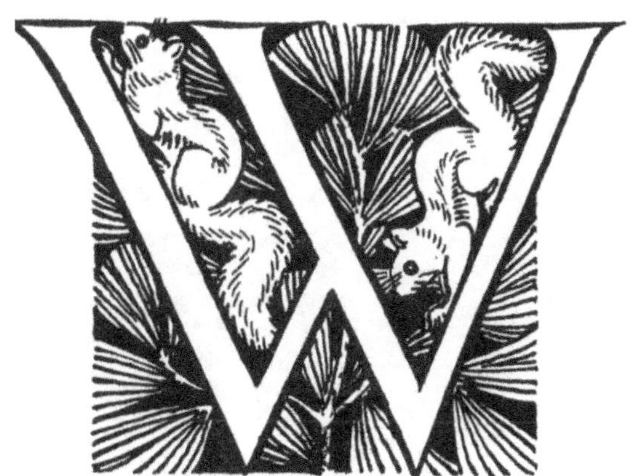

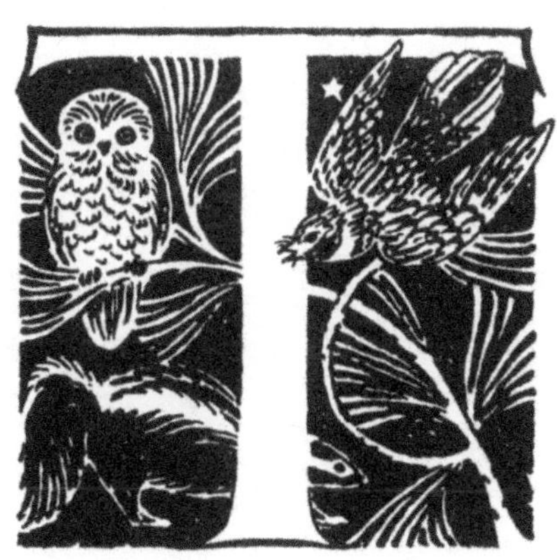

Exhibitions

For the sake of brevity the following abbreviations have been used:
CNE: Canadian National Exhibition; OSA: Ontario Society of Artists; AGT: Art Gallery of Toronto; AGO: Art Gallery of Ontario; CGP: Canadian Group of Painters; NGC: National Gallery of Canada; RCA: Royal Canadian Academy

1924

AGT Exhibition of Canadian Graphic Art
228 Two woodcuts
229 Two woodcuts
230 Northern Lights (pen drawing)
231 A Japanese Artist (brush drawing on silk)

1925

OSA
269 Winter Night (pen drawing)
270 March Wind (pen drawing)

CNE International Graphic Art
717 Wild Geese by the Shore (pen)
718 Island in Moonlight (pen)
719 Loons under water (pen)

British Empire Exhibition, London, England
Moose Crossing a Point
Frozen Lake

1926

OSA
160 Loons on the Coast (pen and ink)
161 Swans and New Snow (pen and ink)

CNE International Graphic Art
866 pen drawing

AGT Invited contributor to the Group of Seven Exhibition
151 North October Evening
152 Spring Light and Ospreys
153 Moose and Northern Lights
154 After the Winter Sunset
155 Winter Morning

NGC Special Exhibition of Canadian Art, 21 January to 28 February
107 A Meteor (drawing)
108 March Wind (drawing)

1927

Exposition d'art canadien, Jeu de Paume, Paris, France
129 Orignal dans la neige (dessin)
130 Lac gelé (dessin)

CNE International Graphic Art
849 drawing
850 drawing

CNE Small Pictures
371 Ospreys
372 Evening and Wild Ducks

OSA Black and White
186 drawing-pen
187 drawing-pen

NGC Annual Exhibition of Canadian Art
147 Loons on the Coast (drawing)
148 Swans and New Snow (drawing)
149 Spring Light and Ospreys (oil painting)
150 Winter Evening (oil painting)

1928

CNE International Graphic Art
826 Hawk and Mink (pen and ink)
827 Deer Leaping (pen and ink)
828 Osprey and Eagle (pen and ink)
829 Marsh Hawk (pen and ink)

AGT Invited contributor to the Group of Seven Exhibition
77 Pine Tree Madonna
78 Winter Evening with Mary and Jesus

1929

OSA Graphic Art
261 Young Rabbits (drawing)
262 Snowy Owl (drawing)
263 Swan & Young Swans (drawing)

1930

CNE Fine Arts
114 Northern Diver
115 White Falcon

CNE Graphic Arts
686 Otter and Pike (pencil drawing)

AGT and Art Association of Montreal, Exhibition of the Group of Seven
100 White Falcon

OSA
105 Morning Song

The Book Plate Association International, Sixth Annual Exhibition
Los Angeles Public Library; catalogue issued
3 plates: George H. Fensom, Maisie Reid Humphries, Hope Holmested (honourable mention)

1931

OSA Black & White
180 An Old House at Thornhill (pen drawing)
181 An Old House at Thornhill (pen drawing)
182 Sleigh Riding (pen drawing)

NGC Annual Exhibition of Canadian Art
181 White Falcon (oil painting)
182 Northern Diver (oil painting)

The Book Plate Association International, Seventh Annual Exhibition, May 1931
Los Angeles Museum Exhibition Park; catalogue issued
1 plate: Robert Holmes, R.C.A.

1932

CNE Fine Arts
239 At Nobleton

OSA
105 Moonlight in the Orchard (oil)

NGC Annual Exhibition of Canadian Art
170 Behind the Cutter (pen drawing)
171 Woodshed Door (pen drawing)

1933

OSA
219 Farmhouse in Winter (pen drawing)
220 Winter Morning (pen drawing)

CNE Graphic Art
614 Rapids at Night (pen and ink)
615 Harvest Afternoon (pen and ink)
616 Winter Morning (pen and ink)

AGT Canadian Society of Graphic Arts
409 Studies of Horses (wash drawing)

NGC Annual Exhibition of Canadian Art
168 Rapids at Night (drawing)
169 Harvest Afternoon (drawing)

The Book Plate Association International, Ninth Annual Exhibition
Los Angeles Museum Exposition Park; catalogue issued
1 plate: H.W. Hardy

CGP, Heinz Art Salon, Heinz Ocean Pier, Atlantic City
34 Hawk
35 Loon

AGT CGP members' work
49 Fall Evening

CGP Art Association of Montreal
40 Fall Evening

1935

AGT Exhibition of Paintings by John Alfsen, Caven Atkins, Thoreau MacDonald, Pegi Nicol, Robert Ross, Carl Schaefer
263 A Wet Barnyard, 1935 (wash)
264 Breaking a Road, 1935 (wash)
265 Fall Ploughing, 1935 (wash)
266 Young Eagle, 1935 (wash)
267 Eagle Stretching, 1935 (wash)

AGT Canadian Society of Graphic Art
95 Illustration for *Walden* (pen and ink)
96 Illustration for *Walden* (pen and ink)
97 Wash Drawing

1936

Canadian Society of Graphic Art, AGT
236 An Old Barn (wash)

1937

OSA
112 Great Horned Owl

London, England, Royal British Colonial Society of Artists
47 Great Horned Owl (oil)
53 Red-Tailed Hawk (oil)

1938

London, England, Tate Gallery, A Century of Canadian Art
149 Ermine
150 Owl and Jay

OSA, AGT

118 Owl and Jay
119 Ermine

CNE Fine Art
168 Hawk Study

CNE Canadian Small Pictures
558 Family Group

AGT Royal Canadian Academy
140 Redtail Hawk
141 Great Horned Owl

1939

New York World's Fair, Canadian Artists in Water Colour
83 Breaking The Road (wash drawing)

*CGP New York World's Fair: Canadian Art
40 Ermine (lent by NGC)

CNE Fine Art
140 Marsh Hawk

Golden Gate Exposition, San Francisco, Fine Bookbinding Exhibition; catalogue issued by Grabhorn Press
Robson *Canadian Landscape Painters*

1941

OSA
97 Redtail Hawk

1942

AGT, Print Room. Artists: Ada G. Killins, Fred H. Brigden, W.J. Phillips, Thoreau MacDonald

Hawk Study (oil) painted 1938
Red-Tail Hawk (oil) painted 1938, lent through the courtesy of Dr Lorne Pierce
Marsh Hawk, Rain (oil) painted 1938
Marsh Hawk, Snow (oil) painted 1939
Owl and Jay (oil) painted 1937
Young Red-Tail (oil) painted 1939
Muskrat (oil) painted 1939
Cow Pasture (oil) painted 1939
Goshawk (oil) painted 1939
Moose Study (wash drawing) painted 1942
Morning Chores (wash drawing) painted 1942
Sunday (wash drawing) painted 1942
Illustration (wash drawing)
Woodshed Door (pen drawing)
Old House at Thornhill (pen drawing)
Old House near Woodbridge (pen drawing)
Fox in November (wash drawing)
Moose Study (wash drawing)
Red Fox on a fence (pencil)
Mink (pencil)

Print Room, Hart House, University of Toronto
Exhibition of original drawings for *Maria Chapdelaine*

The American Institute of Graphic Arts, International Book Illustration 1935-1945
Pierpont Morgan Library, New York
Illustration for *Maria Chapdelaine*

1949

Book Jacket Designers Guild, Inc, Second Annual Exhibition
A-D Gallery, New York
Jacket Design for *Northern Farm*

CNE Fine Art
40 Hawk over the Pasture (oil on canvas) (lent by AGT)

1952

London Public Library and Art Museum
Exhibition of two hundred drawings; no list of individual items

1959

AGT
Exhibition of drawings for *West by East*

1960

AGT Canadian Drawings
Young Moose

1967

Barrows Print Room, Hopkins Center, Dartmouth College, Hanover, New Hampshire
Exhibition of the collection of Professor and Mrs Ray Nash; no list of individual items

Tom Thomson Memorial Gallery, Owen Sound, Ontario. The Jennings Young Collection
50 MacDonald House, Thornhill (drawing) executed 1964
51 Two Houses (drawing)
52 Barn, Pioneer Village (drawing)

1971

Thornhill Public Library, Thornhill, Ontario
Exhibition of the collection of L.B. Pierce; no list of individual items

References in Print

1926

The Canadian Forum. vol 7, no 74 (1926)
'The Happy Isles,' unsigned review of the *Happy Islands, Stories and Sketches of the Georgian Bay,* by Marlow A. Shaw

The Canadian Forum. vol 6, no 69 (June 1926)
Bertram R. Brooker, 'Canada's Modern Art Movement,' p 276-9

Rochdale Observer. Lancashire, Eng. (May [12 or 15] 1926)
column, 'Canadian Art' (second notice). Review of 1925 British Empire Exhibition on tour

1927

Canadian Homes and Gardens. August 1927
F. Maud Brown, 'Canadian Art in Paris'
Article on exhibition and photograph showing poster

Journal des Débats. Paris, (11 April 1927)
Paul Fierens, Review of Canadian Exhibition at the Jeu de Paume; mention of poster

1928

Toronto Daily Star. (14 April 1928)
'Youth and Art,' review of Portfolio of Forum Drawings. Unsigned

The Publishers' Weekly. New York, vol 113, no 25 (23 June 1928)
Norah Thomson. 'Illustrated Books that Interpret the Canadian Spirit,' p 2516
Reproductions.
Includes a list of the twelve best produced Canadian books selected by a committee of three for the Booksellers' Association in 1927 (six of the twelve have work by Thoreau MacDonald)

1929

Construction. Toronto, vol 22, no 3 (March 1929)
Whole issue devoted to the Claridge Apartments; 12 signs of the zodiac in foyer ceiling designed by TM

Construction. Toronto, vol 22, no 5 (May 1929)
Whole issue devoted to the Concourse Building. Five reproductions on 138 incorrectly attributed to J.E.H. MacDonald

Yearbook of the Arts in Canada, 1928-1929. Toronto, Macmillan of Canada, 1929. Bertram Brooker (ed.)
Plate 34 (p 274) reproduction of a drawing and a note

1930

Melvin O. Hammond. *Painting and Sculpture in Canada.* Toronto, Ryerson Press, 1930. p 70

1931

Onward: a Paper for Young Canadians. vol 41, no 39 (26 September 1931)
Blodwen Davies, 'Famous Canadian Pictures: Harvest by Thoreau MacDonald,' article and reproduction

1932

Albert H. Robson. *Canadian Landscape Painters.* Toronto, Ryerson Press [1932]. p 179

1933

Saturday Night. 21 October 1933
Review of CGP Exhibition, Heinz Art Salon, Atlantic City

1934

Saturday Night. 17 November 1934.
B.K. Sandwell, 'Book Notes'
A note on the Woodchuck Press and its productions; reproduction

Saturday Night. 30 June 1934
Reproduction of a photograph 'Old House, Thornhill,' shown in a competition

1935

Mail and Empire. Toronto. 6 December 1935
Pearl McCarthy, review of Group Show, MacDonald, Schaefer, Nicol, Ross, Alfsen, Atkins, at the Art Gallery of Toronto

Saturday Night. 14 December 1935
G. Campbell McInnes, review of Group Show at the Art Gallery of Toronto

1938

Telegram. Toronto. 29 June 1938
Column 'At the Galleries' on the forthcoming Macmillan edition of *Maria Chapdelaine*

1939

Graham McInnes. *A Short History of Canadian Art.* Toronto, Macmillan of Canada, 1939. p 94-5

1940

Bridle and Golfer. Toronto. November-December
William Colgate, 'Personality of a Painter,' Review of *J.E.H. MacDonald* by E.R. Hunter

Print. vol 1, no 1 (June 1940)
'Books in Canada,' p 107, unsigned review

Ontario Library Review. 1940
Margaret E. Hughes. 'A Guide to Canadian Painters'

1941

Maritime Art. vol 2, no 2 (December 1941)
E.R. Hunter, 'Thoreau MacDonald': reproductions

1942

Lorne Pierce. *Thoreau MacDonald.* Toronto, Ryerson Press [1942] 8 p (The Beverley Papers, 6)
Reproductions

E.R. Hunter. *Thoreau MacDonald.* Toronto, Ryerson Press [1942] 43 p (Canadian Art Series)
Reproductions

The Varsity. 11 February 1942
William Nichols, 'Hart House Revolution: Thoreau MacDonald,' a review of the exhibition of original drawings for *Maria Chapdelaine* at the Hart House Art Gallery

The Star. Toronto. 26 December 1942
Unsigned appreciation of TM; reproduction 'Farmhouse, Ontario'

1943

The Gazette. Montreal. 16 January 1943
St. George Burgoyne, review of *Thoreau MacDonald* by E.R. Hunter

Globe and Mail. Toronto. 9 January 1943
Unsigned review of *Thoreau MacDonald* by E.R. Hunter; reproduction 'Harvest'

Halifax Star. 9 January 1943
Unsigned review of *Thoreau MacDonald* by E.R. Hunter

Daily Star. Windsor. 9 January 1943
Valerie Conde, 'Thoreau MacDonald's Place in Art,' review of *Thoreau MacDonald* by E.R. Hunter

William Colgate. *Canadian Art: Its Origin and Development*. Toronto, Ryerson Press [1943] p 100, 202, 221, 224, 244, and 246; reproductions, p 241 and 245

1944

The Gazette. Montreal. 9 September 1944
Tracy S. Ludington, 'Folklore Made Alluring,' a review of *Mountain Cloud* by Marius Barbeau; reproduction

1945

Globe and Mail. Toronto. 23 June 1945
William Arthur Deacon, 'Atmosphere and Character in Scott's Early Stories,' review of the Ryerson Press reprint of *In the Village of Viger* by Duncan Campbell Scott

American Artist. vol 10, no 1 (January 1946) p 22
Norman Kent, 'Thoreau MacDonald, Canadian Illustrator,' no 8 in a series on book illustrators; reproductions

Canadian Art. vol 3, no 3 (May 1946)
'Thoreau MacDonald: Canadian Illustrator,' quotation and reproduction from Norman Kent's article in *American Artist*, vol 10, no 1 (January 1946)

Print. vol 4, no 3 (1946)
Woodchuck Press Gathering: unsigned review of a specimen book of cuts used by the Woodchuck Press

1947

Print. vol 5, no 1 (1947)
Note under Contributors, p 90

1948

New York Herald Tribune Weekly Book Review. 7 November 1948
Richardson Wright, 'Higher North,' review of *Northern Farm* by Henry Beston; reproductions

Halifax Daily Star. 23 August 1948
Percy Ghent, 'Canadian Artist is also a Naturalist'

Brandon Daily Sun. 14 October 1948
'Canadian Artist Prints Brochures Aids Conservation,' unsigned

1949

The Canadian Bookman. summer 1949
Marsh Jeanneret, 'Author's Friend: the Book Editor,' p 11

Saturday Night. 31 May 1949
York Reed, 'Down North,' review of *The MacKenzie* by Leslie Roberts

Saturday Night. 20 December 1949
Unsigned review of *Young Bush Pilot* by Jack Hambleton

1950

Donald W. Buchanan. *The Growth of Canadian Painting.* London and Toronto, Collins 1950. p 33

Graham McInnes. *Canadian Art.* Toronto, Macmillan of Canada, 1950. p 90-1

1951

Saturday Night. 25 September 1951
'Work in Bloom,' review of *Woods and Fields,* signed P.D.

Mayfair. July 1951
Unsigned article, 'What makes the MacDonalds Paint'

The Bulletin, Federation of Ontario Naturalists. no 54 (1951)
E.M. Walker, review of *Woods and Fields,* p 3-4

Paul Duval. *Alfred Joseph Casson.* Toronto, Ryerson Press, 1951. p 11

Globe and Mail. Toronto. 1 September 1951
William Arthur Deacon, 'Thoreau MacDonald, Canadian Illustrator,' review of *Woods and Fields*

1952

The Windsor Art Association, Members' Letter, April 1952
Notice of London, Ontario, circulating exhibition

The London Evening Free Press. 26 January 1952
Notice of exhibitions at the London Public Library and Art Museum

The Leader Post. Regina. 4 October 1952
'Black and White Book Illustrations on Show,' unsigned review of London, Ontario, circulating exhibition

Paul Duval. *Canadian Drawings and Prints.* Toronto, Burns and MacEachern, 1952. plate 56 (Minessing Swamp)

Daily Star. Windsor. 29 March 1952
Review of London, Ontario, circulating exhibition

Daily Star. Windsor. 5 April 1952
David Mawr, 'Thoreau MacDonald's Pen-Ink drawings and Quebec Art showing at Willistead,' review of London, Ontario, circulating exhibition

The Calgary Herald. 16 December 1952
'Nature Scenes Feature Coste House Display,' unsigned review of London, Ontario, circulating exhibition

1953

Hans Vollmer. *Allgemeines Lexikon der bildenden Künstler des XX. Jahrhunderts: Unter Mitwirkung von Fachgelehrten des In- und Auslandes.* Leipzig, Seemann, 1953-62. 6v

Victoria Daily Times. 8 April 1953
'Noted Canadian Illustrator shows pen drawings here,' unsigned review of London, Ontario, circulating exhibition

1954

The Educational Record. Quebec. vol 80, no 3 (July-September 1954)
E.R. Hunter, 'J.E.H. MacDonald'

1955

J. Russell Harper. *Canadian Paintings in Hart House.* Toronto, University of Toronto Press [1955]. p 71

1958

A.Y. Jackson. *A Painter's Country.* Toronto, Clark, Irwin, 1958. p 156

1959

R.E. Watters. *A Checklist of Canadian Literature.* Toronto, University of Toronto Press [1959]. p 625, 659

1960

R.H. Hubbard. *National Gallery of Canada, Catalogue of Paintings and Sculpture. Vol 3: Canadian School.* Toronto, University of Toronto Press [1960]. p 202-3

1961

Provincial's Paper. vol 26, no 2 (1961)
Paul Duval, 'Word and Picture; the Story of Illustration in Canada'

1965

MacLean's Magazine. vol 78, no 21 (1 November 1965)
John Maclure, 'Hidden Treasures of a Shy Rebel,' article on J.E.H. MacDonald

Paul Duval. *Group of Seven Drawings.* Toronto, Burns and MacEachern, 1965
Plates 4, 5, 6, and 9 by TM. Plate 2 the combined work of J.E.H. MacDonald and TM

American Artist. vol 29, no 10 (December 1965) p 36
Norman Kent, 'The Line Drawings of Thoreau MacDonald': reproductions

1966

Bulletin of the National Gallery of Canada. vol 4, no 1 (1966) p 6
Sybille Pantazzi, 'Book Illustration and Design by Canadian Artists 1890-1940': reproductions

Emily Carr. *Hundreds and Thousands: The Journal of Emily Carr.* Toronto, Clark, Irwin, 1966. p 7

1967

Hanover Gazette. 9 March 1967
'This Week at Hopkins Center,' unsigned notice of exhibition

The Dartmouth. 7 March 1967
F. Byrd, 'Two Galleries Feature MacDonald's Paintings,' review of exhibition

Valley News. Hanover. 3 March 1967
'Rural Ontario Theme of Art at the Center,' notice of exhibition

1968

Naomi Jackson Groves. *A.Y.'s Canada.* Toronto, Clarke, Irwin, 1968. p 102

1969

Carl Schaefer. 'Personal Reminiscences,' in *Catalogue for the Carl Schaefer Retrospective Exhibition: Paintings from 1926 to 1969*

Jeremy Adamson. *The Hart House Collection of Canadian Paintings.* Toronto, University of Toronto Press [1969]. p 98

1970

The Art Gallery of Ontario. *The Canadian Collection.* Toronto, McGraw-Hill [1970]. p 285-8

Peter Mellen. *The Group of Seven.* Toronto, McClelland and Stewart, 1970. p 49, 144, and 184 (p 184, quote by TM)

The Canadian Forum. vol 50, no 591/2 (April-May 1970) p 42
Joan Murray, 'Graphics in the Forum, 1920-1961'

1971

Creative Canada: A Biographical Dictionary of Twentieth-Century Creative and Performing Artists. Vol 1. Compiled by Reference Division, McPherson Library, University of Victoria, B.C. Published in association with McPherson Library by University of Toronto Press [1971]. p 203-4

L. Bruce Pierce. *Thoreau MacDonald: Illustrator, Designer, Observer of Nature.* Toronto, Norflex Limited, 1971. 48 p. cover title, reproductions

1972

Paul Duval. *Four Decades: The Canadian Group of Painters and their Contemporaries, 1930-1970.* Toronto, Clarke, Irwin [1972]. p 11-12, 14

J.H. Granatstein and Peter Stevens. *Forum: Canadian Life and Letters 1920-1970.* Toronto, University of Toronto Press [1972]. illustration p 39

Colin MacDonald. *Dictionary of Canadian Painters.* vol 4. Ottawa, Canadian Paperbacks Publishing. forthcoming

1972

R.E. Watters. *A Checklist of Canadian Literature.* second edition, Toronto, University of Toronto Press [1972]. p 884, 928

Index

www.ingramcontent.com/pod-product-compliance
Lightning Source LLC
LaVergne TN
LVHW082158080826
844660LV00046B/1281

* 9 7 8 1 4 8 7 5 7 2 1 3 6 *